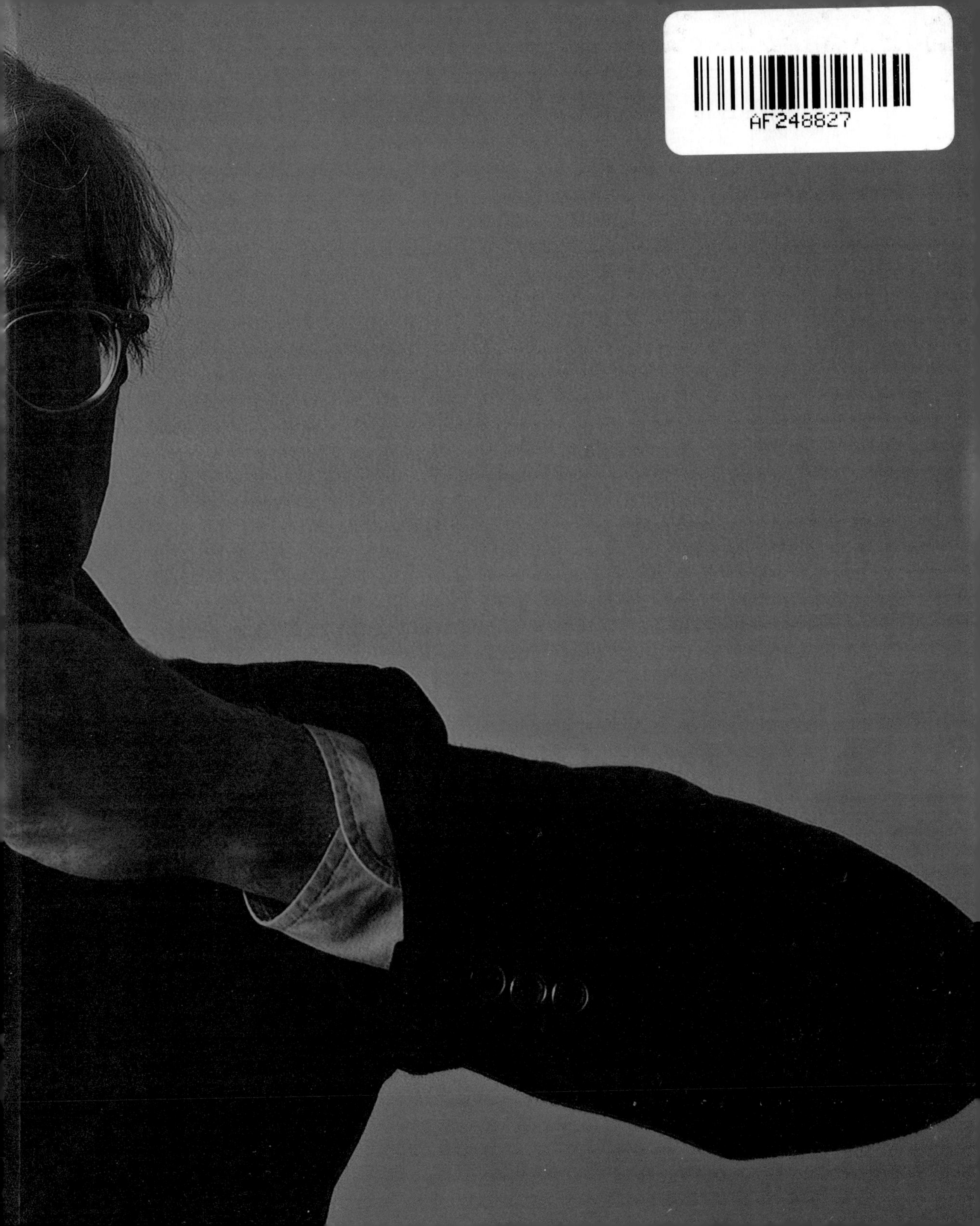

AF248827

Polaroid Now

THE HISTORY AND FUTURE OF POLAROID PHOTOGRAPHY

CHRONICLE CHROMA

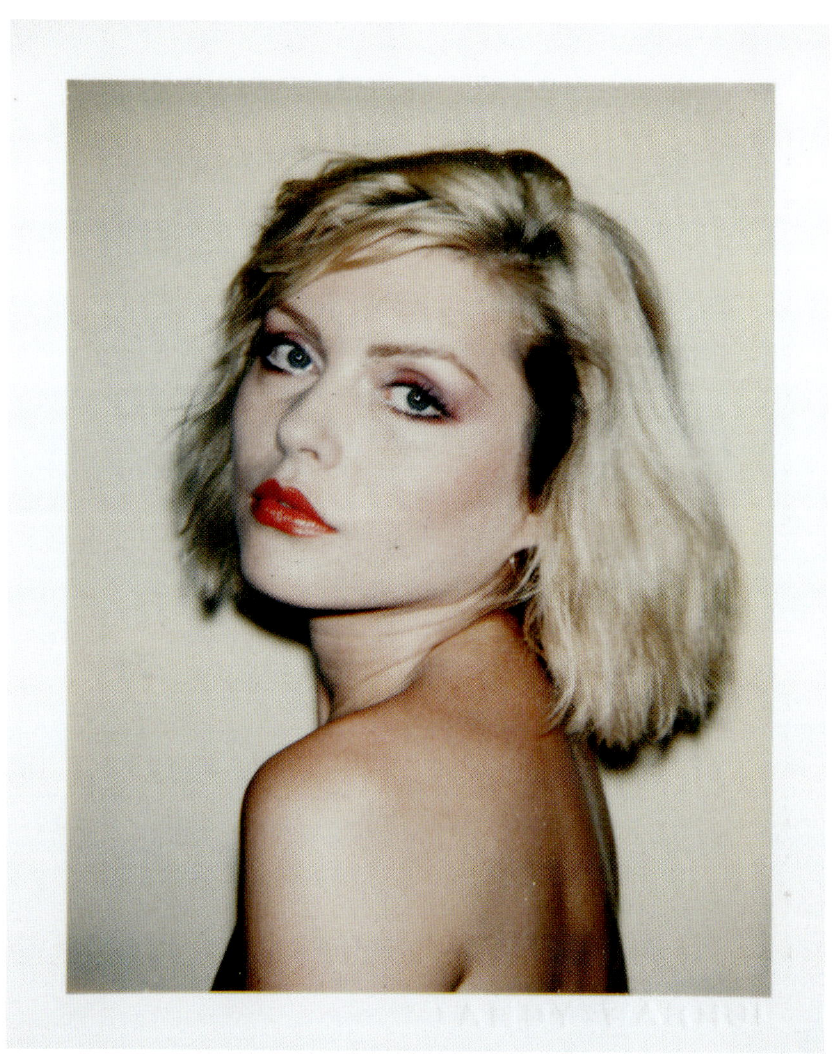

4   Andy Warhol, *Debbie Harry*

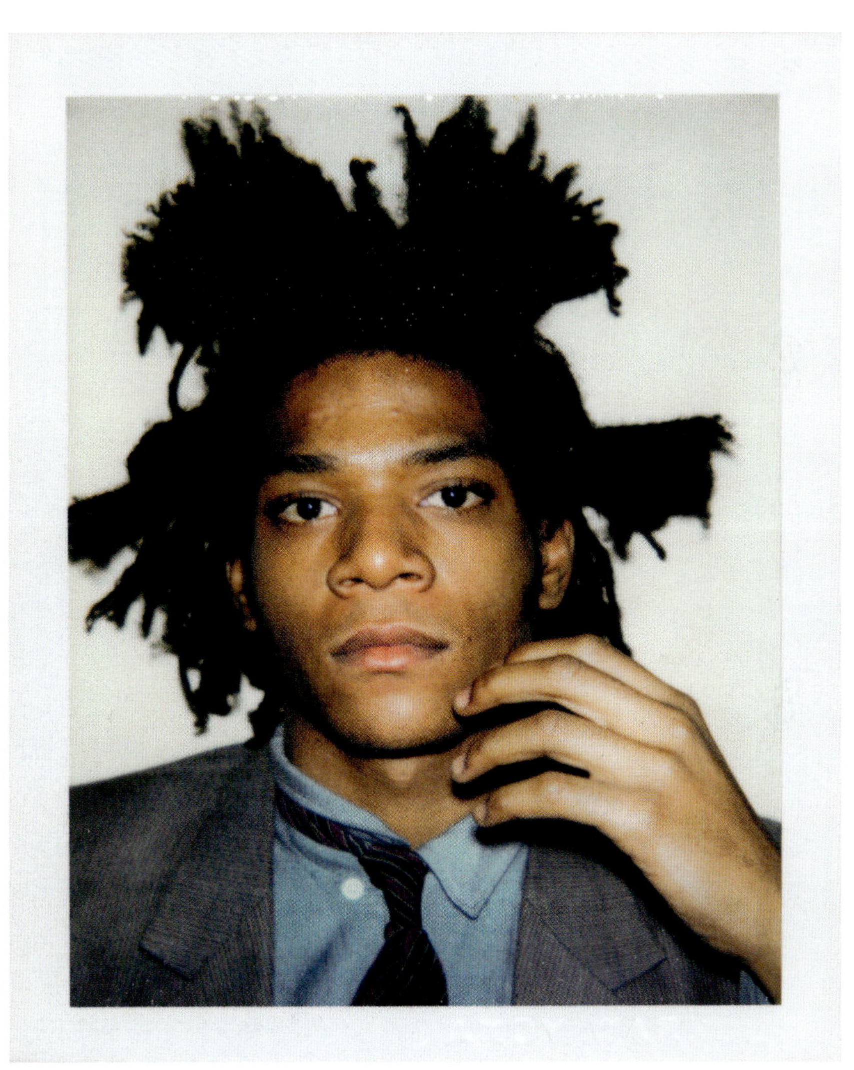

Andy Warhol, *Jean-Michel Basquiat*   5

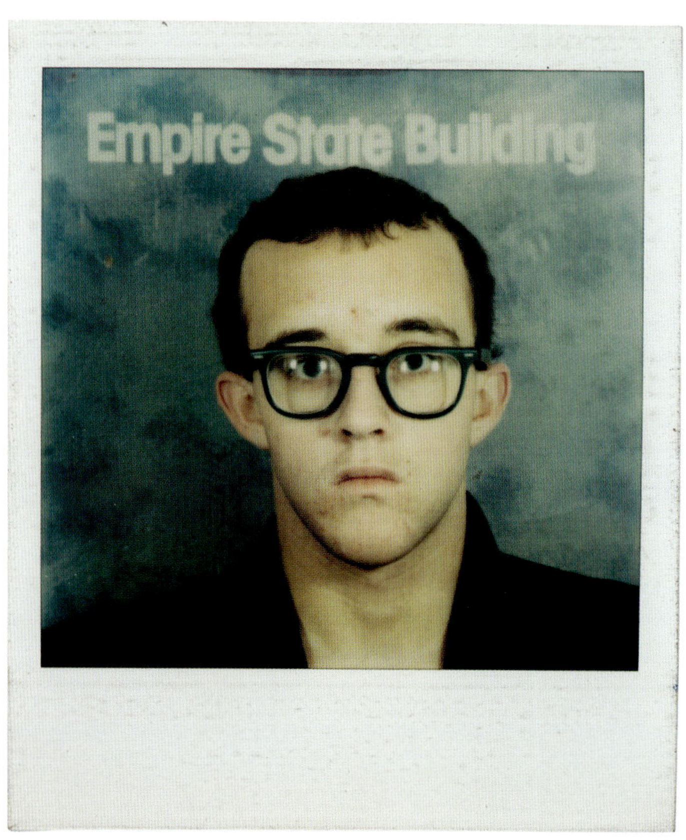

6   Keith Haring, *Self Portrait*

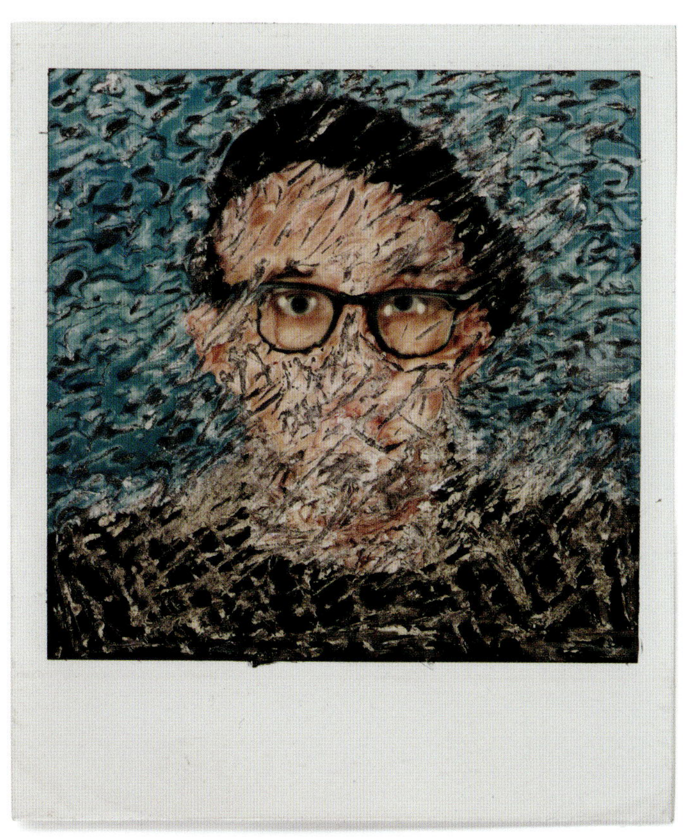

Keith Haring, *Self Portrait*   7

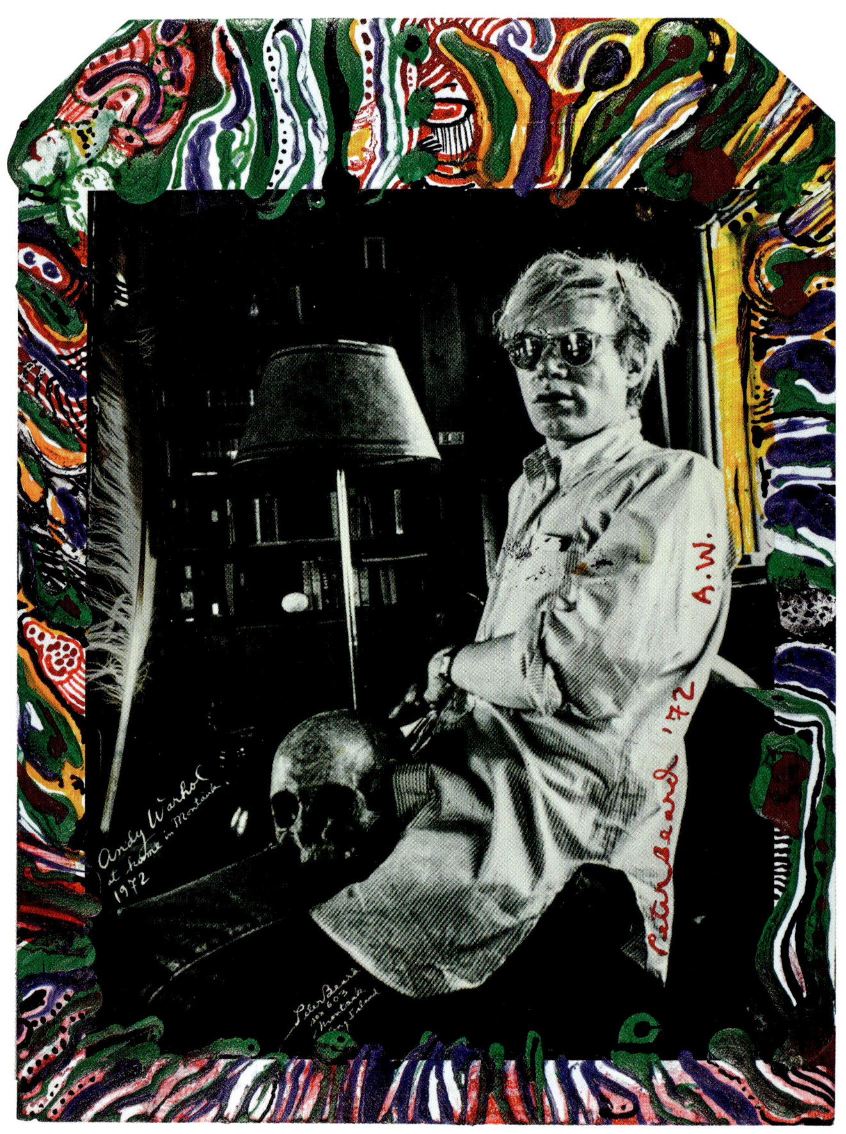

Andy Warhol
at home in Montauk
1972
A.W.
Peter Beard '72

    Chuck Close, *9-Part Self Portrait*

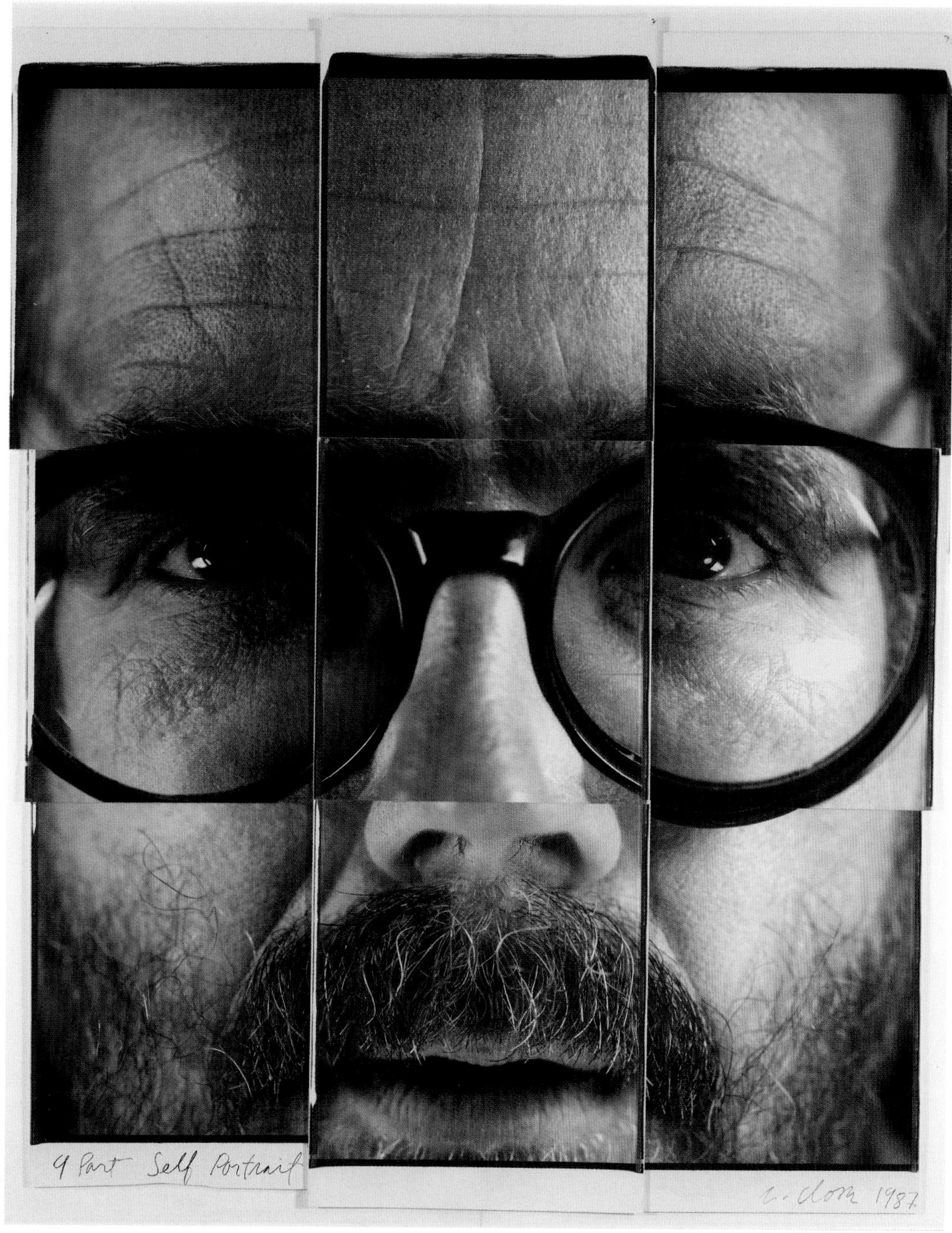

4 Part Self Portrait
C. Close 1987

Polaroid Now

by Steve Crist

I stepped through the gates of the Polaroid Corporation in Waltham, Massachusetts, back in 2004. Upon presenting myself at the fortress-like entry point, a retirement-age security guard snapped a quick portrait. A few minutes later, my personalized visitor badge was created and laminated—produced entirely on Polaroid-brand materials.

By today's standards, it's hard to recall what instant photography was like back in 2004. Digital cameras were being sold at the time, but they had yet to be fully adopted by all consumers, and there was no easy way to share digital photographs. Cell phones with poor-quality cameras had been launched in the United States in 2002. Apple's first iPhone had yet to be released, and wouldn't be until 2007. Many professional photographers still held tight to their comfortable, film-based cameras and analog film stocks, and weren't quick to make the transition to digital that a younger generation soon would. Back in 2004, photography was standing at the crossroads between analog and digital.

Edwin Land, and his team of engineers and scientists, created a behemoth of a company by literally inventing its way into our modern society. With the introduction of the first Polaroid instant camera in 1947, Polaroid owned the instant-photography space; and for many decades, its presence and brand name was seen just about everywhere around the globe. Millions of consumers had at least one Polaroid camera somewhere in their homes, and almost every type of professional seemed to need a Polaroid camera occasionally in their workplace.

Professional photographers and average consumers alike seemed to love the magic of Polaroid photography. The famed Polaroid SX-70 cameras emitted a loud, analog noise, and just a few minutes after clicking the shutter, something you personally created would develop beautifully in your hands. It was a magical and addicting experience for many, and Polaroid benefitted handsomely from the success of its many cameras and film formats.

Yet, by 2004, serious financial pain was already being felt inside analog technology brands, such as the venerable Polaroid Corporation. I began my tour of the Polaroid campus that day guided by Barbara Hitchcock, who, at the time, was the company's influential cultural affairs director and keeper of the Polaroid Collection archive. Barbara curated and kept watch over this famous art collection for many decades. It contained many of the finest photographs ever created on Polaroid film, and included museum-grade works that came to be worth a small fortune.

The purpose of my visit was to start the editing process for *The Polaroid Book*, which was to be published the following year. Over a course of many days, I pored over thousands of originals carefully housed in the temperature-controlled vaults. These images had been thoughtfully chosen—a byproduct of a wealthy and successful company that could afford to purchase and underwrite the very best works from influential photographers and artists everywhere.

But changes were happening rapidly; Polaroid had already entered its first bankruptcy and was attempting to reorganize. Barbara mentioned that the workforce had been reduced many times over previous years. Early retirements were being taken, and as we visited, the cavernous and beautifully designed employee cafeteria was devoid of people, but filled with expensive decor and hundreds of precious, mid-century Eames chairs. Barbara was giving me the tour of a huge, industrial-scale property that was the Google campus of its day. But sadly, by 2004, she was one of the few longtime employees left who kept the Polaroid company alive. To the young outsider and new visitor, Polaroid felt like a company that was about to die.

Digital everything was starting to take over our lives—and classic photography brands, such as Polaroid and others, were losing cash and struggling. With their founders long gone, these once great names struggled mightily to reinvent. Due to the times, Polaroid as we knew it was destined to scale down and eventually die in yet another bankruptcy—an unthinkable event to the thousands of employees around the world who enjoyed its halcyon days.

Some years later, after a sequence of events that ultimately tore the old company apart, a new Polaroid would emerge. In 2008, The Impossible Project was started in the Netherlands by a group that risked much energy and capital to try to save a film process (and the manufacturing machinery) as they instinctively knew that millions of people still loved the process.

Oskar Smolokowski and his team of like-minded, Polaroid-obsessed fans rekindled a spirit that still lives on. The new Polaroid operates globally—with a team that passionately makes the film with rescued and reengineered equipment once destined for the scrapyard. New processes and chemistry had to be reinvented to live up to society's new ecological requirements. There were still many millions of those old Polaroid cameras living in closets around the world, and even a few die-hard fans buying up any old film stocks they could get their hands on. It must have seemed very much impossible, but just like Land's old Polaroid team, the new Polaroid managed to make it happen.

Once again, and after years of efforts by many, the Polaroid camera and film formats were again being manufactured and sold. Elsewhere, the classic, large-format 20 x 24 camera was still being operated from studios in New York and Berlin, and new Polaroid products were in development for a different marketplace willing to receive them in a now-fully-digital world.

Photographers—both amateur and professional alike—are now discovering (or rediscovering) a love for all types of analog photography processes that fans won't seem to let die. There are thriving communities of new Polaroid users, groups gathering on Instagram and Facebook, and Polaroid Week events happening in cities and online in many languages. Once again, artists are using Polaroid materials, and the new work is hanging in galleries. A completely new generation of photographers can be seen carrying Polaroid cameras while walking on the High Line in New York City and on the Bund in Shanghai.

But why would anyone want to use a Polaroid camera these days, when they likely have a smartphone in their pocket that can already take great photographs? The answer is complicated.

Our current day is moving at rocket-ship speed, and people of all ages have become fatigued by a glossy and electronic world that is so instantly at their fingertips. A new generation of photographers has emerged; they are looking for unique methods of individual expression, and techniques that yield a much different result than the easy-to-use digital smartphone that everyone seems to carry. A deep yearning to create and stand out as an individual drives many Polaroid users today. They love the analog process and are (still) excited by the results.

This book—*Polaroid Now*—is a celebration of recently created images made by Polaroid artists from around the world. It's impossible to share all the great Polaroid photography you can find online these days; it is coming from every country, and it's being posted every day.

When reaching out and meeting people through the editing process for this book, I found many excited and generous artists who were quick to share their enthusiasm for their Polaroid work. Most now scan and post their new work to share on digital platforms, such as Instagram and Flickr—something that could not have been imagined when the old Polaroid Corporation was facing its last days.

In the early 2000s, book publishers heard rumblings that eventually most analog experiences would become electronic, and we should prepare, as physical books were soon to become a thing of the past. Yet, here we are in the year 2021, and physical books, analog records, and Polaroid cameras and film are still valued and desired. It seems the electronic experience can't quite feed us everything we desire. We still love to create and see art, experience spaces and architecture, listen to live music, and collect and handle objects that don't plug in. Humans are very much tactile creatures, and our universal love for creating, and even enjoying, a messy process continues to live within each of us. Personally, I think that is the very human spirit you can see alive in the photography contained in these pages.

Our Polaroid Artists are our heroes and contributors, and hail from countries around the world. This book celebrates the Polaroid of NOW—a physical medium and group of people that is very much alive and well. Creative types still love analog and physical photographic processes. With Polaroid, many are just as addicted to the magic that was introduced back in 1947. My hope is that this book will inspire you to venture forth and try your hand at creating your own Polaroid photographs, and experience an analog process of real photographic film that still magically develops in your hands.

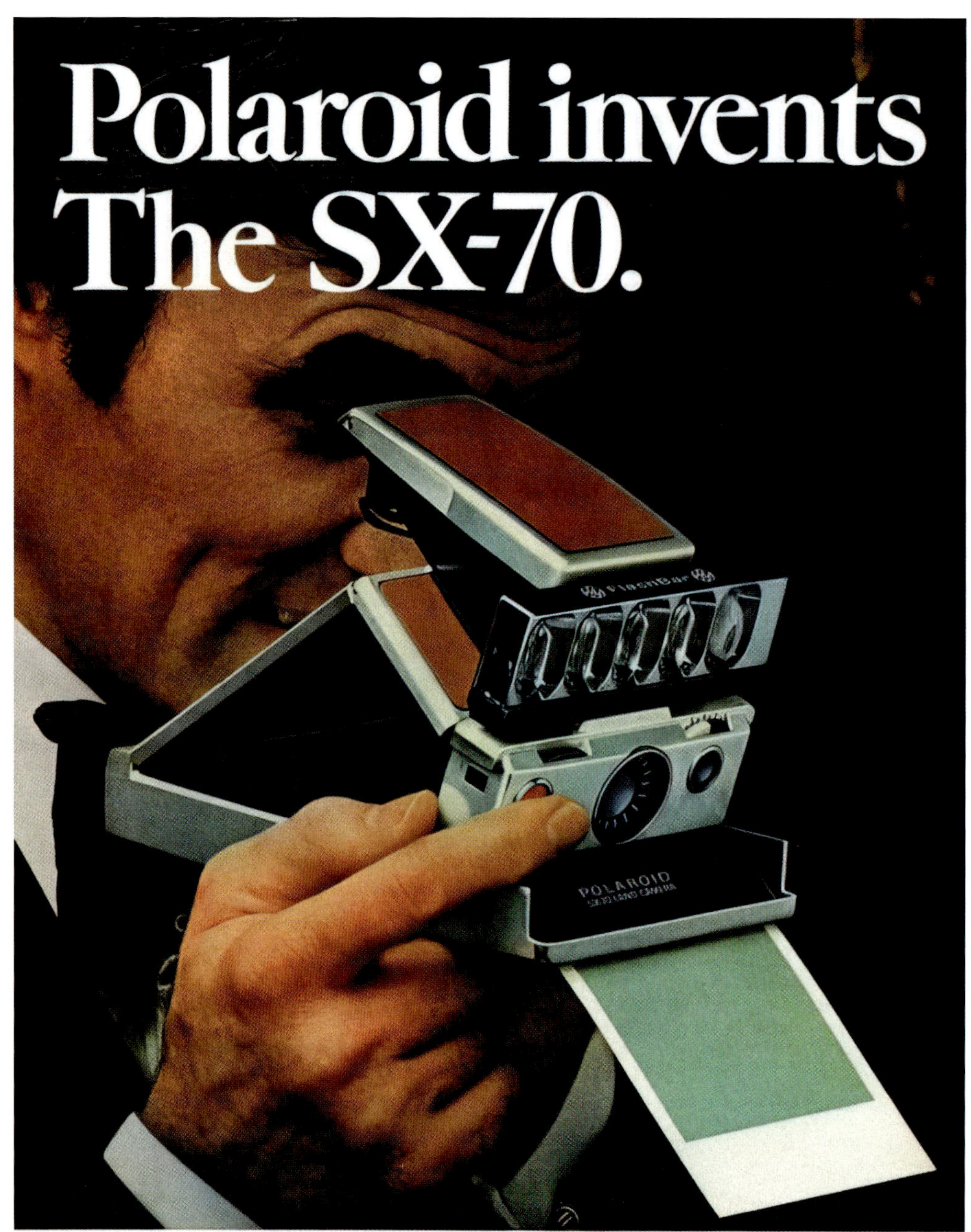

Polaroid invents
The SX-70.
Just touch the red electric button and...

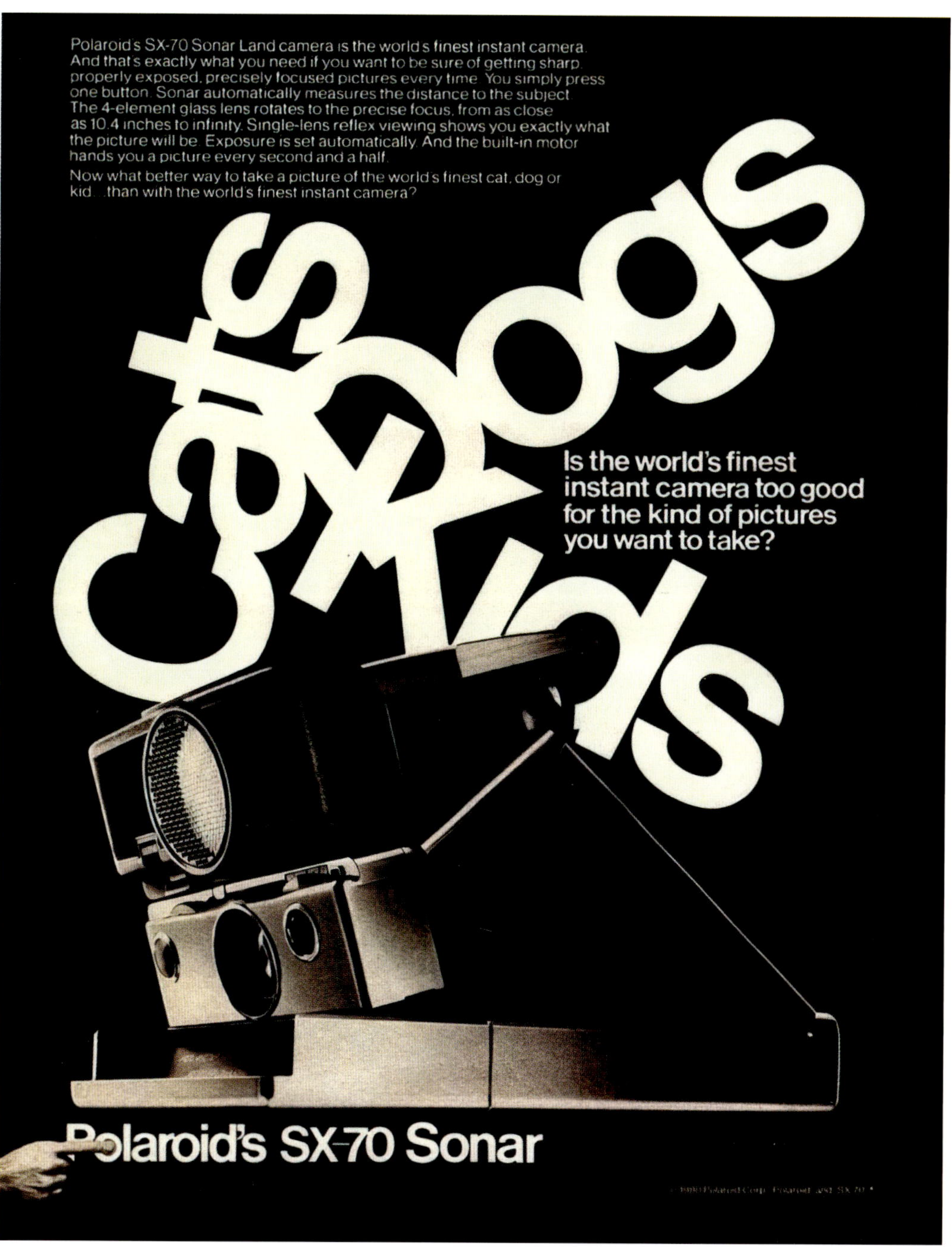

Polaroid's SX-70 Sonar Land camera is the world's finest instant camera. And that's exactly what you need if you want to be sure of getting sharp, properly exposed, precisely focused pictures every time. You simply press one button. Sonar automatically measures the distance to the subject. The 4-element glass lens rotates to the precise focus, from as close as 10.4 inches to infinity. Single-lens reflex viewing shows you exactly what the picture will be. Exposure is set automatically. And the built-in motor hands you a picture every second and a half.
Now what better way to take a picture of the world's finest cat, dog or kid...than with the world's finest instant camera?
Cats Dogs Kids
Is the world's finest instant camera too good for the kind of pictures you want to take?
Polaroid's SX-70 Sonar

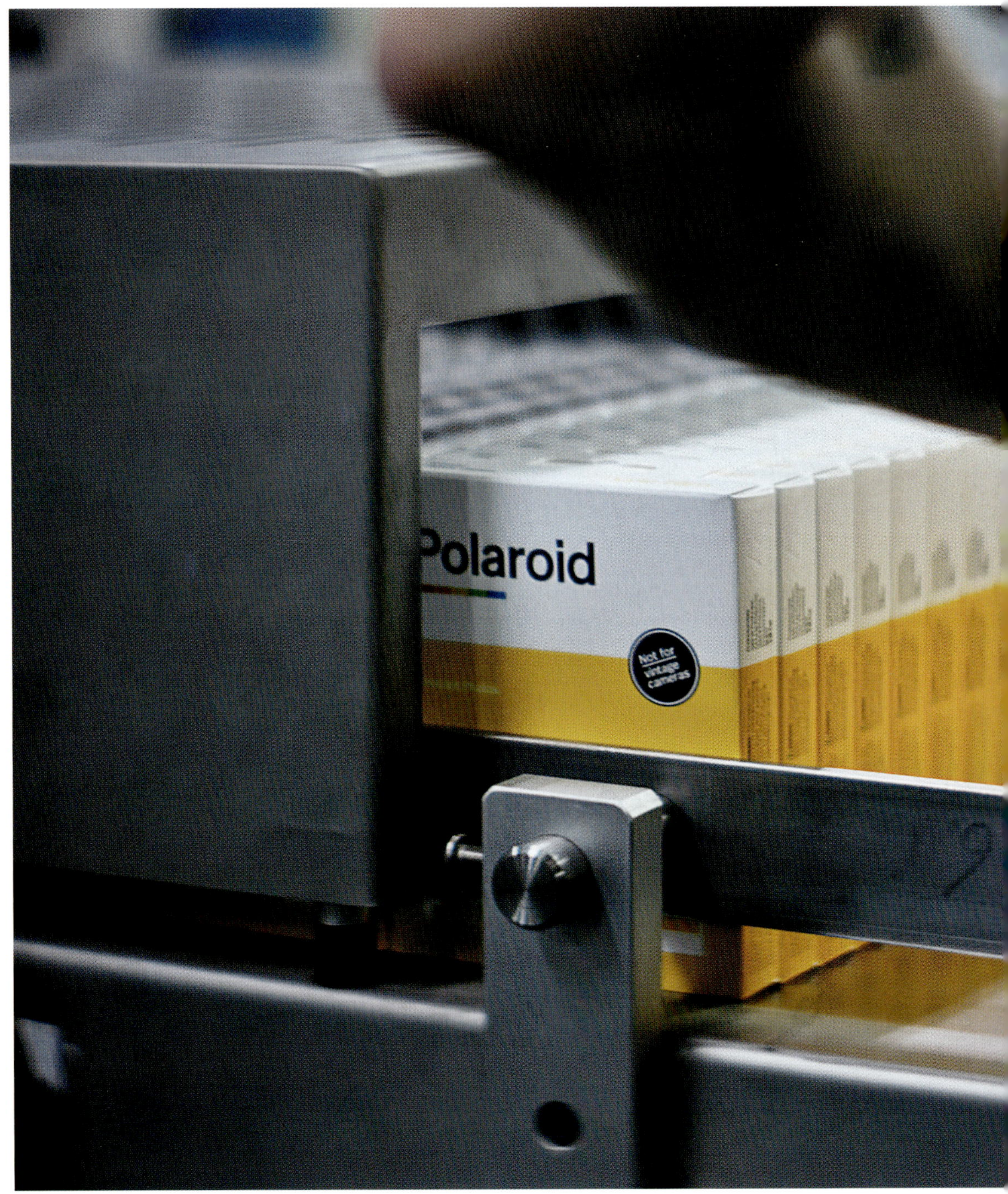
Polaroid
Not for
vintage
cameras

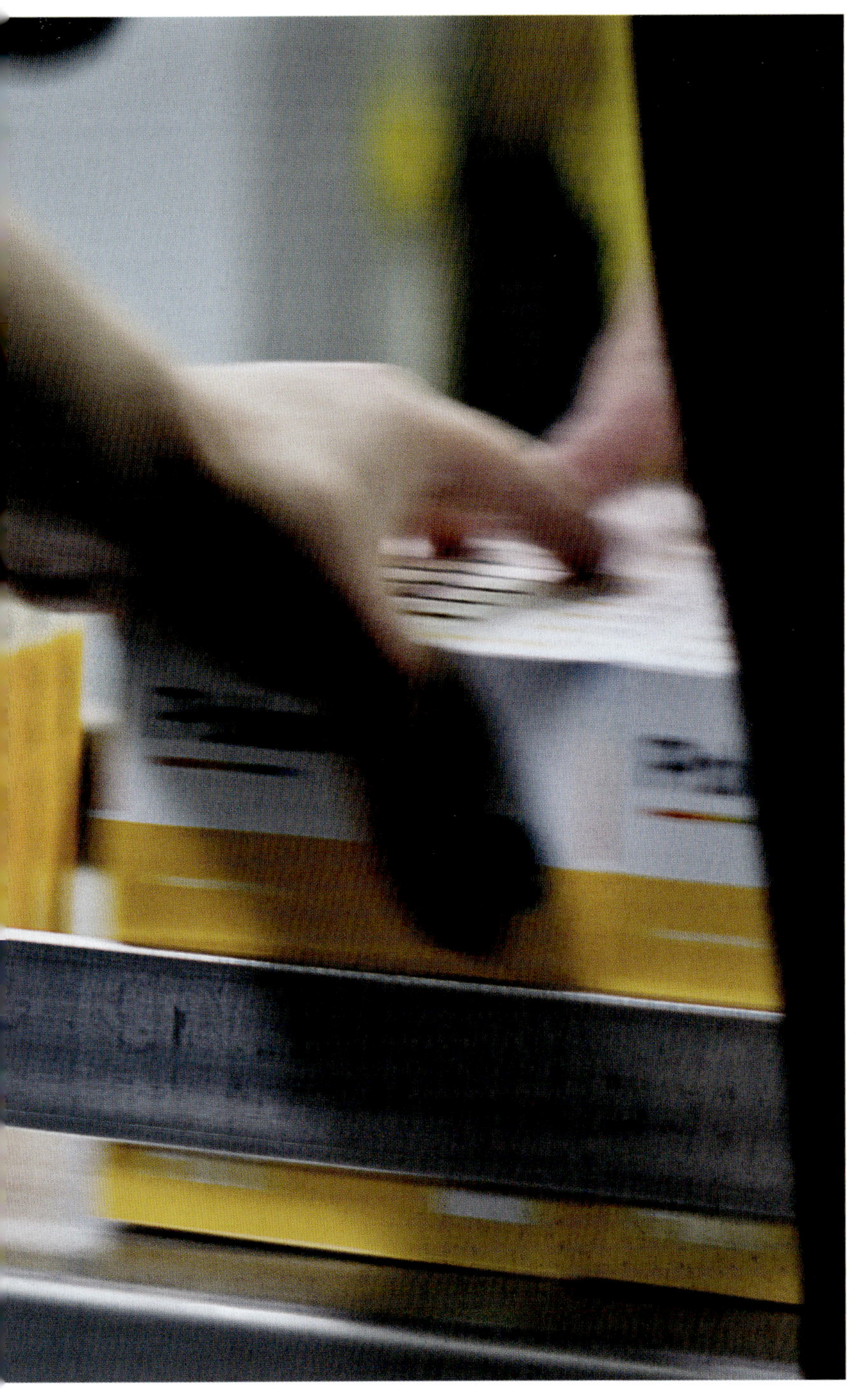

Polaroid Then and Now

by Oskar Smolokowski

Polaroid is one of the few companies in the world that can truly say it invented magic.

I discovered this magic for myself in 2011, in a store hidden away in a fifth-floor loft in lower Manhattan. Walking around the beautiful space with huge Polaroid photo enlargements covering the walls, and the legendary SX70 in my hands for the first time, I could immediately feel the significance of what was on display—even though I knew nearly nothing about it back then. I was twenty-two and completely unaware that my life was about to change forever. My journey to ensure a future, and fight for these incredible products and this incredible brand was about to start. There are many books and articles written about the history of Polaroid and its legendary founder Edwin Land, and my short introduction is not meant to be a match for them. Instead, I'd love to share the parts of the story that captured the hearts and minds of myself and our new team at Polaroid: the reason we continue to work hard at Polaroid now, eighty-three years after the company was founded.

The first thing that jumped out at me when I learned about Polaroid's history was Edwin Land's incredible drive and curiosity. He was relentless in his pursuit of answering questions and inventing ways the world could be better. He would often sleep in his lab to keep working on projects that were "manifestly important and nearly impossible," as he himself put it. Polaroid was founded on this insatiable curiosity. The technical inventions that came out were then turned into products that were useful, magical, and most of the time extremely profitable. Throughout Land's life, his curiosity never faltered. He never stopped exploring new ideas and meticulously patenting all of them, which resulted in 535 patents to his name!

Land's first big breakthrough invention was the thin sheet polarizer: a core technology that is used to this very day in LCD screens, sunglasses, and countless other applications. This is where the name Polaroid comes from, and the invention's commercialization is what the company was focused in its first years after founding in 1937. It would be more than ten years later until Polaroid would first bring the idea of instant photography to the world.

The story of how Polaroid got into the business of inventing instant photography goes more or less like this: In 1943, after a day out walking around and taking pictures on a Rolleiflex camera with her dad, Land's three-year-old daughter simply asked, "Why can't I see the pictures now?"

They were sitting at home with no pictures to look at as a camera like this (and all cameras made at the time) required developing the pictures in a darkroom lab, a process that takes at least a few days and lots of specialized chemistry and equipment. This question got Edwin Land thinking about the problem. In true Edwin Land style, he thought deeply, recruited the best scientists to the project, and worked day and night until the first instant-photo product from Polaroid was launched in 1948. This new instant camera was revolutionary: bringing the magic of creating a photograph right in front of your eyes to the world for the first time. It was a product right at the intersection of art and science, powered by incredibly complex chemistry and enabling a world of creativity. This idea of business being at the intersection of art and science became a guiding north star for Polaroid - a star we still look toward today. In fact, it was such a winning formula that it inspired another famous company visionary at Apple, Steve Jobs, who baked their version—"the intersection of liberal arts and technology"—deep into the values of his company as well.

By 1972, Land and his team at Polaroid transformed instant-photography products from the initially giant and heavy cameras that required peel-apart film to the now legendary, incredibly slim SX70 camera that used integral film with no need for peeling anything apart. Just point, shoot, and watch the magic happen as the photograph develops in front of your eyes. This is when the most-iconic Polaroid format was born, the one I was holding in my hands in the gallery in New York, taking it all in. The legendary white frame, with its unique proportions and incalculable impact on culture and art. Armed with this new and revolutionized instant technology, Polaroid took the world by storm, growing to a two-billion-dollars-a-year business. The impact on culture was impressive; artists from Warhol to Hockney and Haring to Basquiat were all using Polaroid regularly—sometimes in their work and often in their personal lives. The company's brand and products permeated pop culture, and nearly fifty years after the invention of this iconic instant photo format it is still recognized, cherished, and used by millions of people around the world.

It was in those fifty years that the momentum of the brand transcended beyond instant photography. Even in the 2010s, at a time when Polaroid instant photography was at its all-time low, brand love and recognition was still as high as ever.

I believe the reason why the Polaroid brand managed to resonate so deeply with people is how the company managed to connect what it did to fundamentally human values. This quote from Land in particular struck me as beautiful and resonating exactly this sentiment, as he described his observations of people using Polaroid products:

"It turns out that buried within us ... there is latent interest in each other; there is tenderness, curiosity, excitement, affection, companionability, and humor. ... [W]e have a yen for, and a primordial competence for, a quiet, good-humored delight in each other: we have a prehistoric tribal competence ... in being partners in the lonely exploration of a once-empty planet."

The tools Polaroid made, the stories that it told, the way it cared about the magic of everyday moments and empowering creativity for all gave it the staying power few brands in history have enjoyed. Unfortunately, after a failed billion-dollar project that was meant to revolutionize instant video capture, called Polavision, Edwin Land's days at the company were numbered. He was forced to step down and retired in 1982 to focus on the science of color and the way we perceive it, called Retinex theory. Polaroid was still a mighty business for years to come, and only started having serious problems in the late '90s into the 2000s.

To tell the next part of the story I need to go back to the loft where my Polaroid journey began. The name above the door wasn't actually Polaroid, it was The Impossible Project. After a series of bankruptcies between 2001 and 2008, and as digital photography took hold, it looked like Polaroid would stop making its iconic film forever, and history would close this chapter in history. But the love created around the world was so strong that it brought some people to the rescue. The heroes came from where you would least expect them—a spider eye PhD named Florian "Doc" Kaps, and his family and friends, managed to purchase the last factory, literally days before it was scheduled for scrapping. They immediately got to work restarting the original instant-film machinery. To make this work, they would need to revolutionize the chemistry inside the film to make it manufacturable at a lower scale, and within today's environmental regulations. That was in 2009, and by 2012 they had managed to make good progress. At the same time, Polaroid the brand lived on as strong as ever, with new ownership developing a successful licensing program.

I joined The Impossible Project shortly after my visit to the store, both as an investor and an employee; and by 2016 we managed to make great progress in setting up the company for success. But we all knew from day one that the mission was to reunite with Polaroid—after all, we were making Polaroid film! In September 2017, on Polaroid's eightieth birthday, we launched Polaroid Originals. We managed to put the pieces back together and reached a deal to reunite the factory and the brand under one roof and ownership.

And that brings us to what Polaroid is now, and where it's going. At the end of the day, we are just a bunch of people who are excited and proud about the opportunity to take the brand and what it stands for forward. We love instant photography; it's still the heart and soul of the brand, and we have big plans for it for years to come. But we also plan on taking the brand further. We've reignited the curiosity of our scientists and are exploring new fields of chemistry that can help the world become a better place. We're looking toward the intersection of art and science to guide us as we plan our next products. We aim to bring tools and initiatives to continue empowering creative culture. And, perhaps most importantly, we want to stay true to contributing to a world that is more human and meaningful, bringing creativity, delight, and magic to anyone who crosses paths with Polaroid.

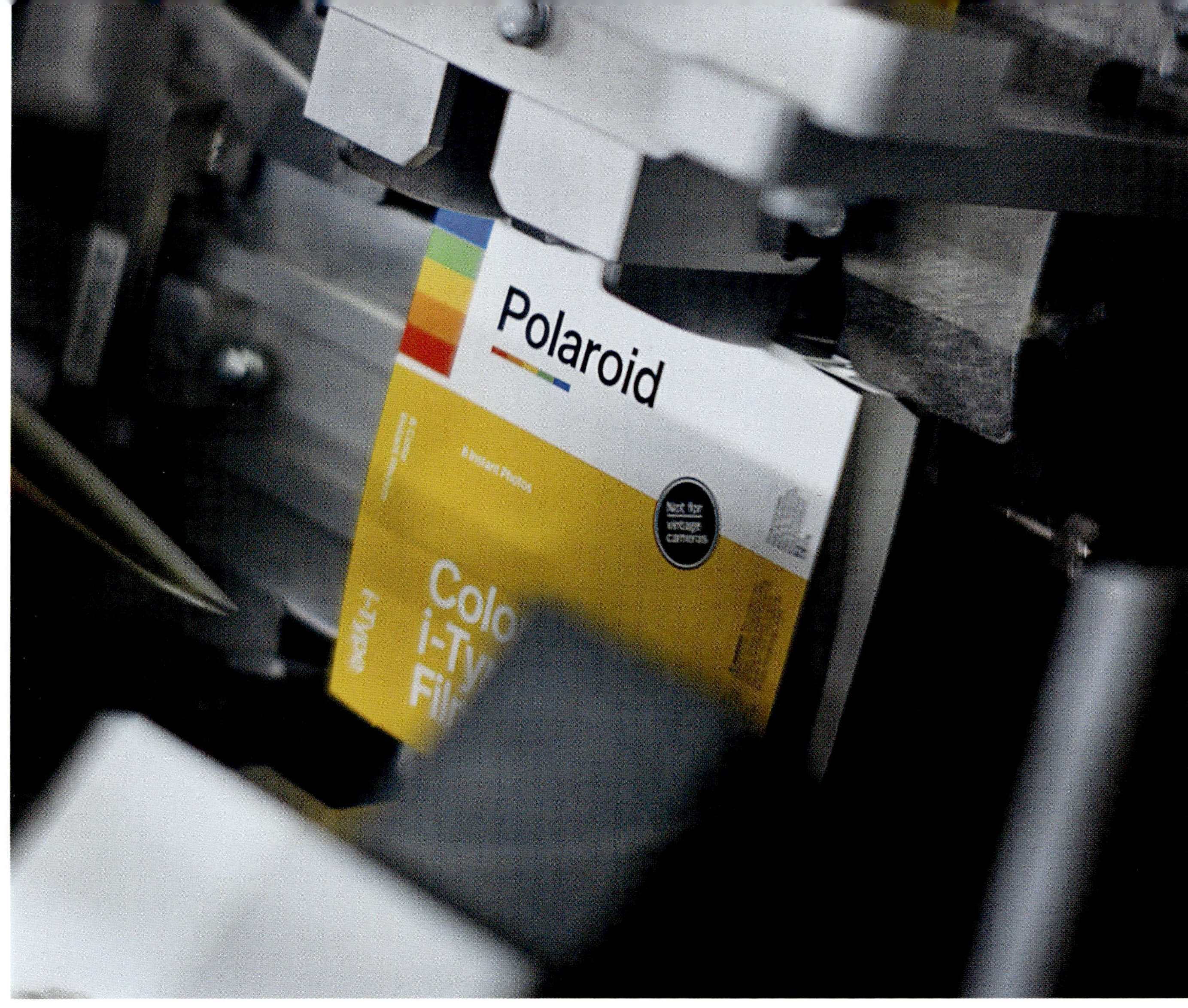

Polaroid
8 Instant Photos
Not for vintage cameras
Color i-Type Film

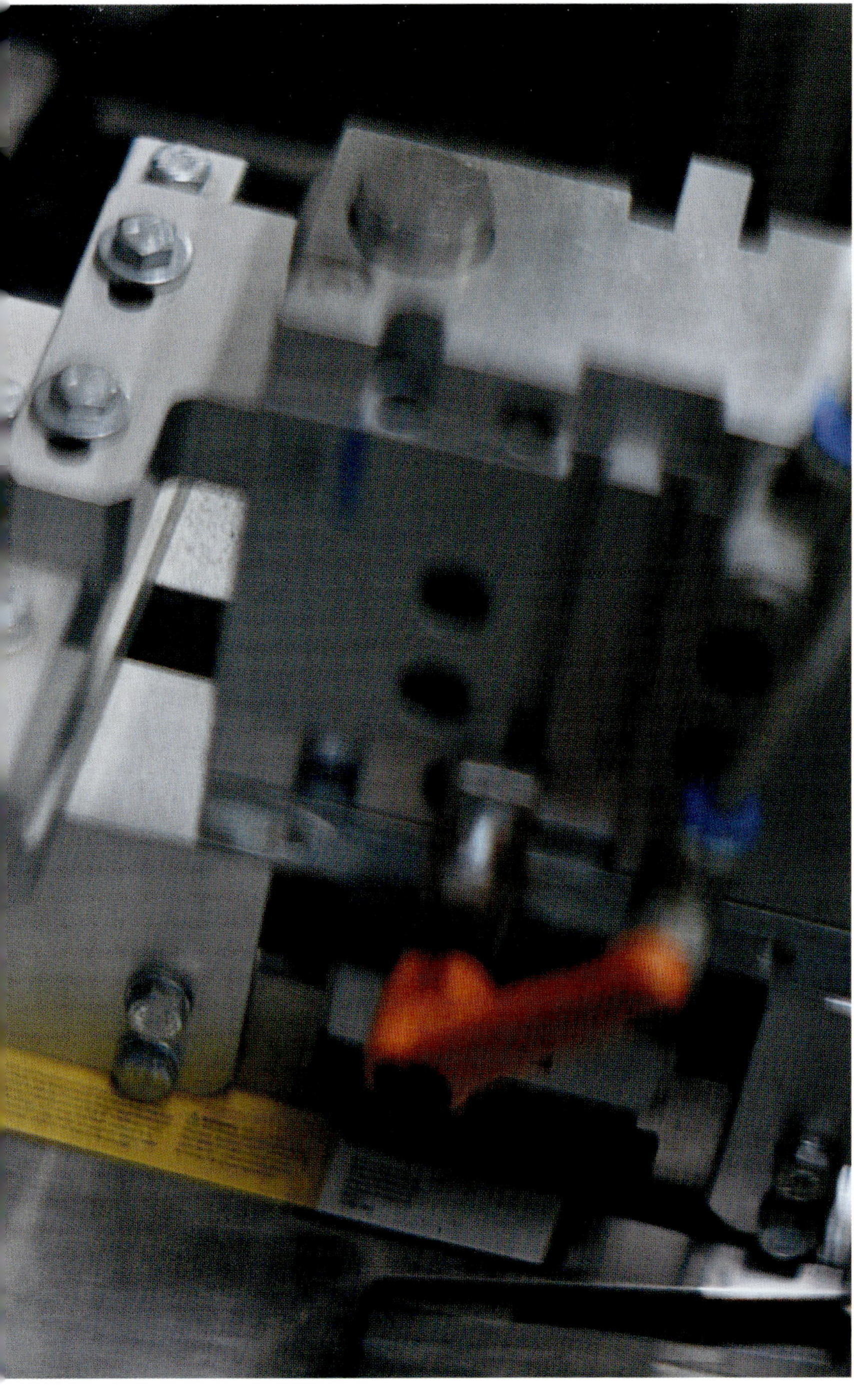

POLAROID
Artists

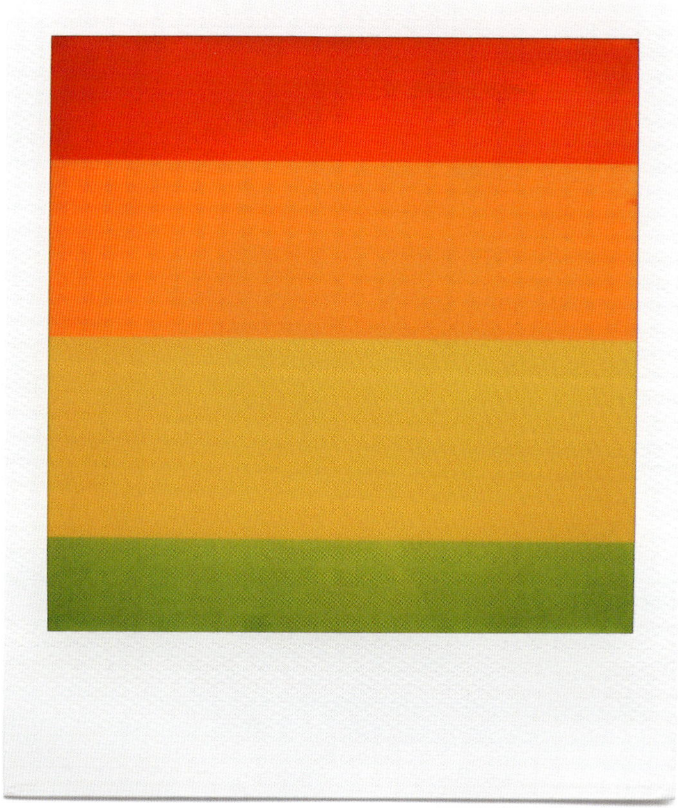

24   Grant Hamilton, *Roy G*

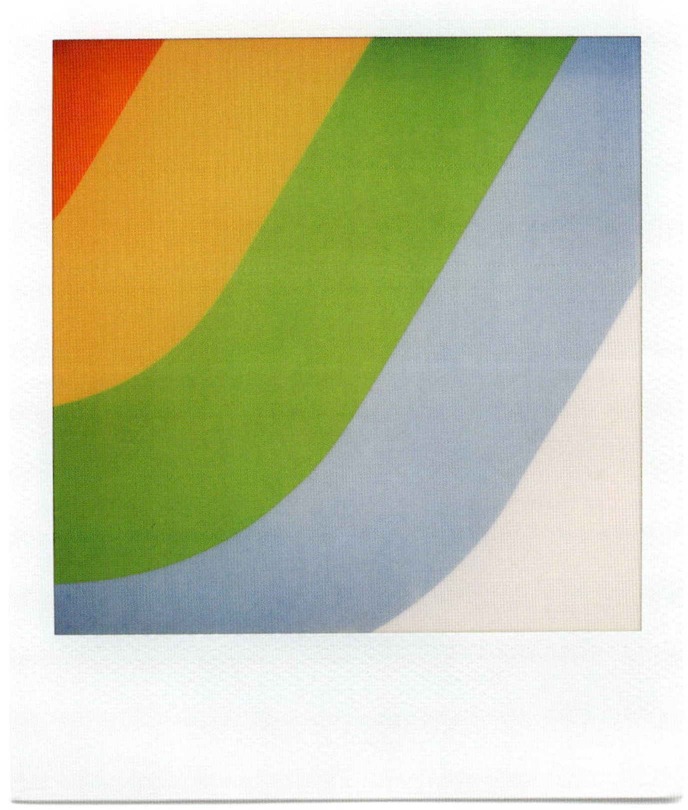

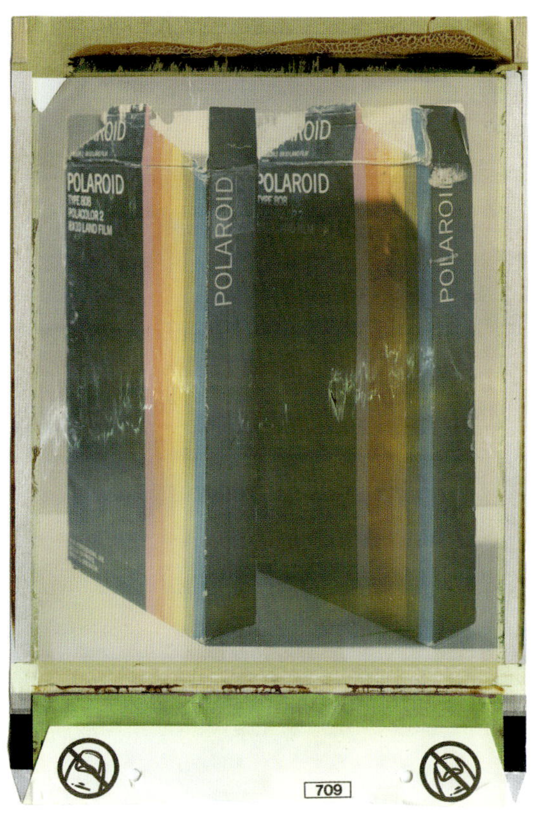
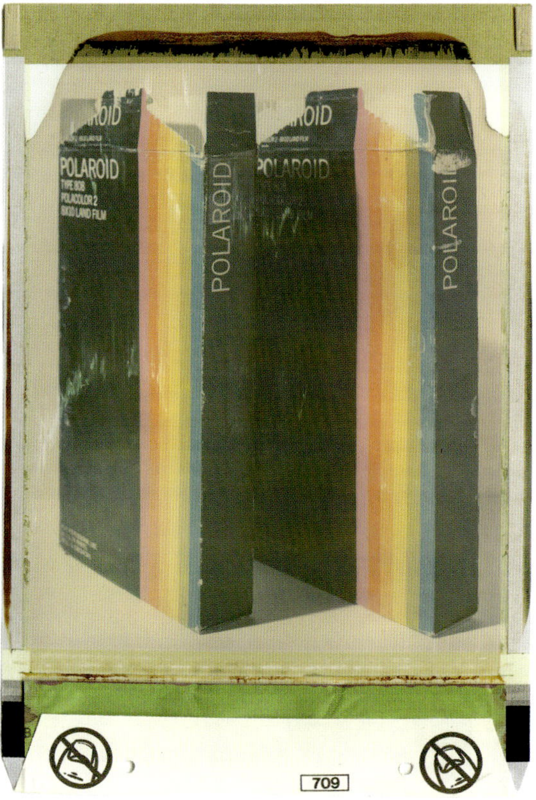

   Matthew Brandt, *A835190387728B, A835190387728A, A835190387728C, A835190387728D*

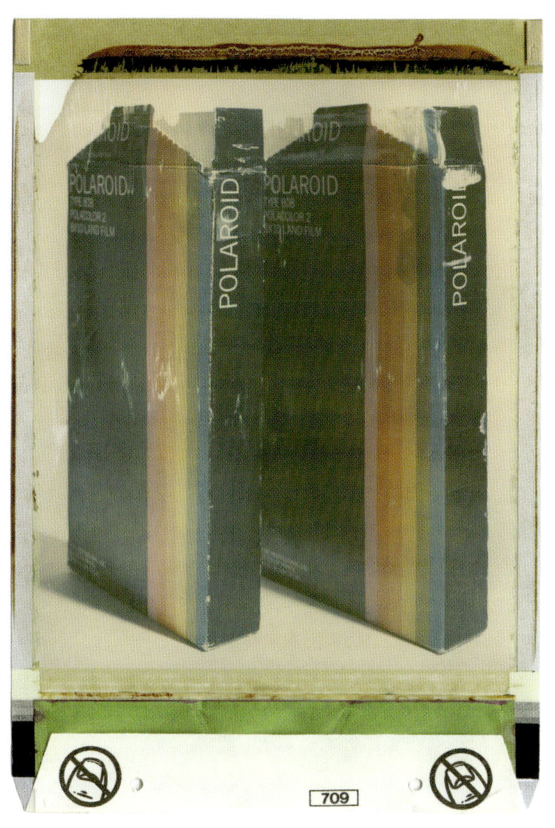
POLAROID
POLAROID
TYPE 808
POLACOLOR 2
8X10 LAND FILM
POLAROID
POLAROID
709
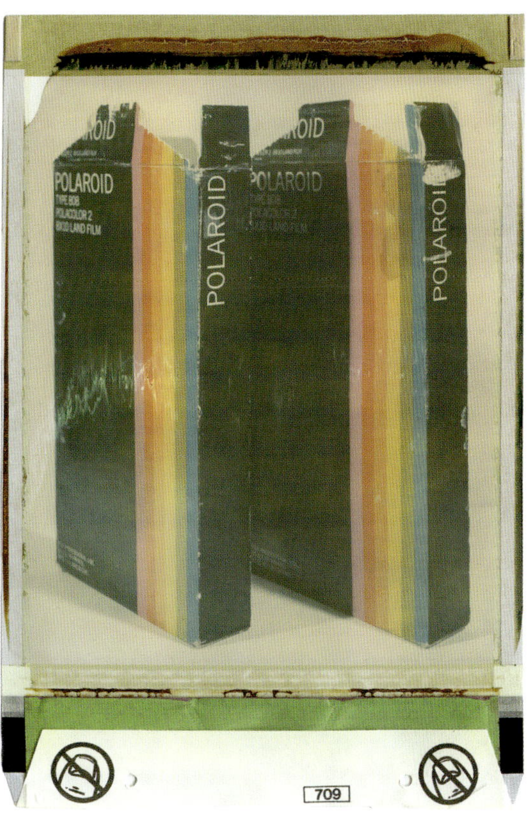
POLAROID
POLAROID
TYPE 808
POLACOLOR 2
8X10 LAND FILM
POLAROID
POLAROID
709

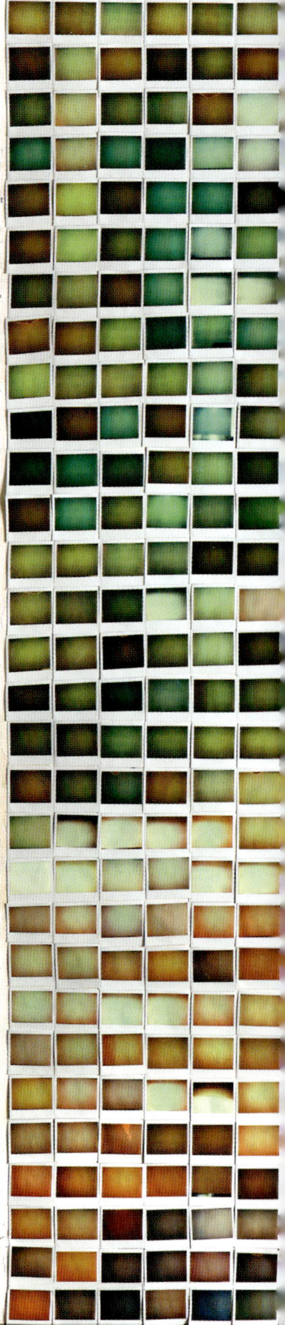

   Matthew Brandt, *Polaroids (Edwin Land Holding Camera)*

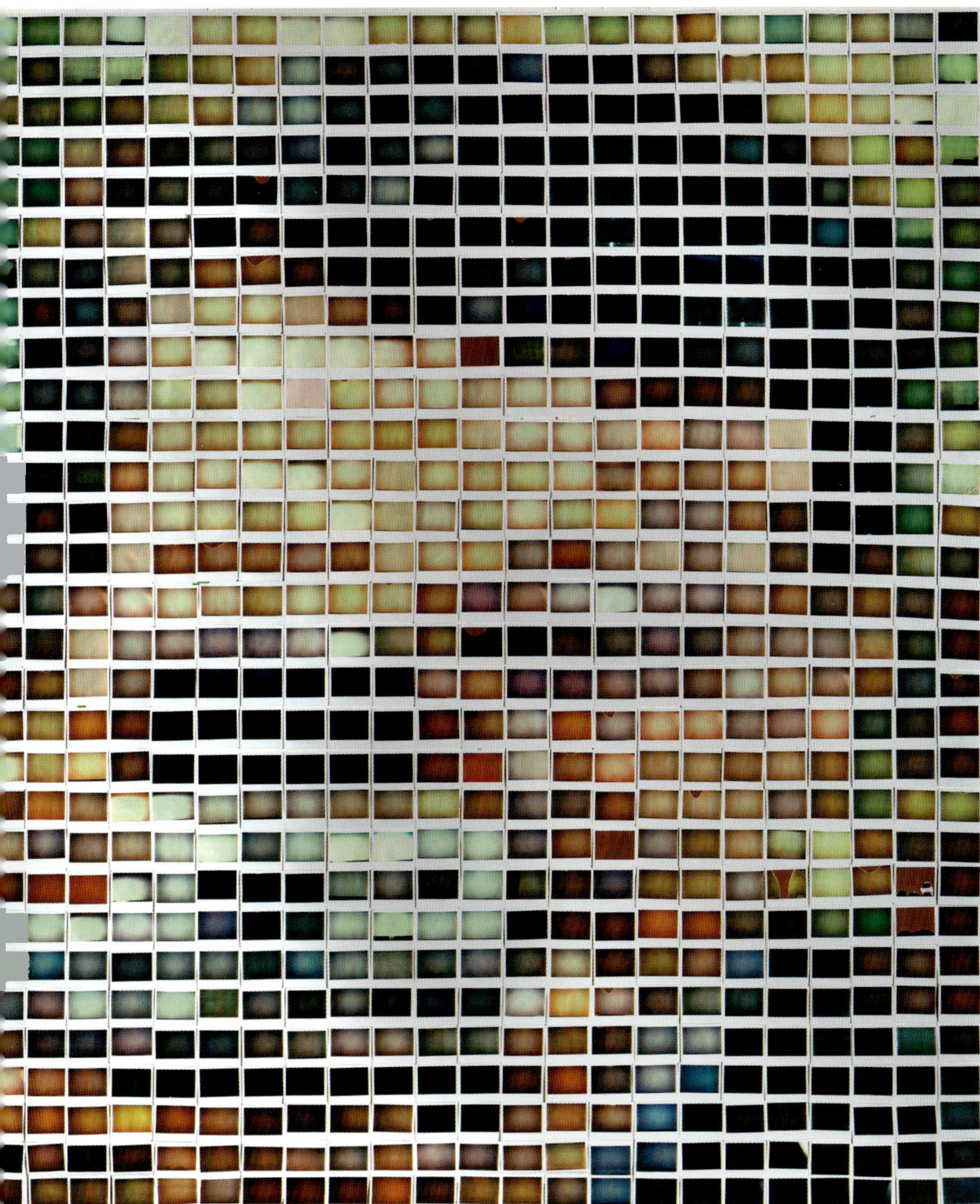

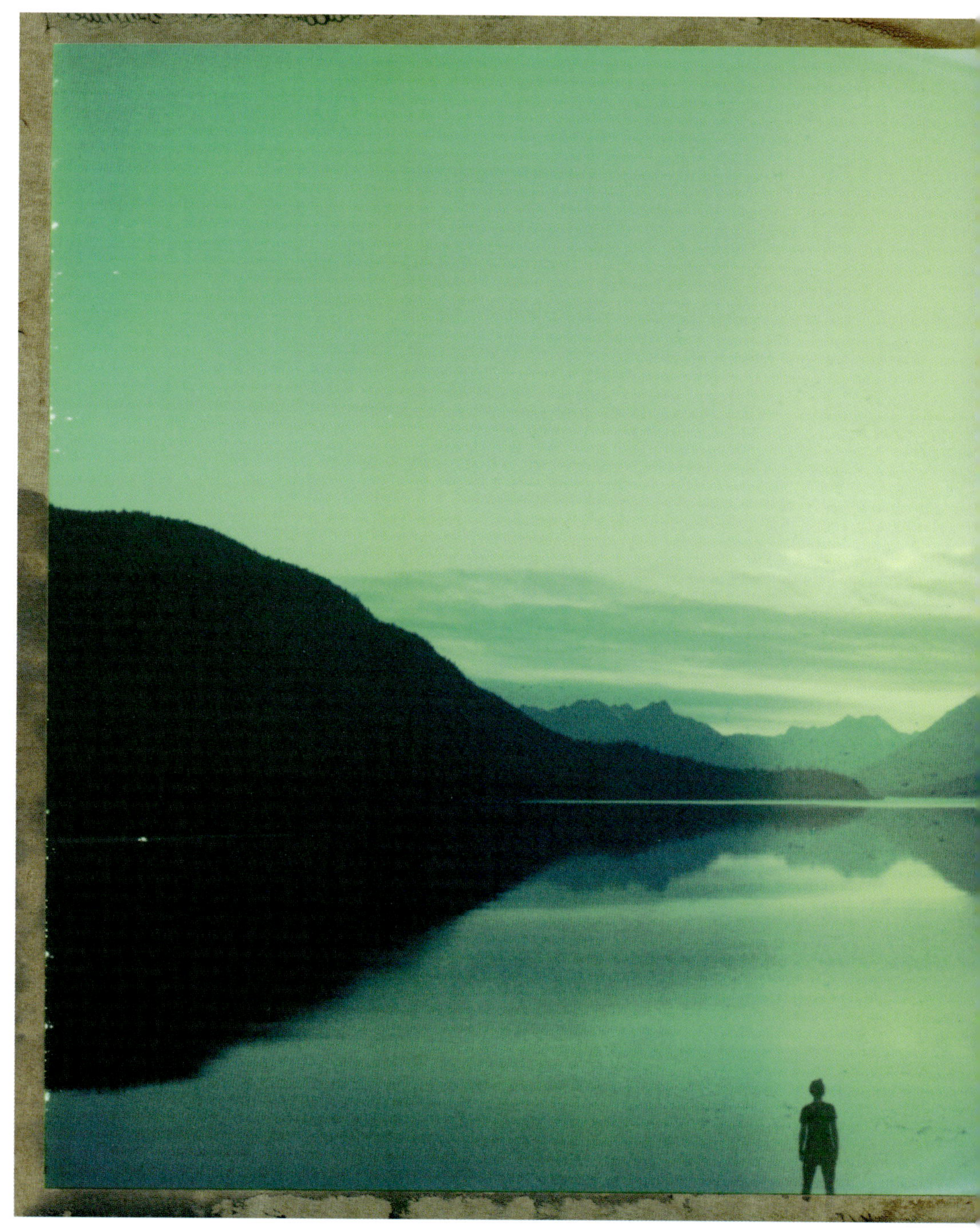

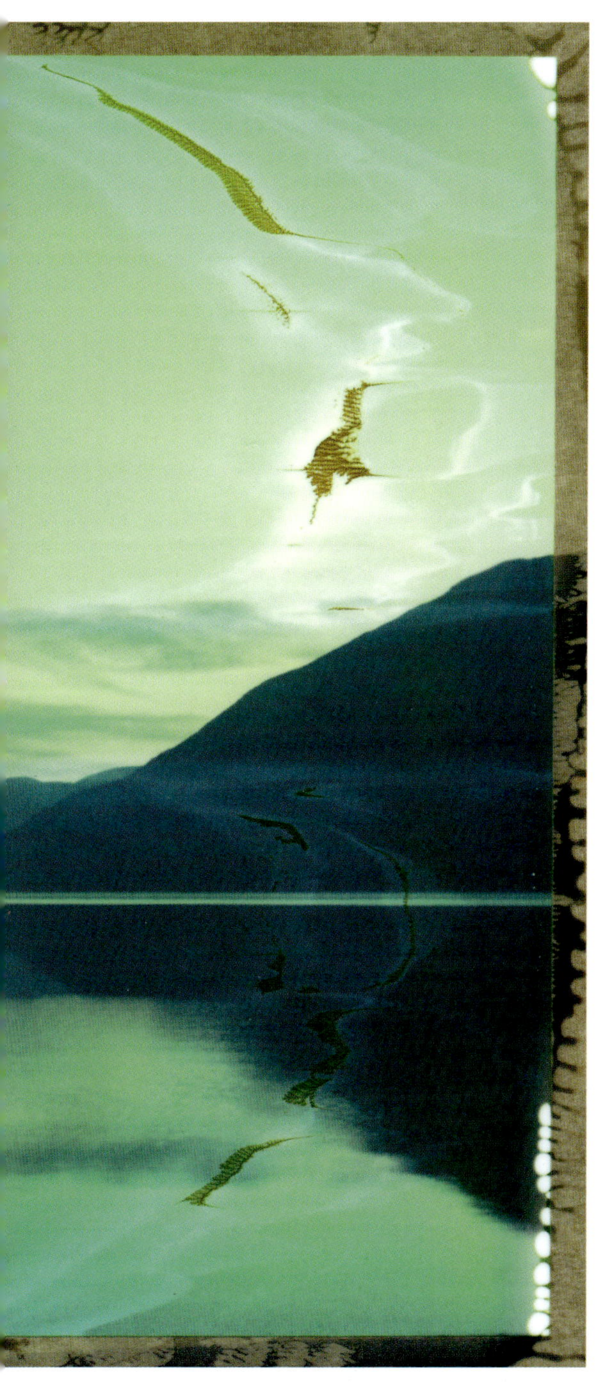

Mikael Bidard, *Untitled* 31

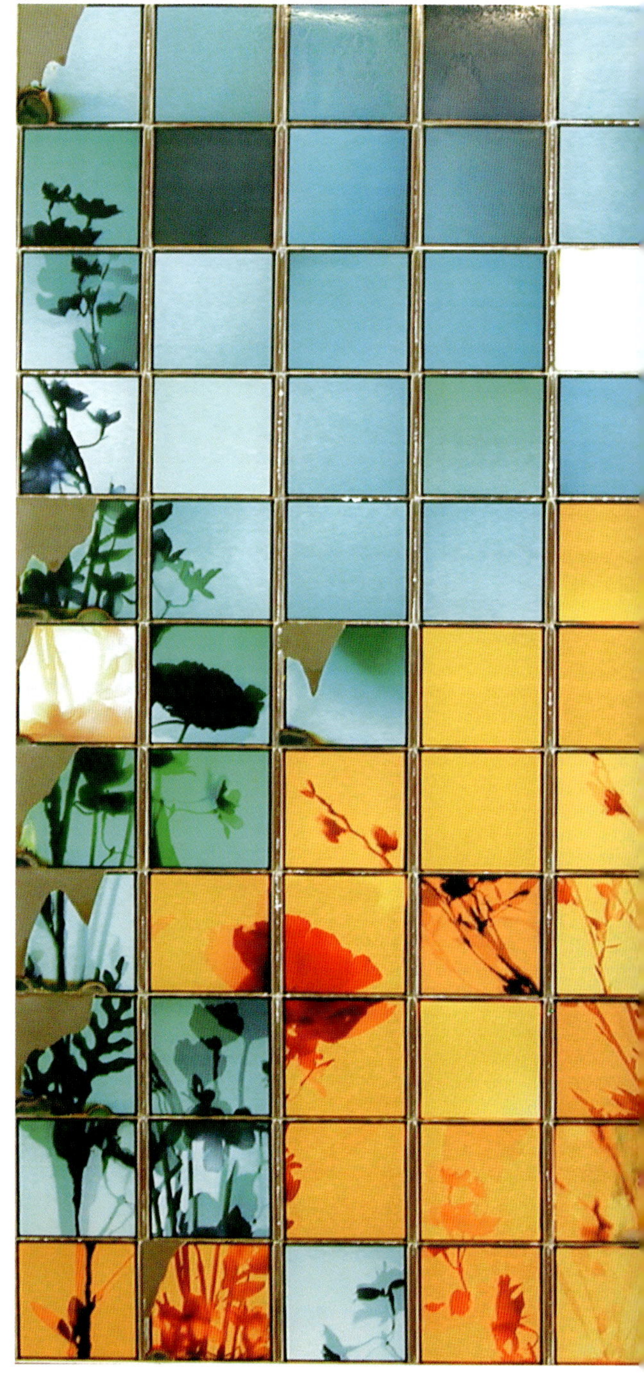

   Patrick Winfield, *Origin 5*

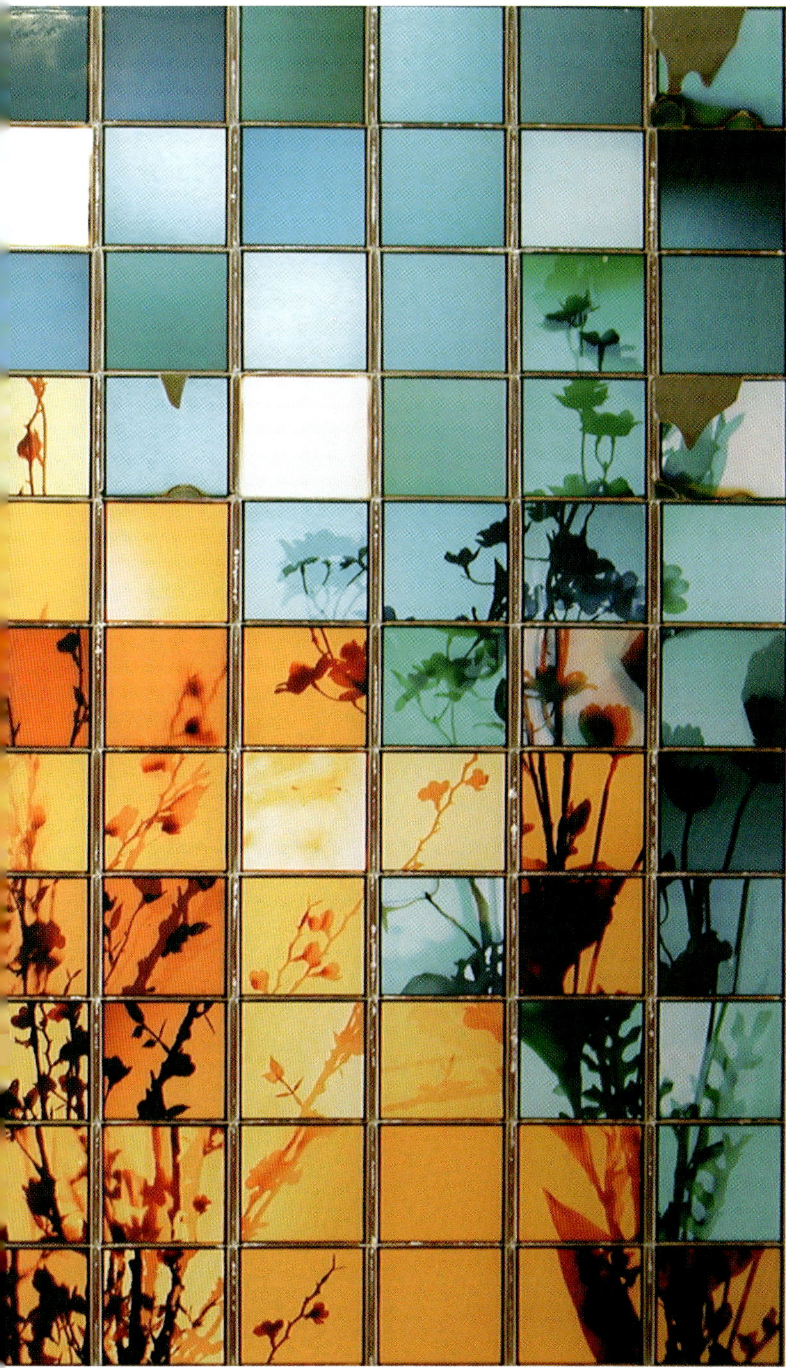

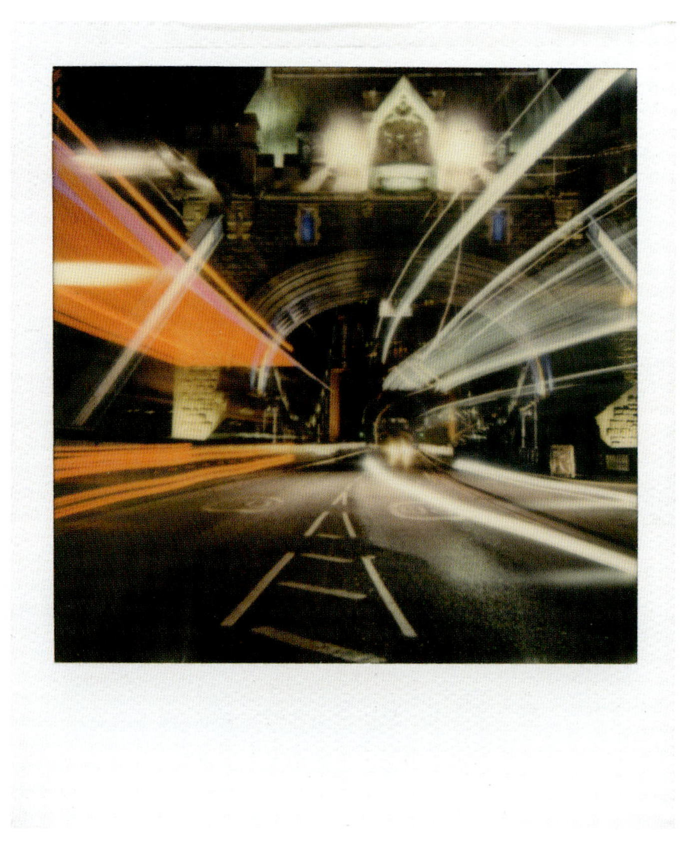

34   Ray Liu, *Lightstreams on Tower Bridge*

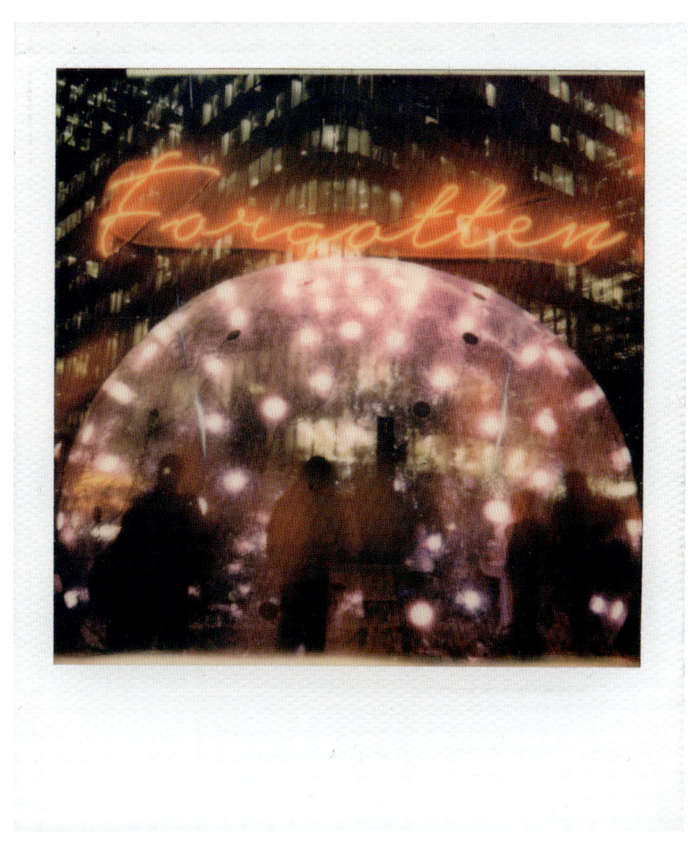

Forgotten

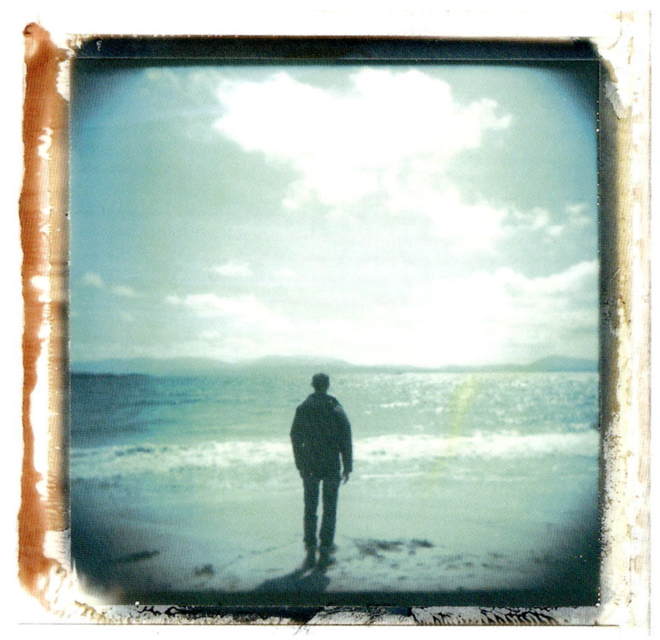

36   Stefano Questorio, *Ocean*

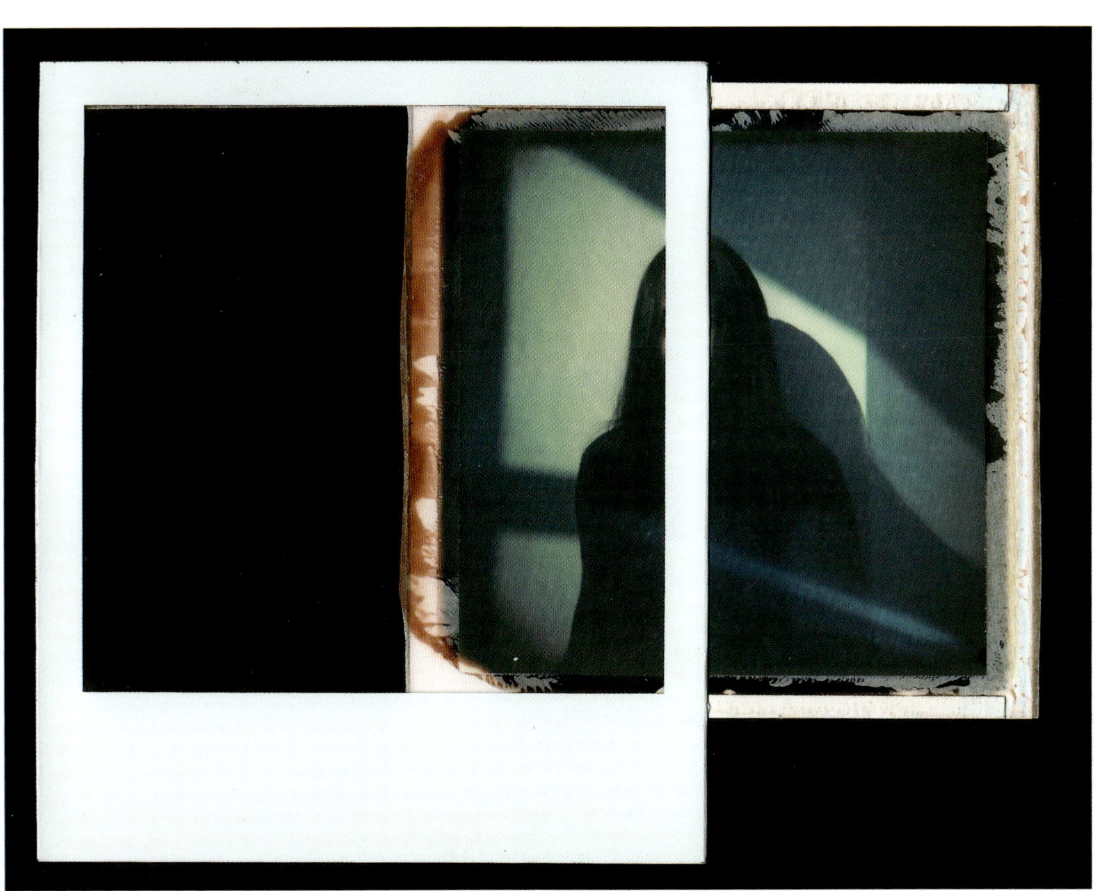

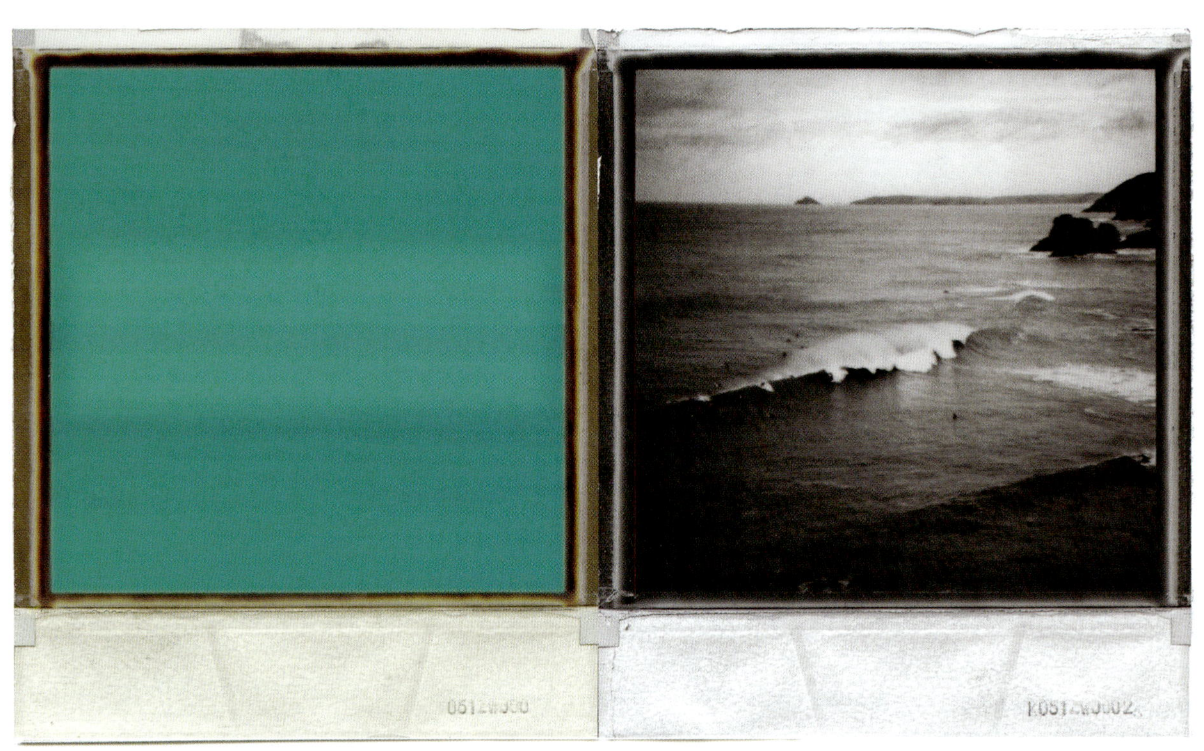

   Robert Reader, *Blue No.1*

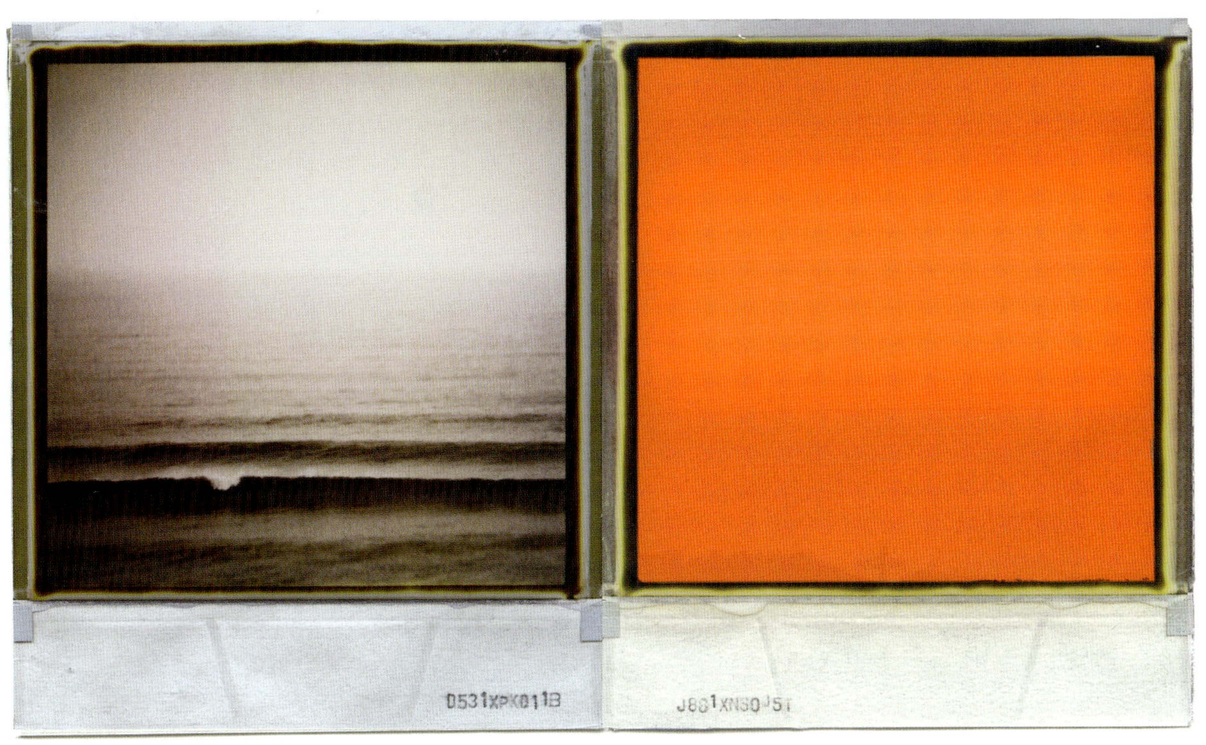

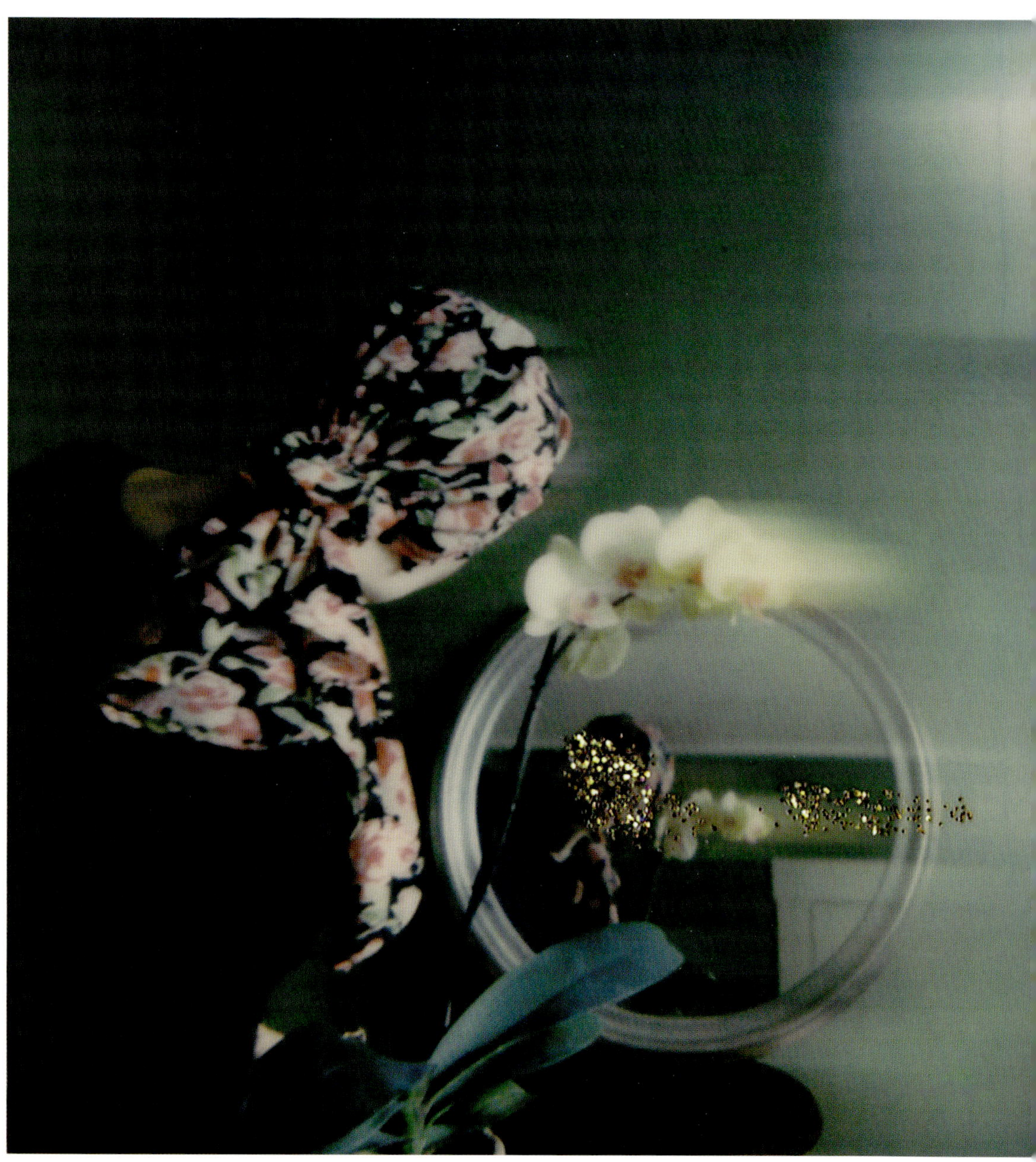

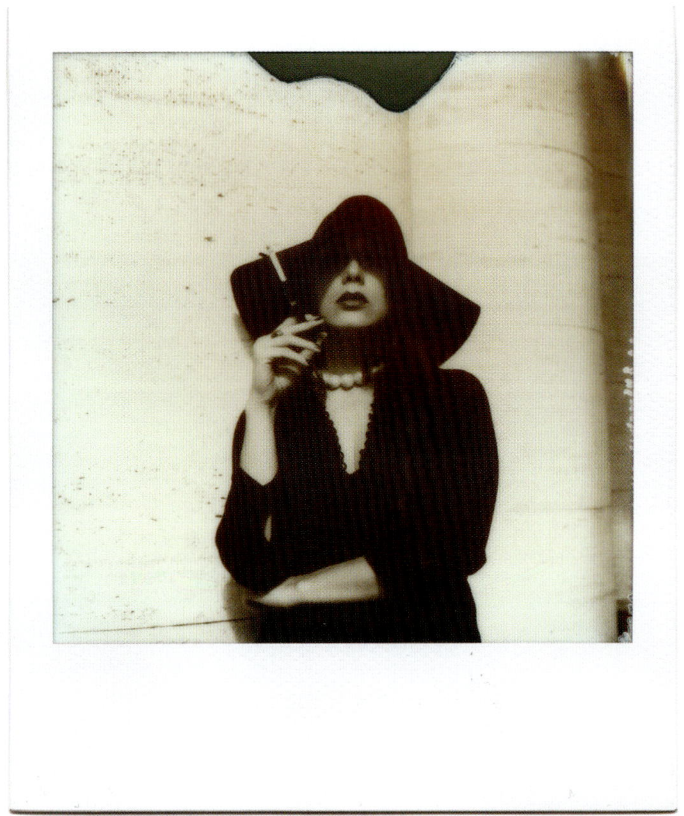

42   Patrizio Cipollini, *Elisa Desoire*

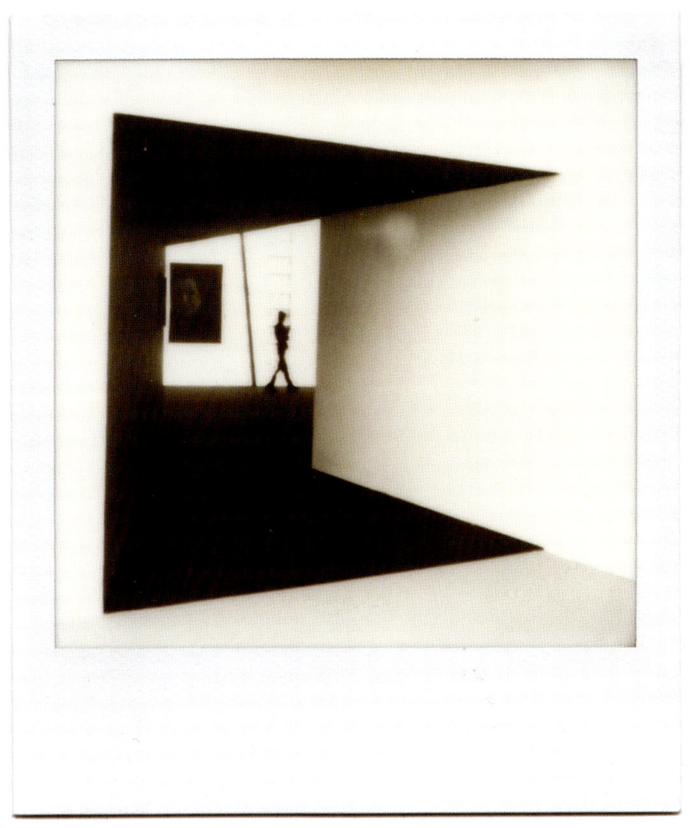

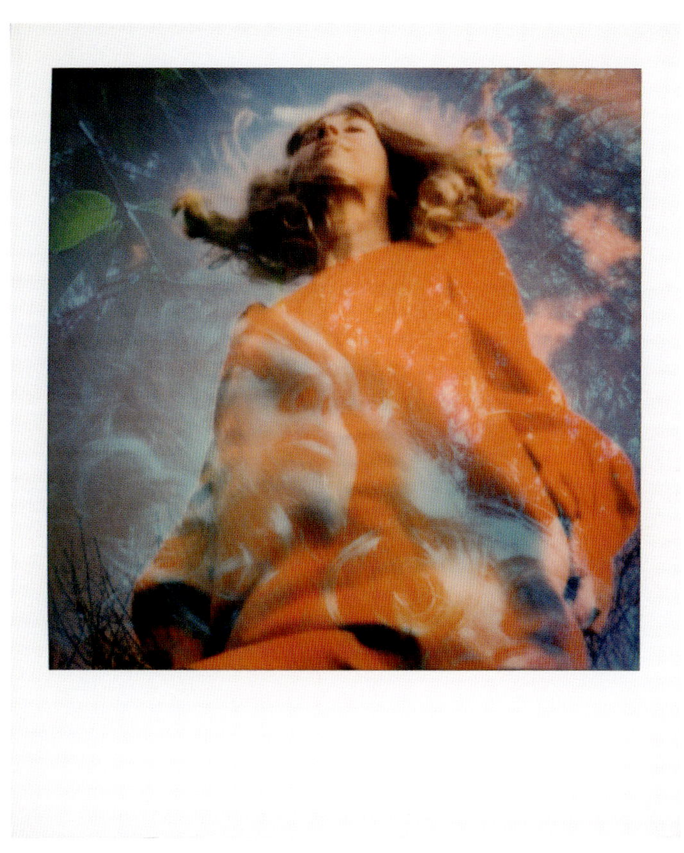

44   Clare Marie Bailey, *Telepath*

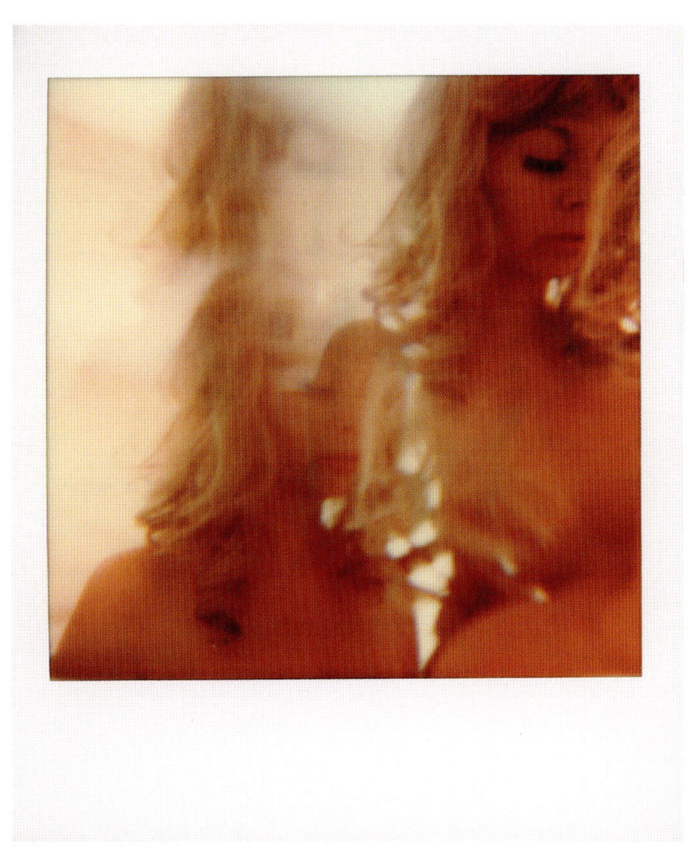

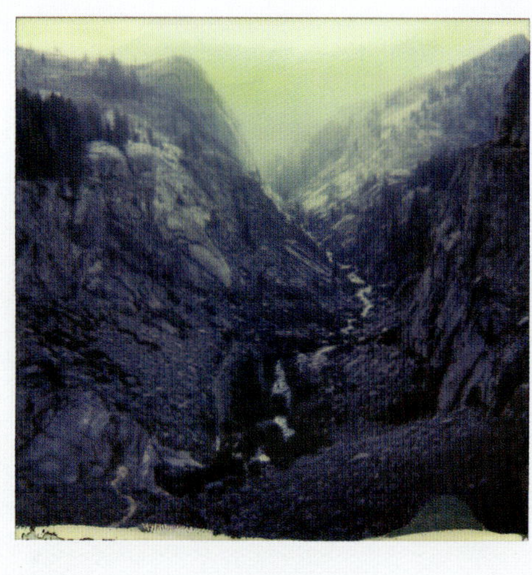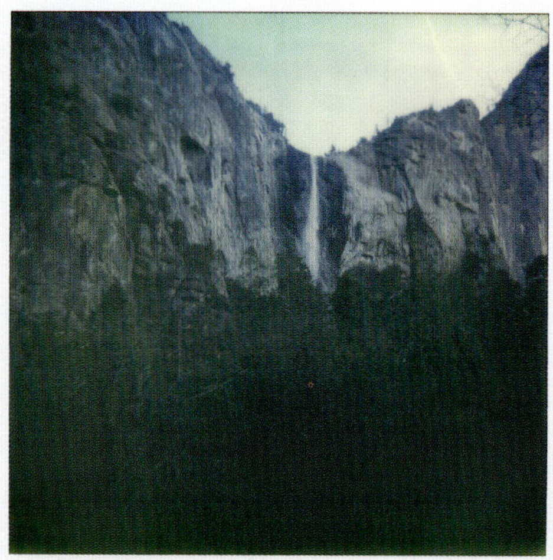

46   Michael Behlen, From the series, *Searching For Stillness Volume II*

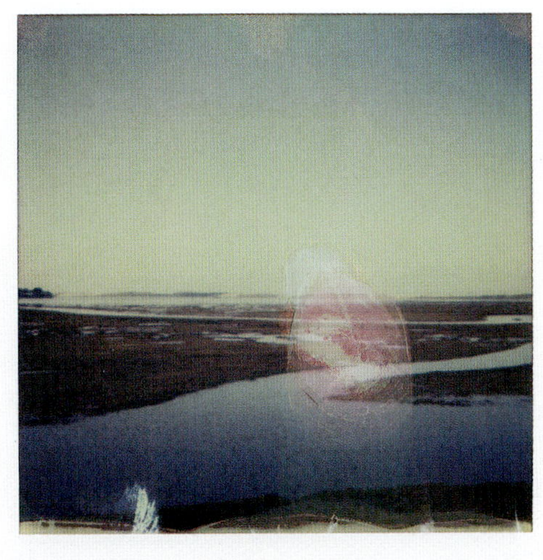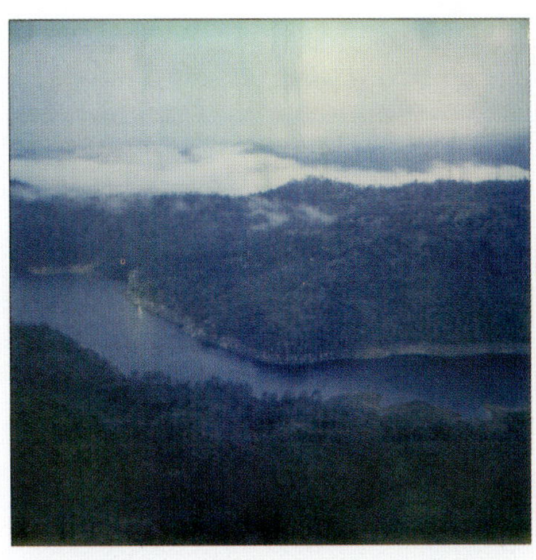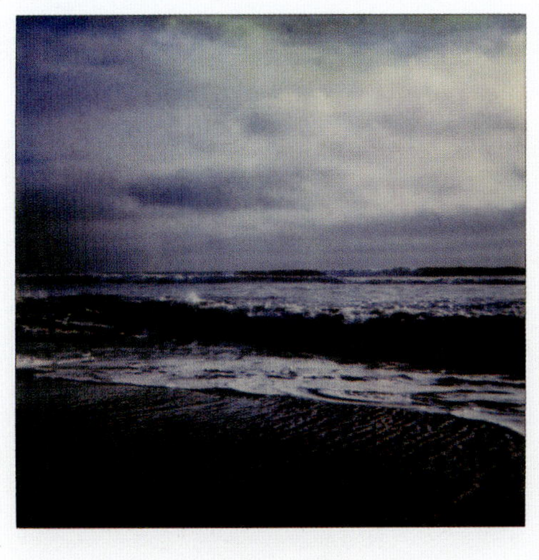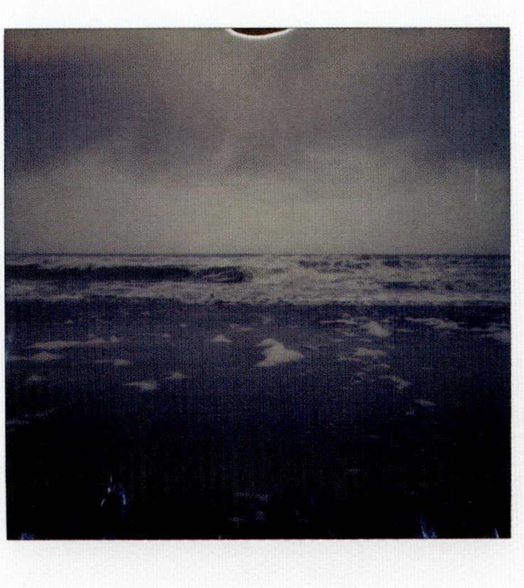

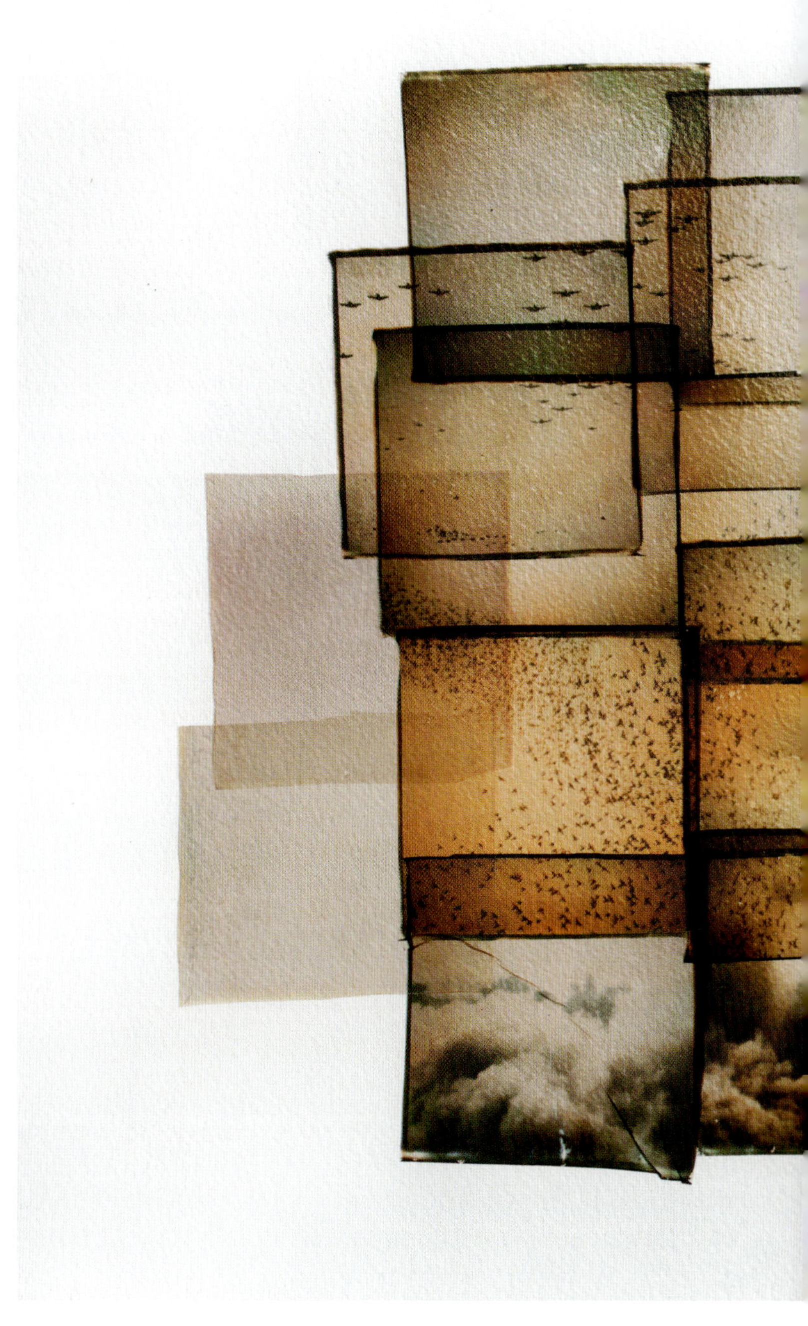

    Rhiannon Adam, *Migration*

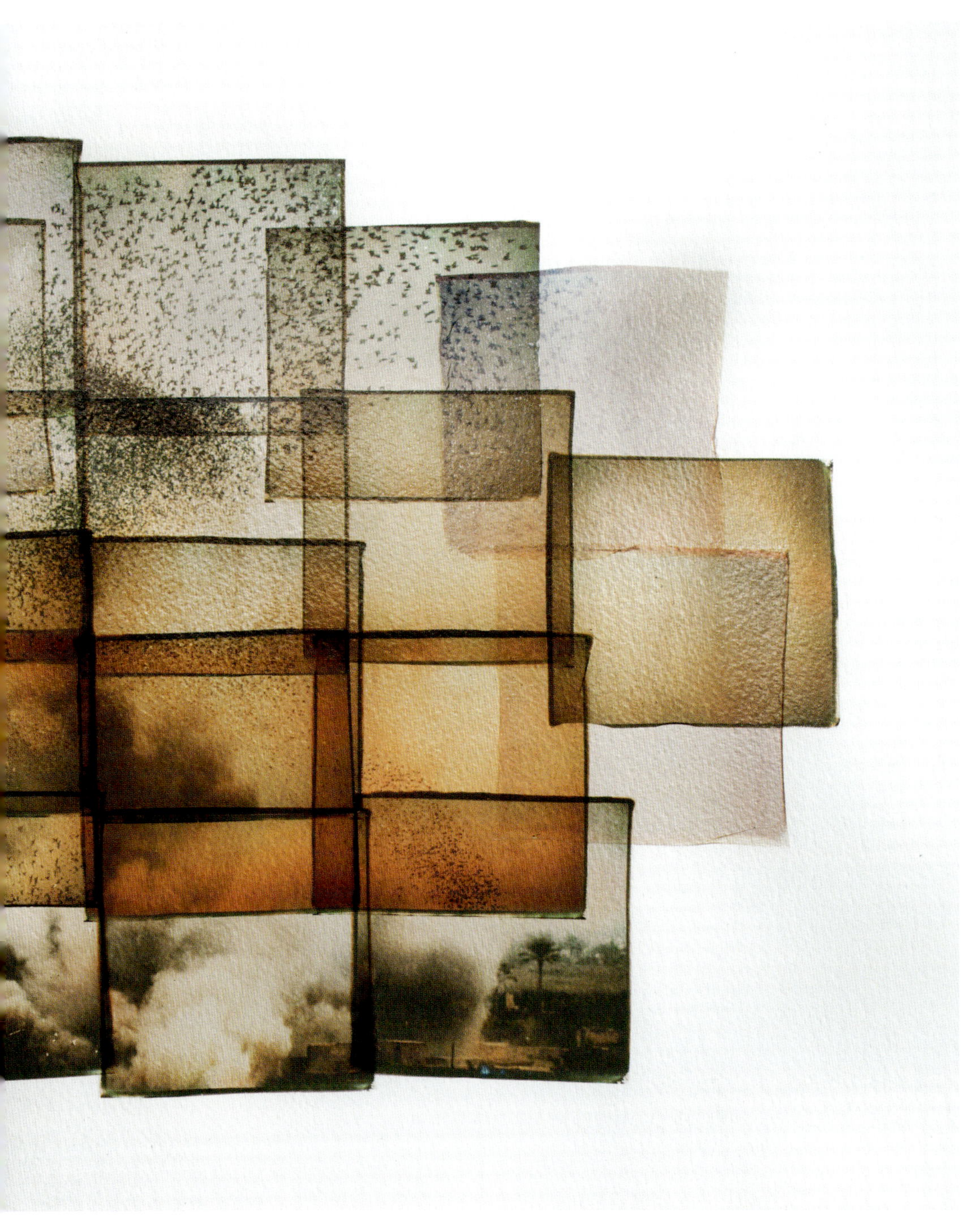

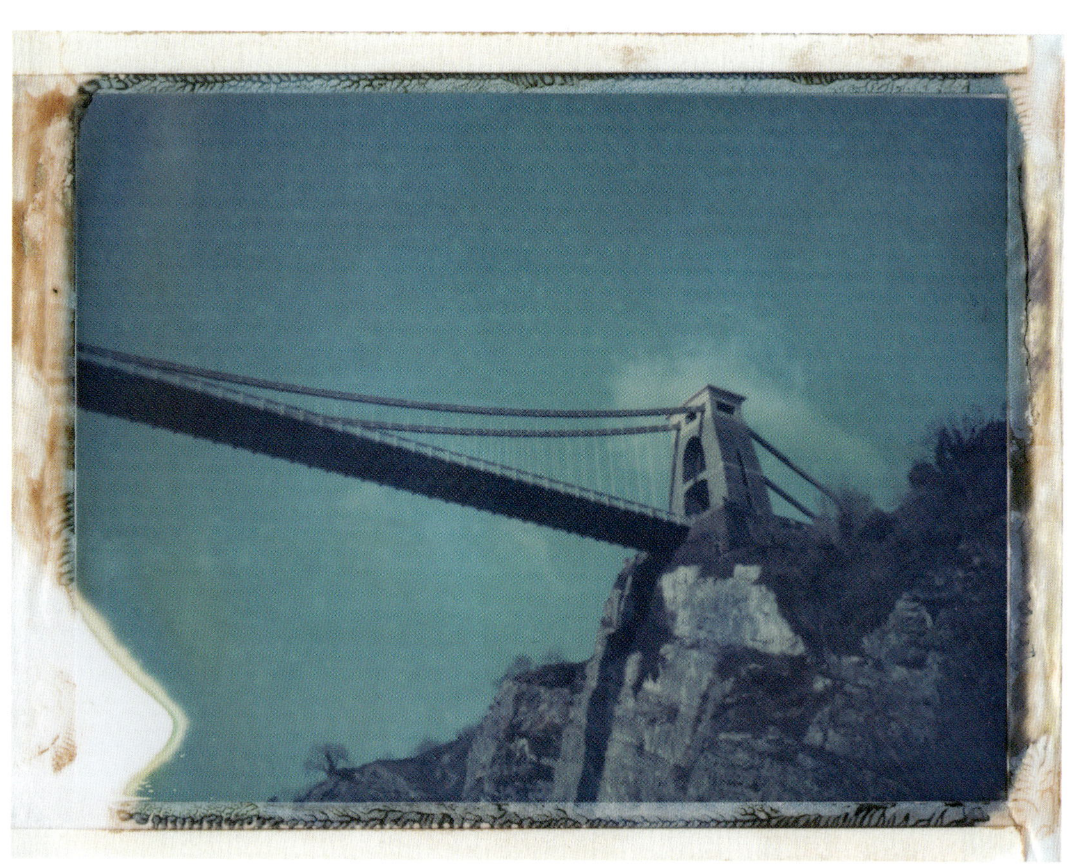

50   Adam Bell, *Untitled*

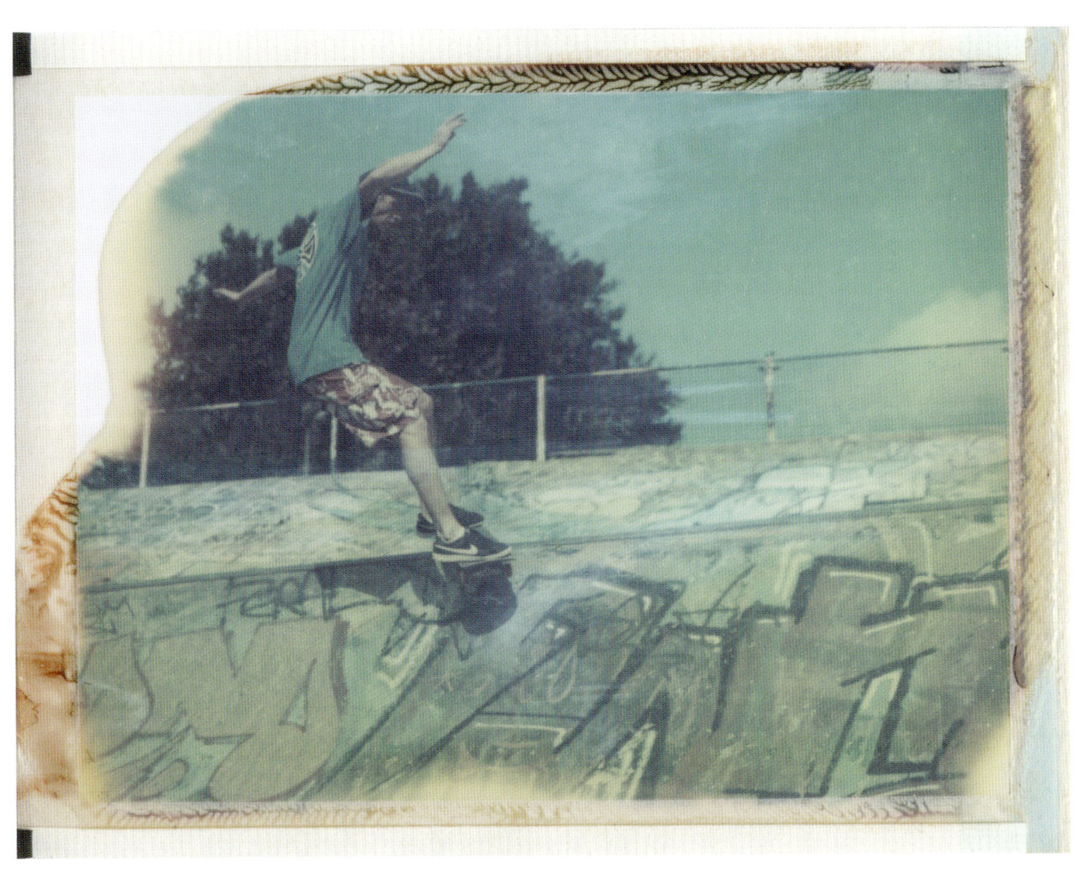

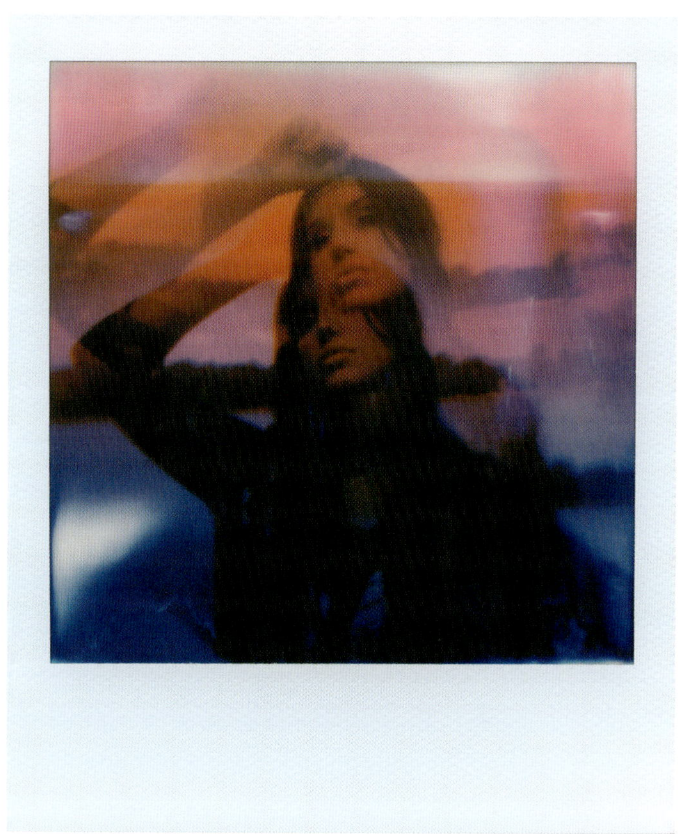

52   Julia Beyer, *Weekend Haze (Sister of the Moon)*

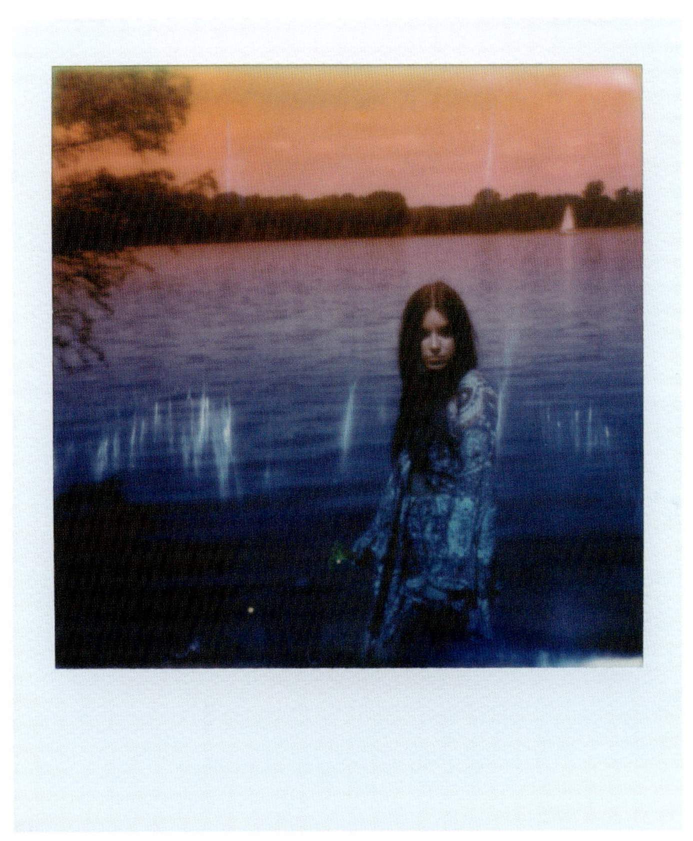

Julia Beyer, *Remember Me (Sister of the Moon)*   53

    Patrick Winfield, *Origin 14*

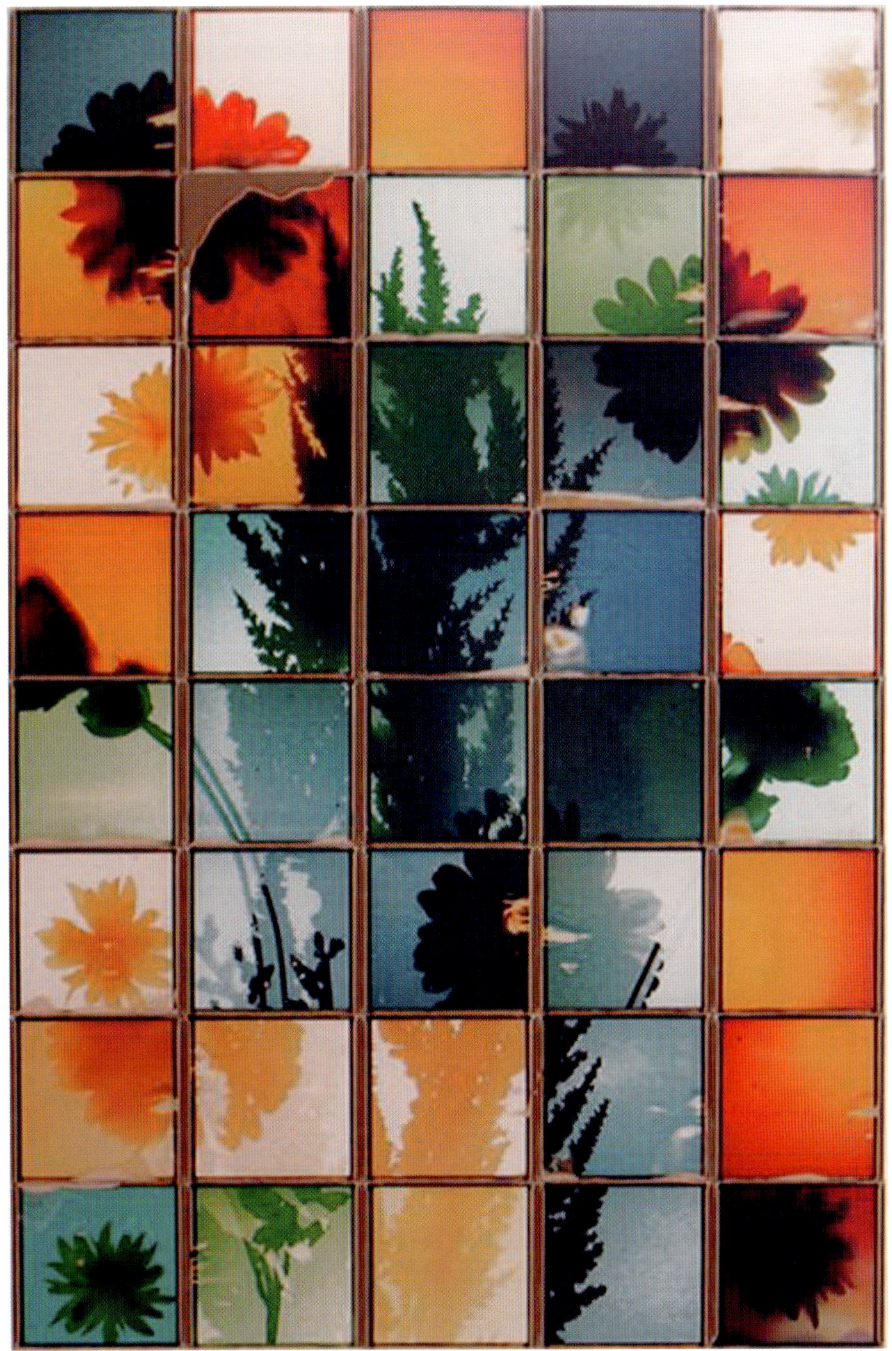

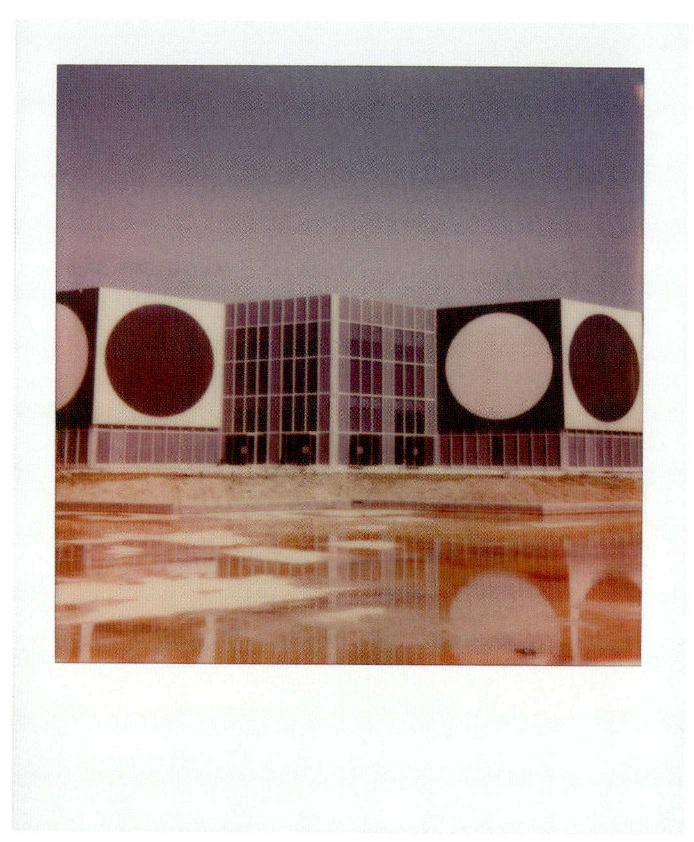

56   Andrea Angelino Catella, *Untitled*

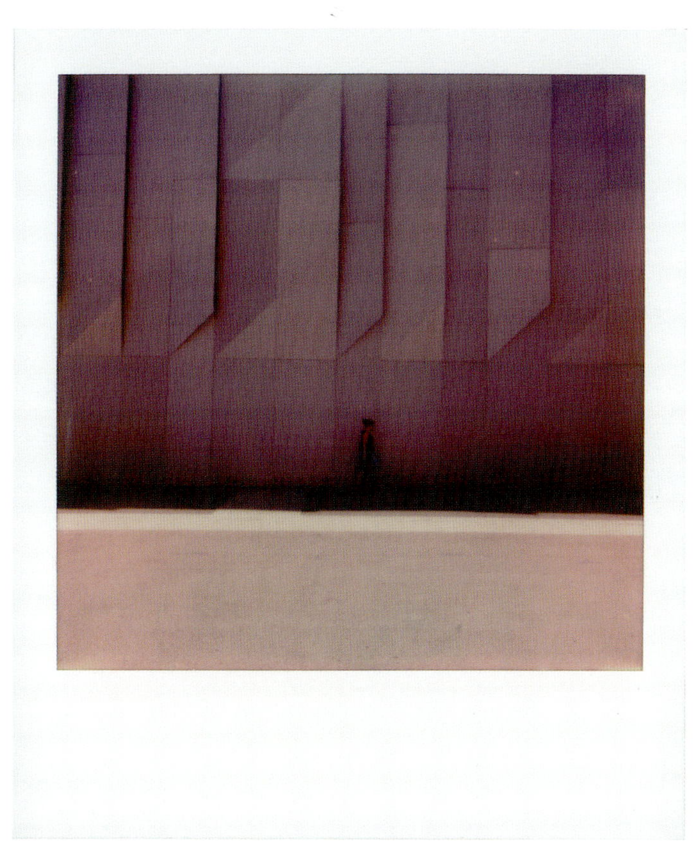

   Philippe Bourgoin, *Untitled*

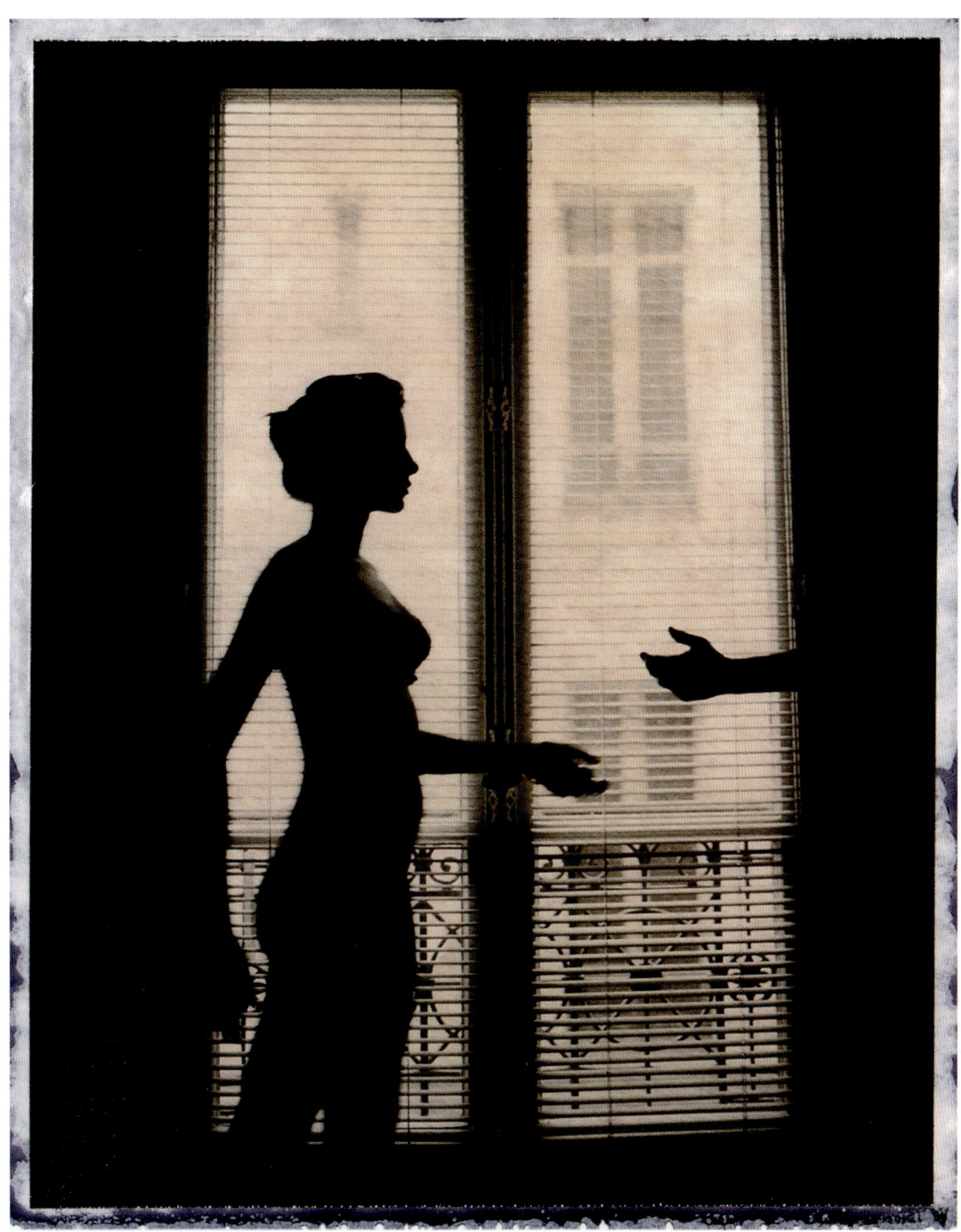

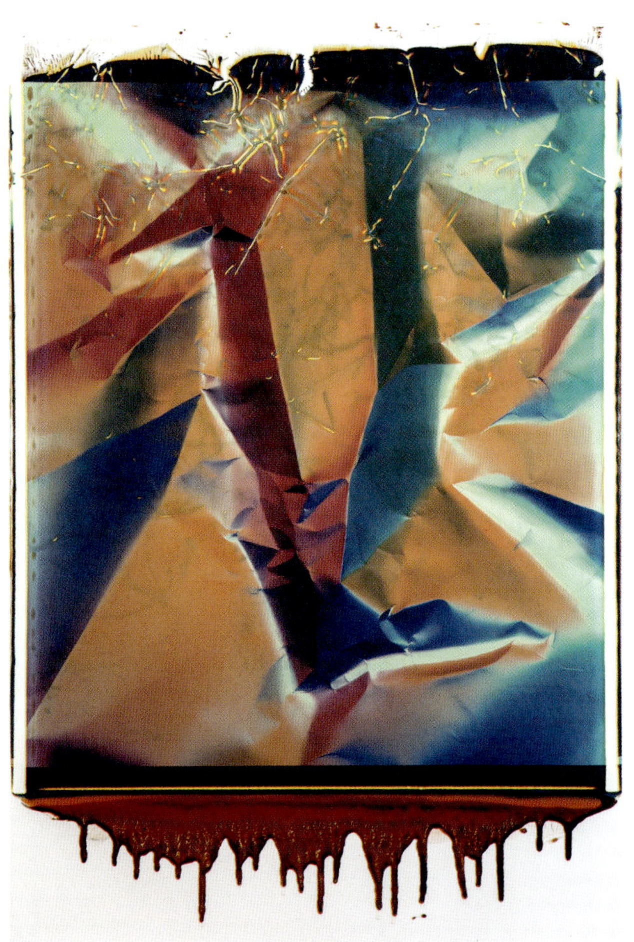

    Ellen Carey, *Crush & Ding*

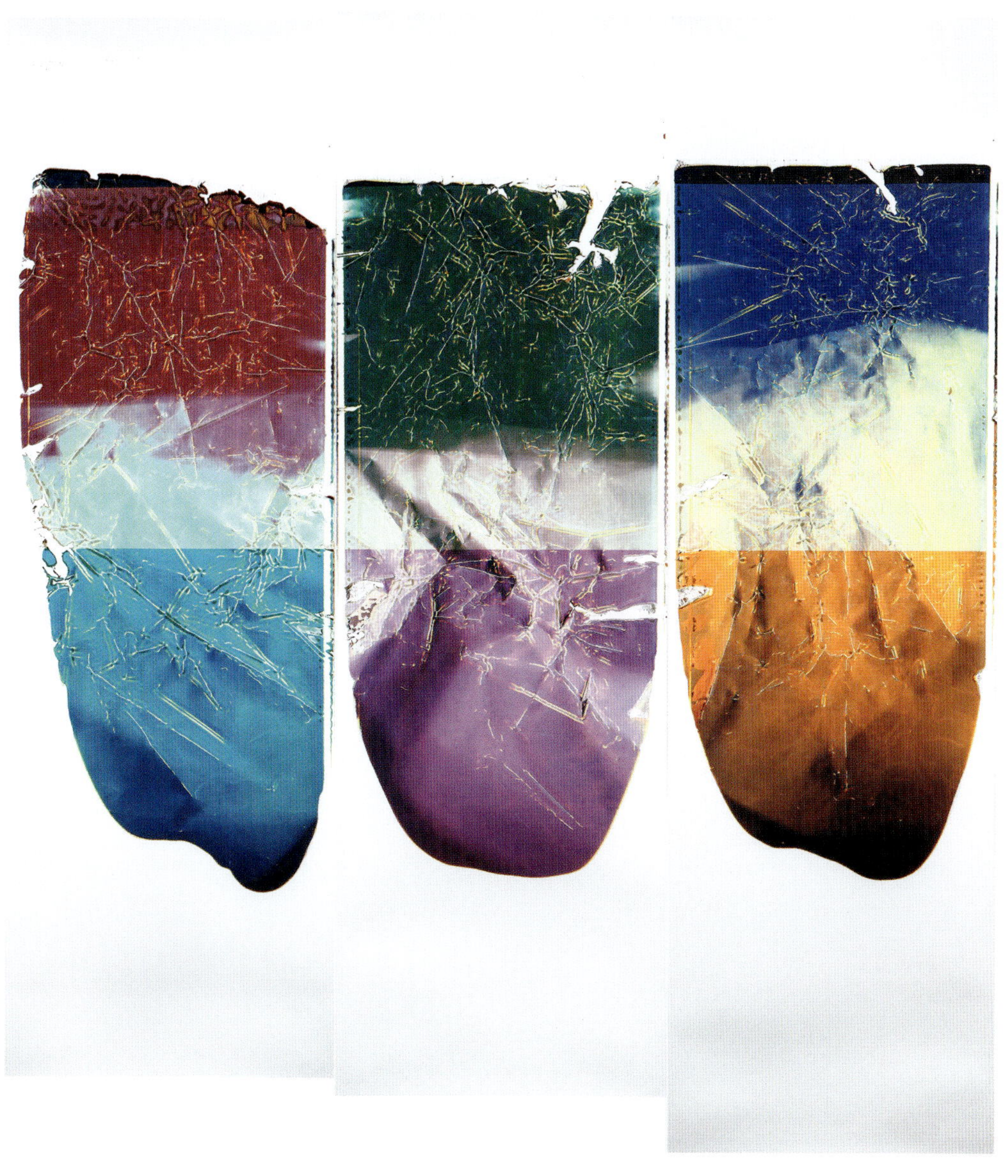

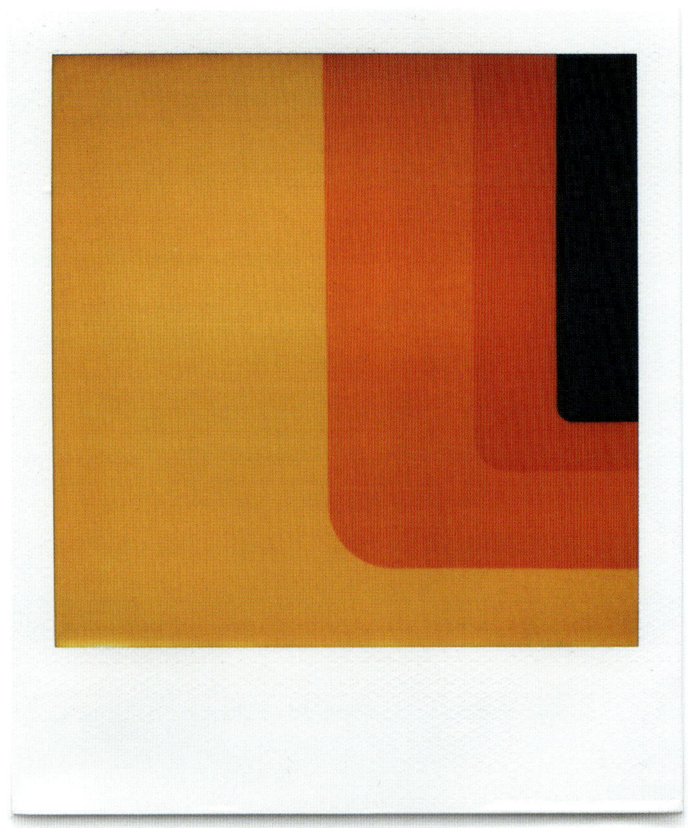

  Grant Hamilton, *Have a Nice Day*

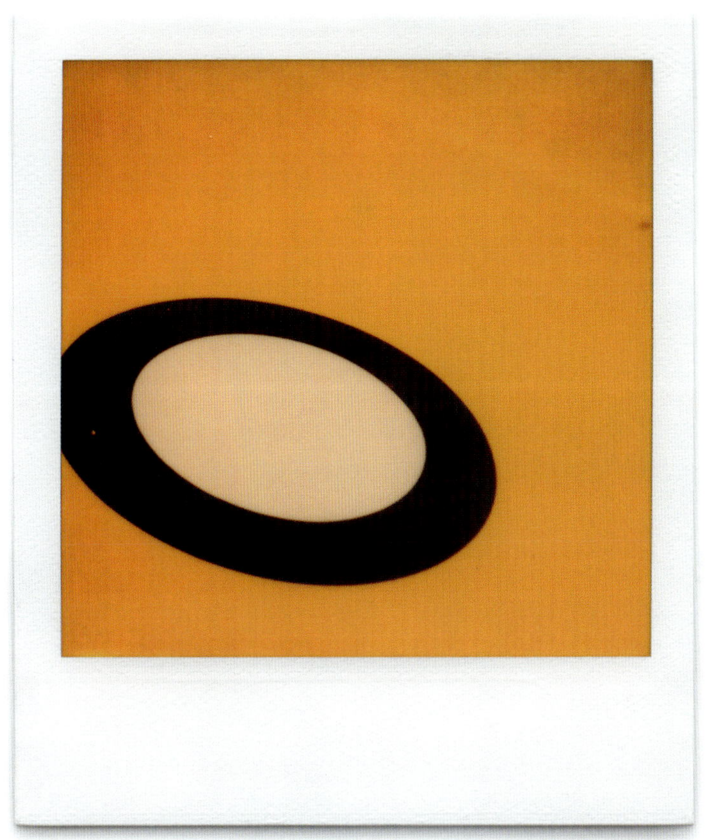

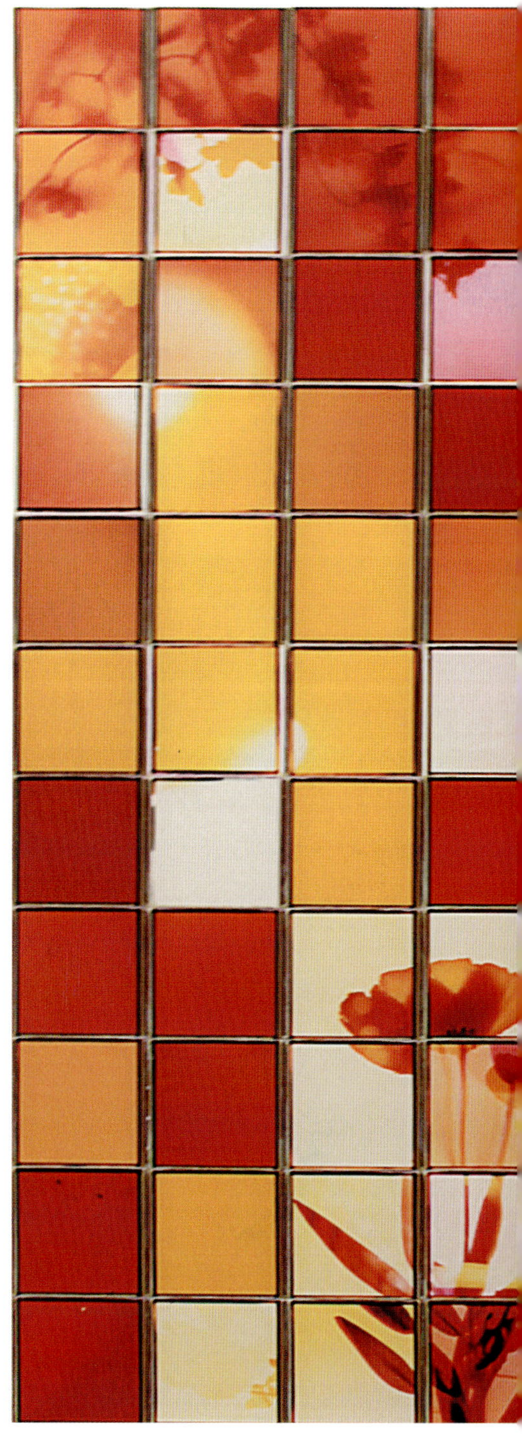

   Patrick Winfield, *Sleep*

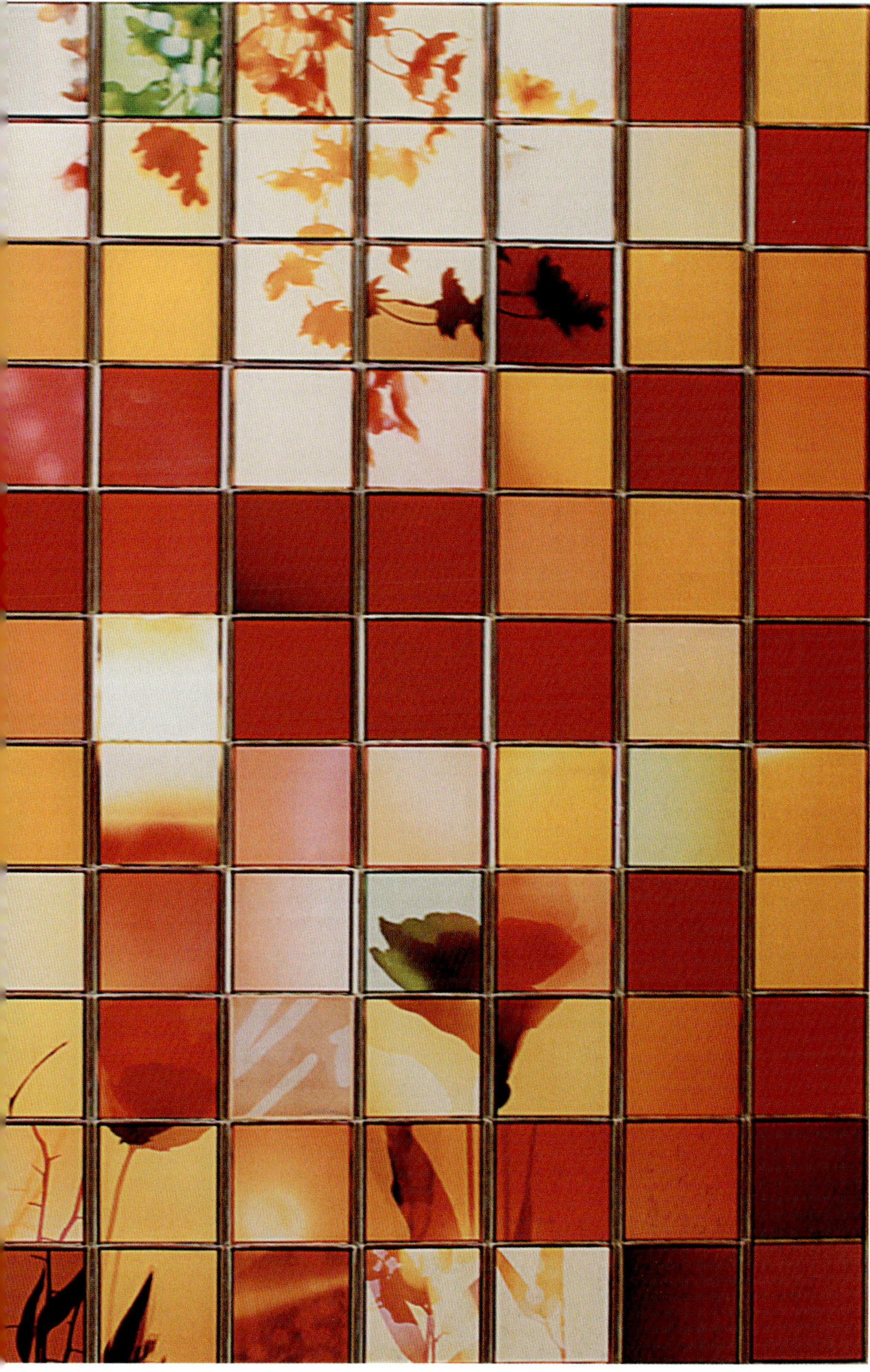

    Julie Cockburn, *Bonsai*

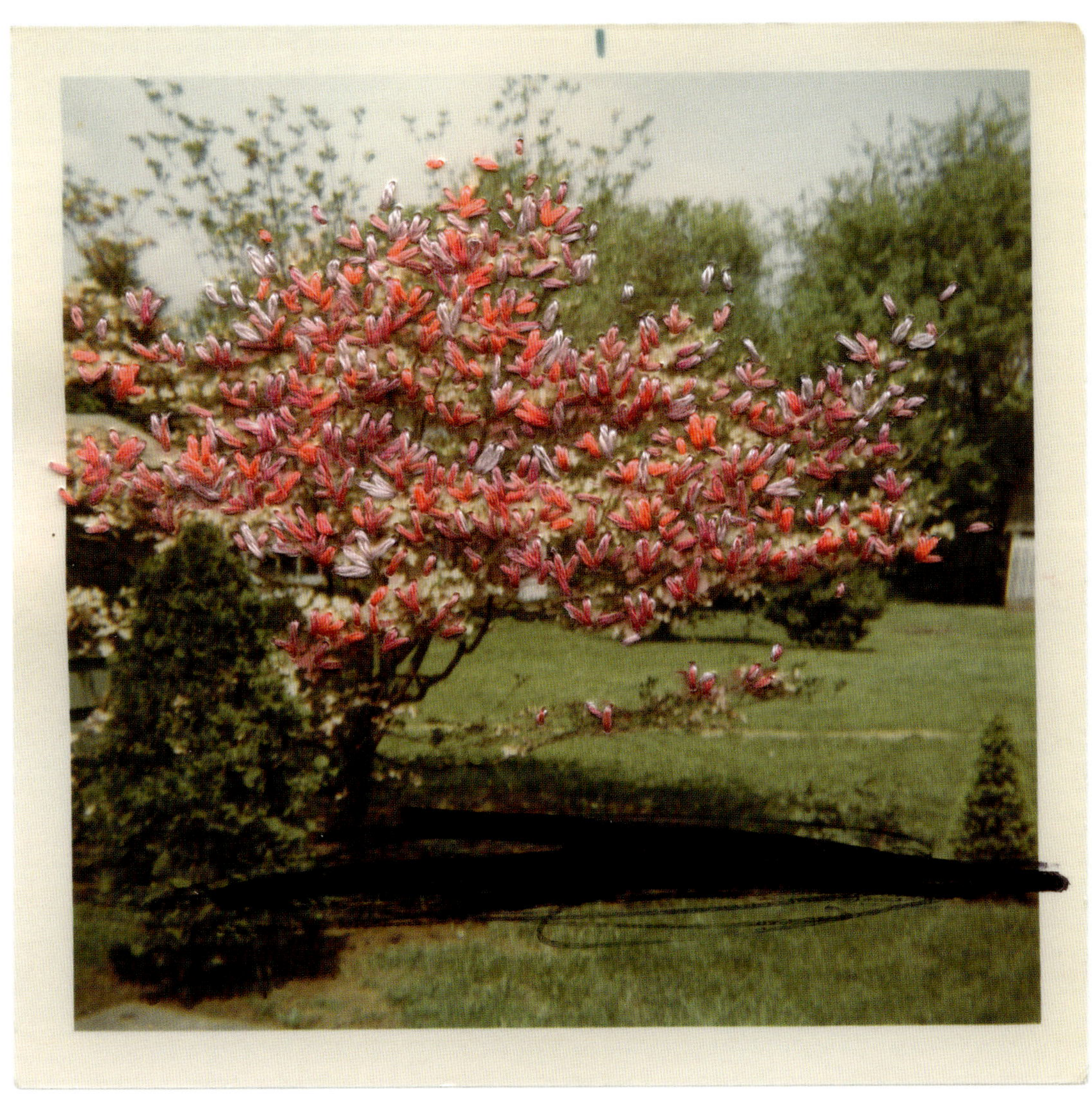

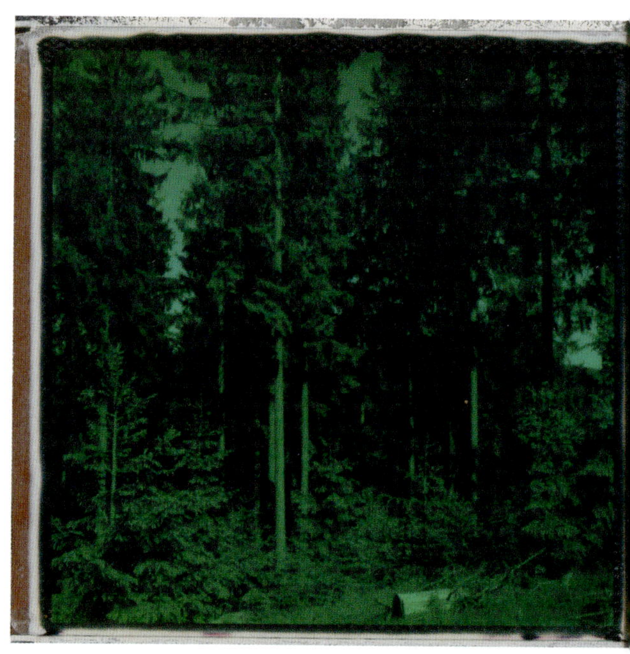

68   Ina Echternach, *The Ants Love The Trunk*, *On The Way To The Summit*, *Green Color of Hope*

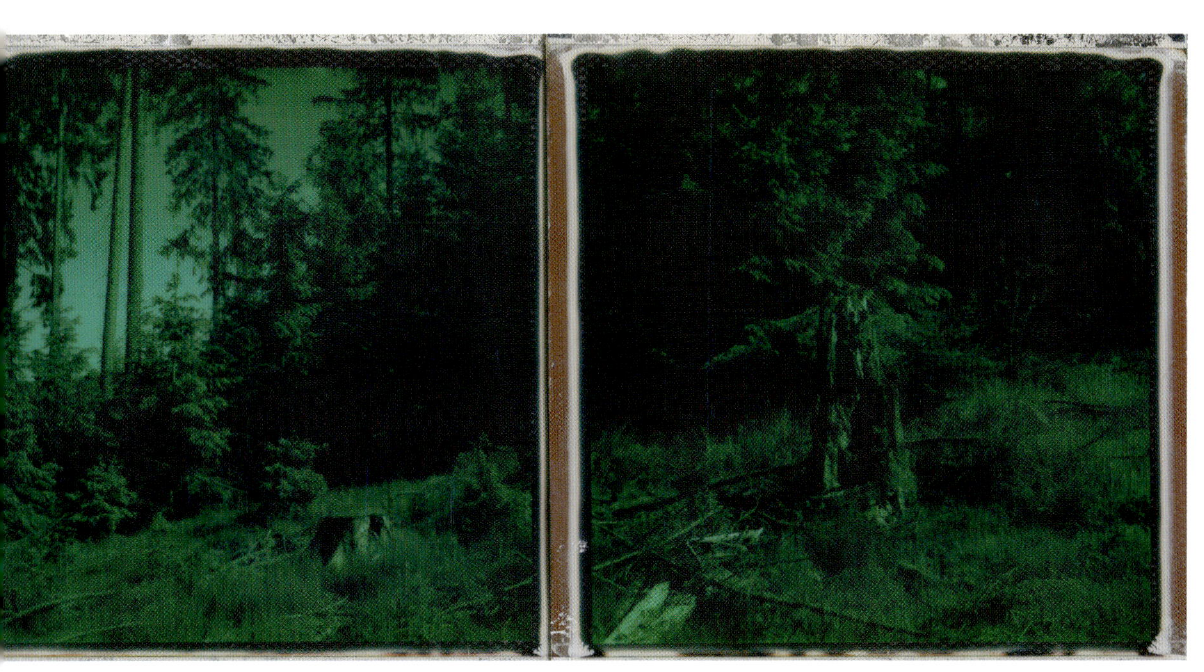

    Ruth Storey, *Sometimes when you look at me it's more than I can stand. I'm not good enough for you to look at me like that*

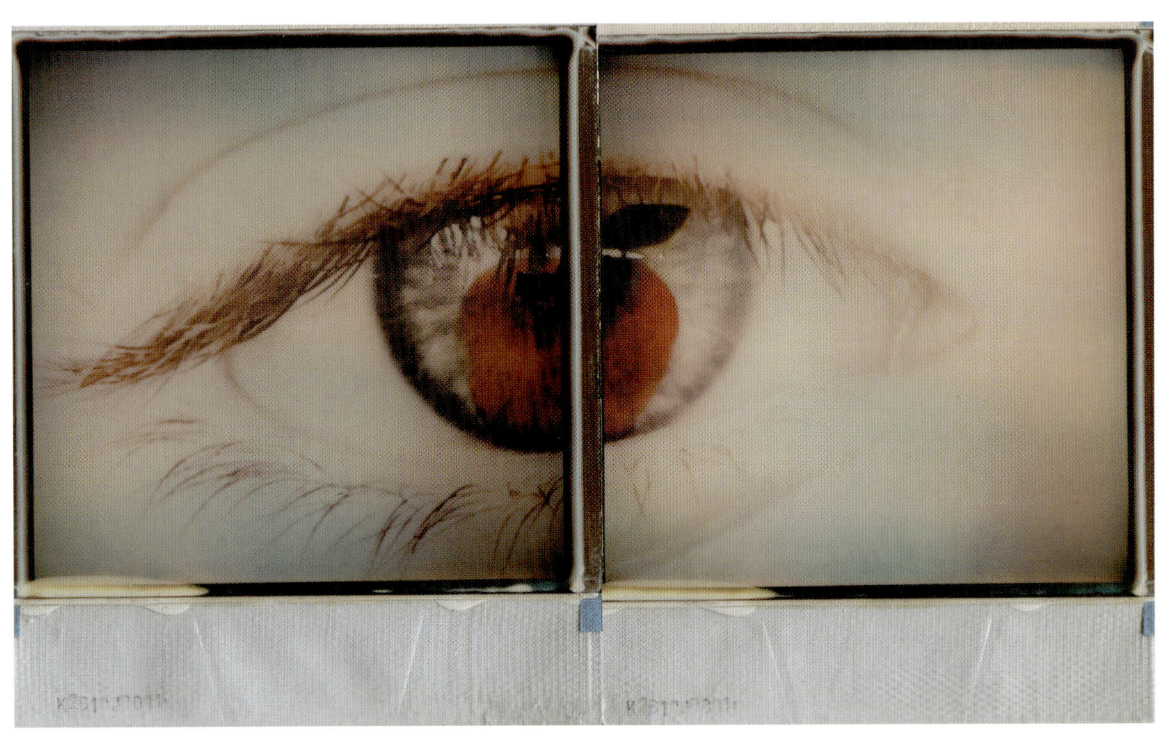

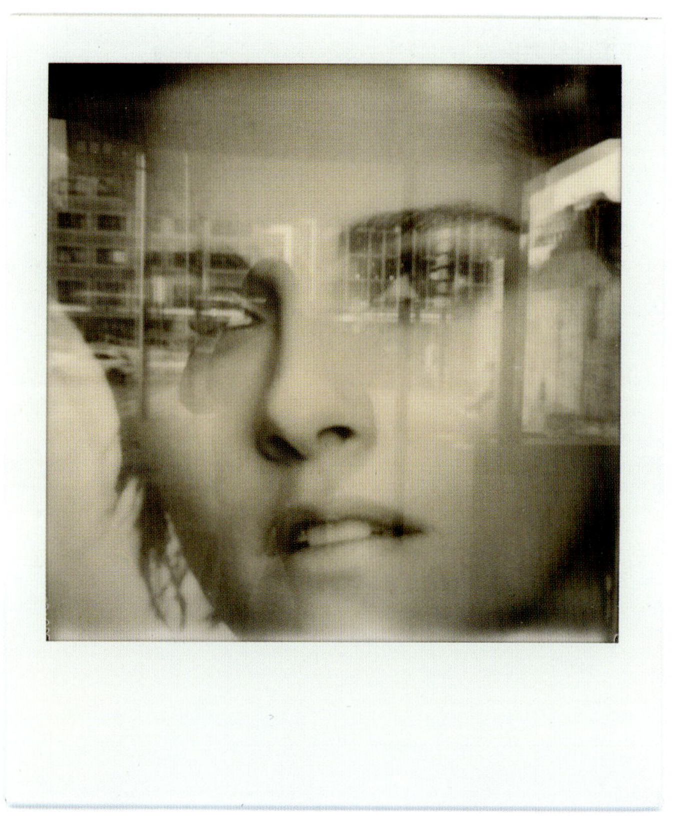

 Andreas Haenni, *Urban Portrait*

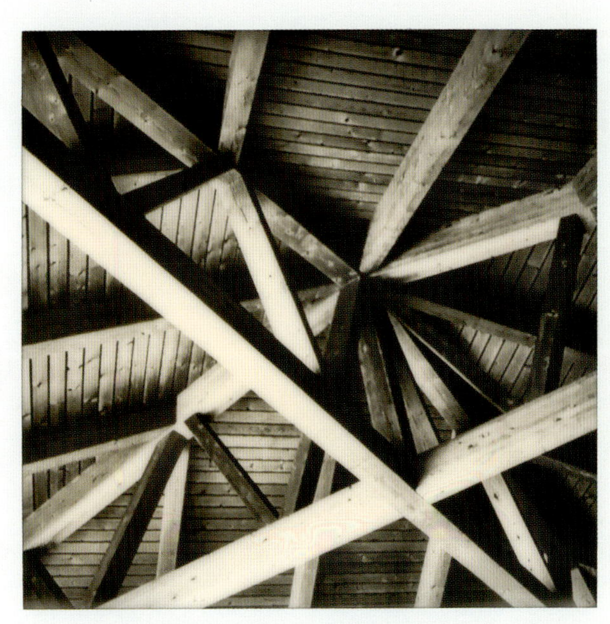

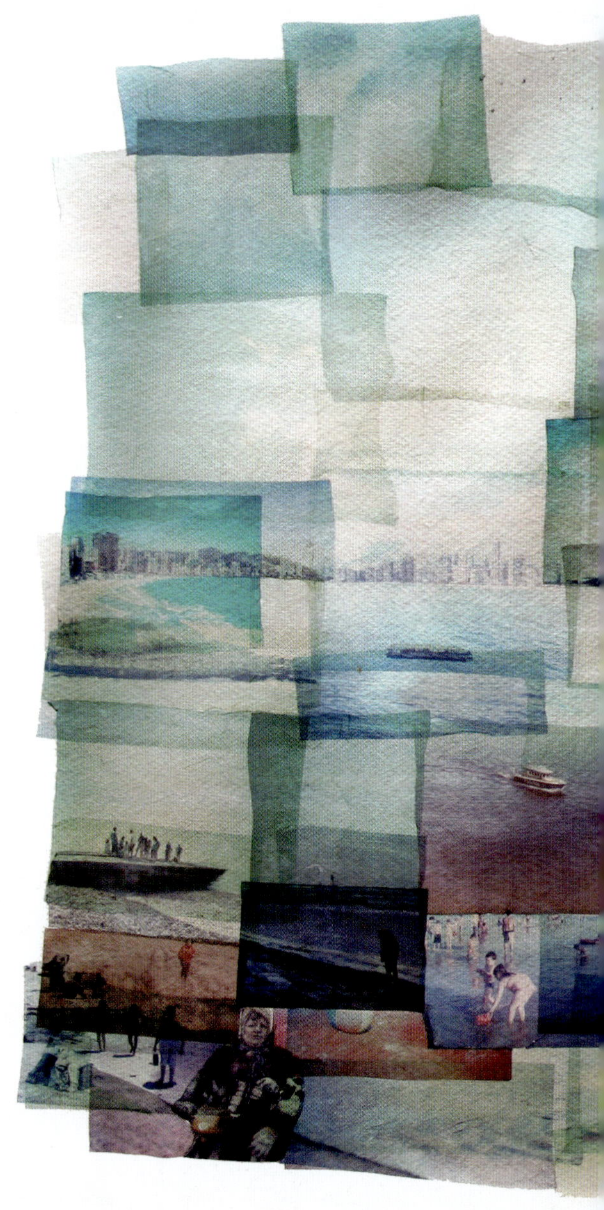

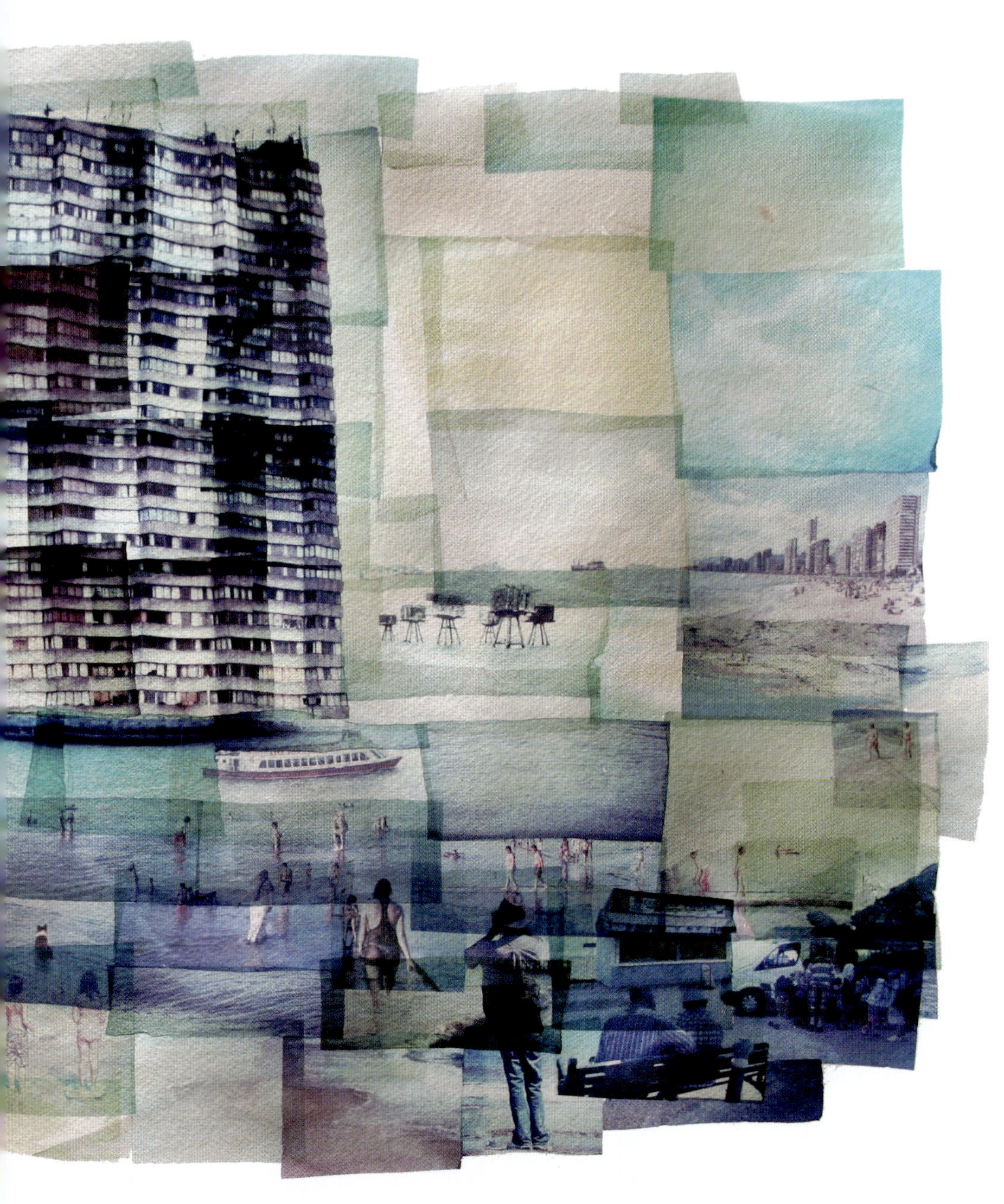

    Heather Polley, *Self Portrait (Eye)*

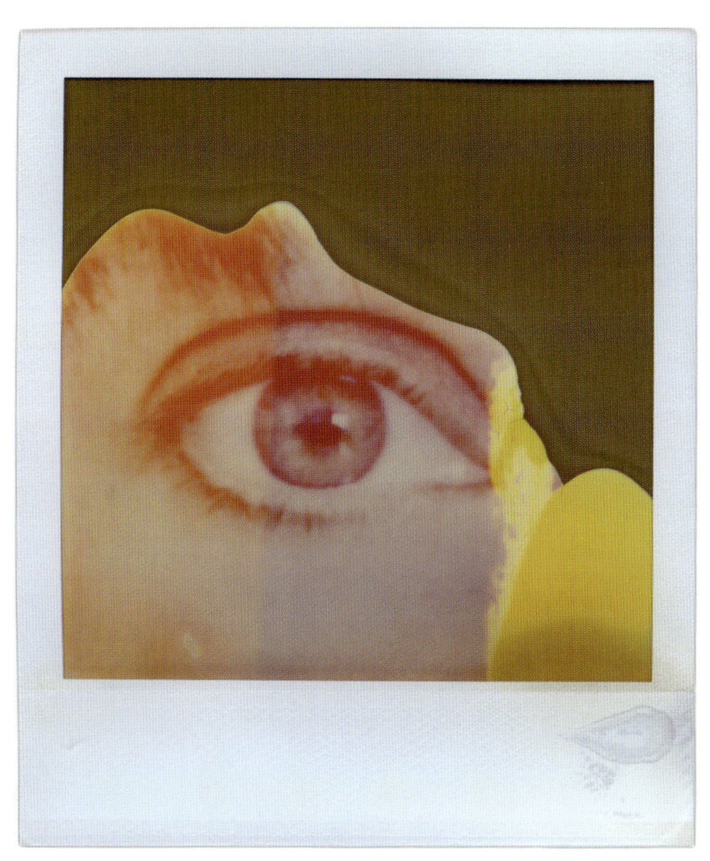

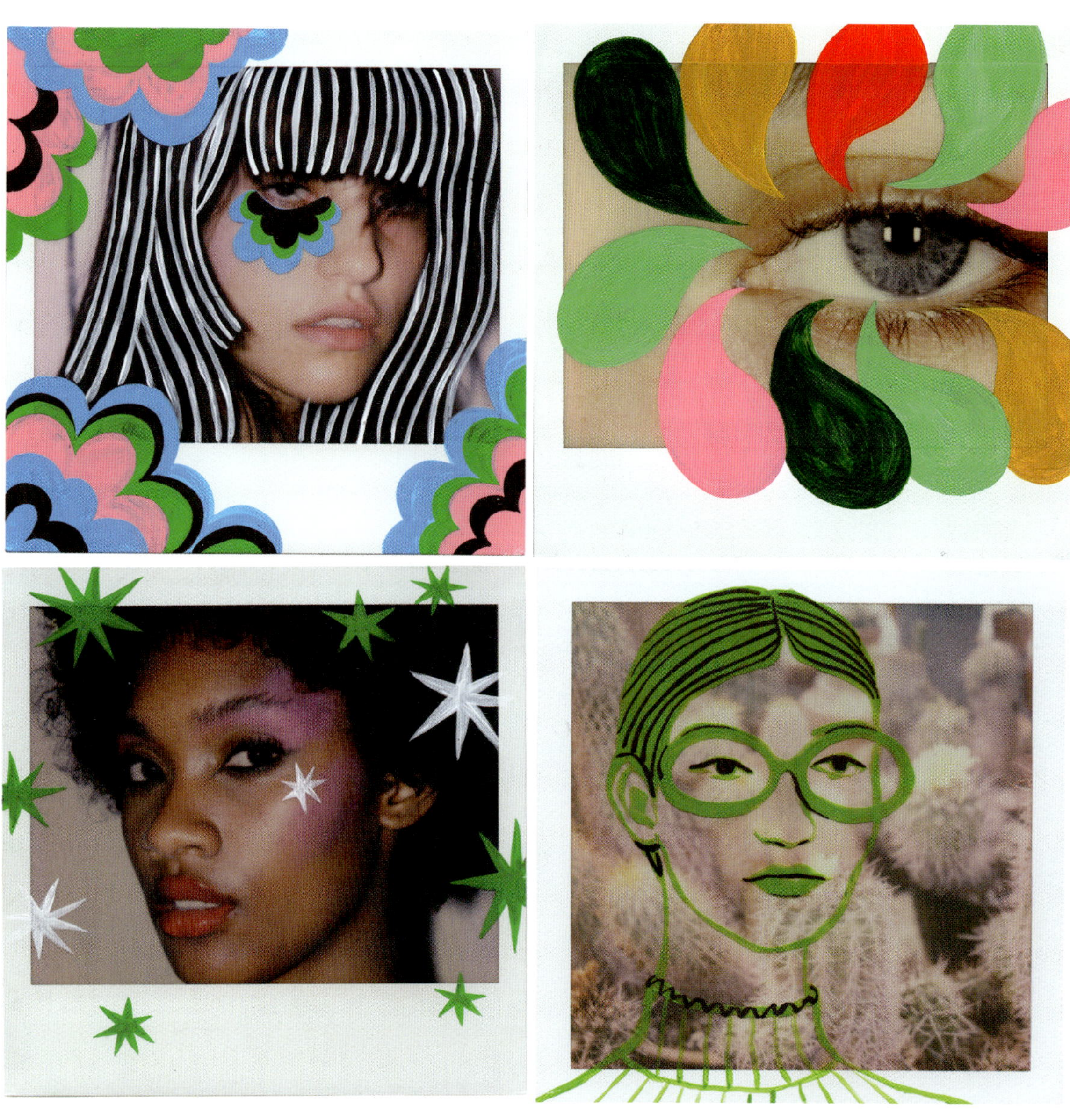

78   David Lekatch and Bijou Karman, *300 Polaroids*

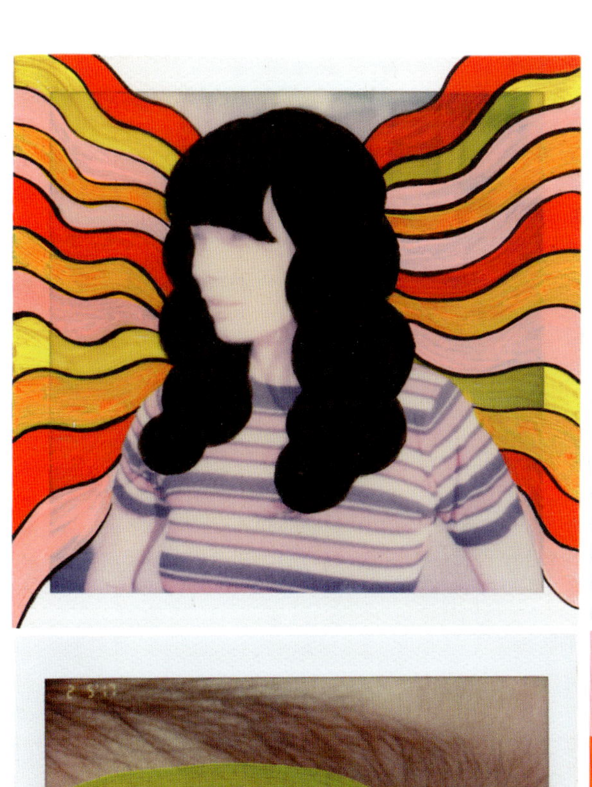
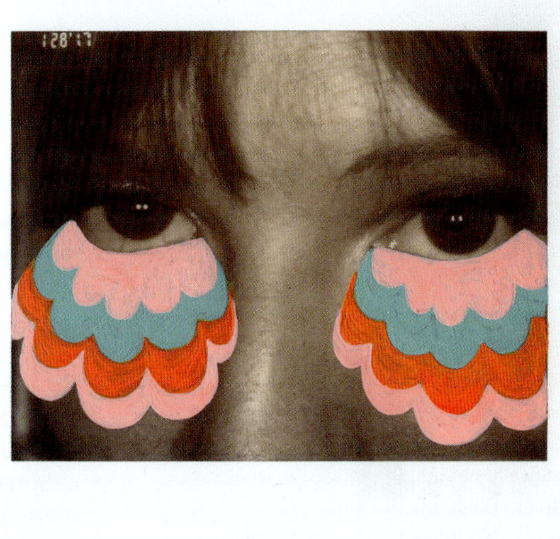
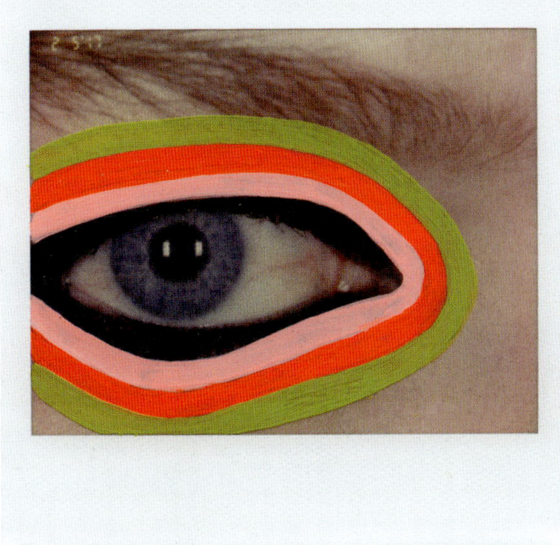
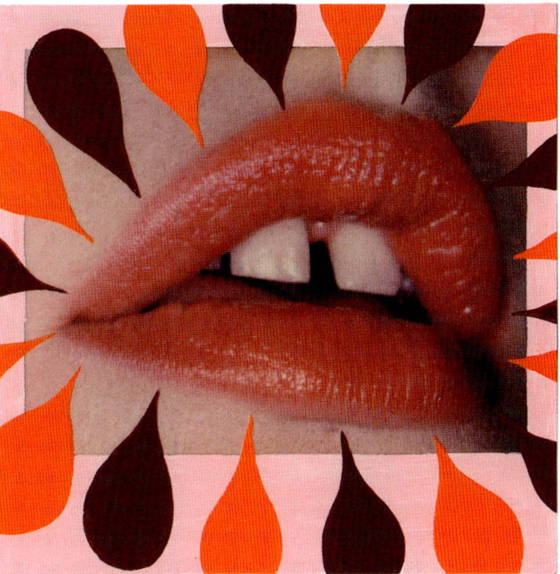

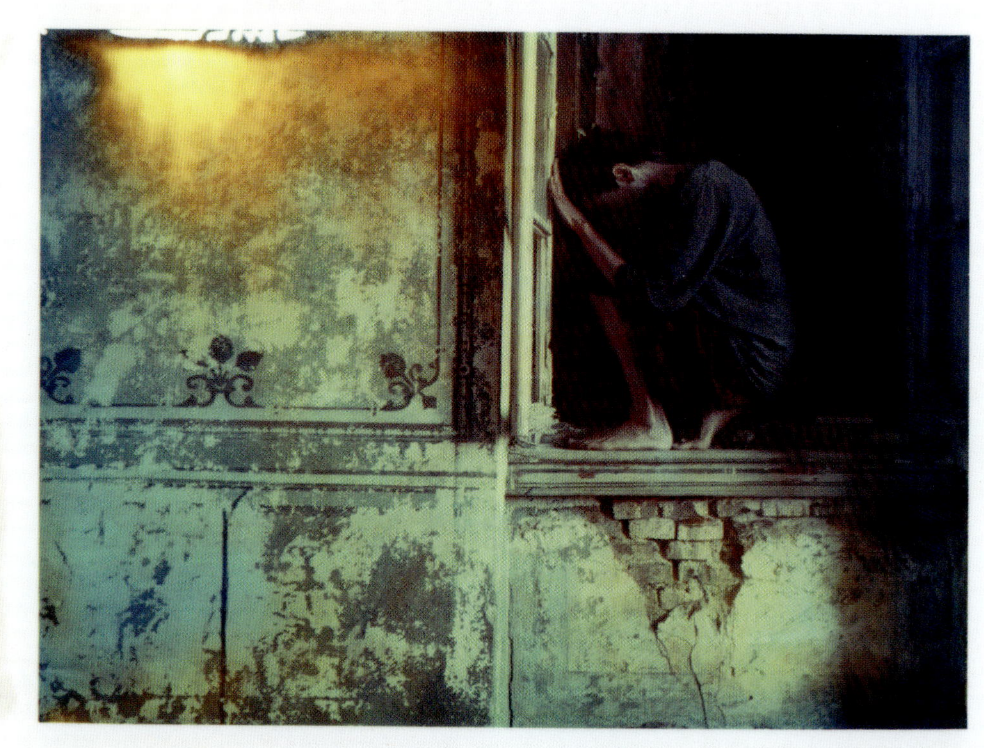

80   Alek Lindus, *Neither Subject nor Object*

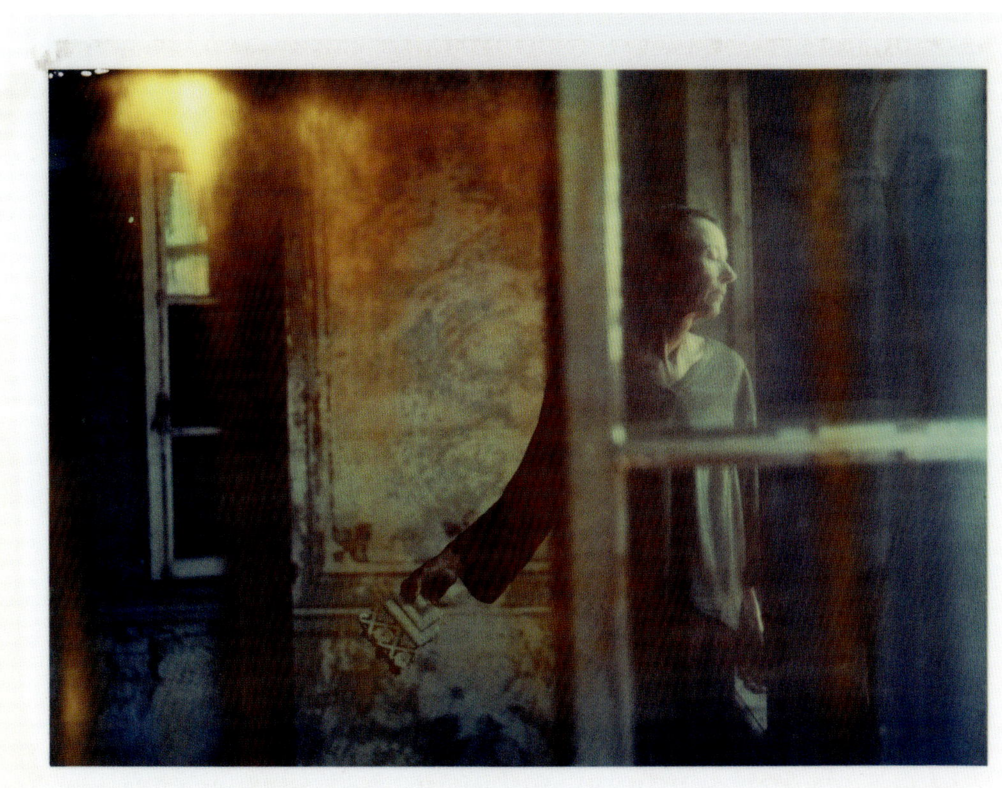

   Leonardo Lussana, *Vertical Square*

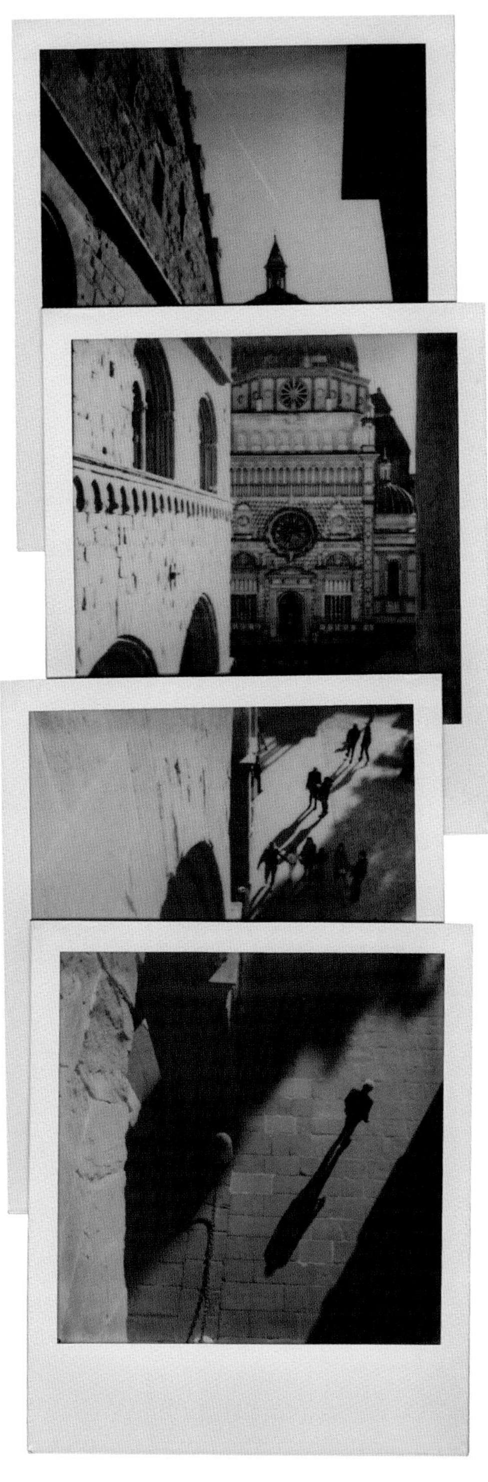

84   Duncan Manning, *Isolation*

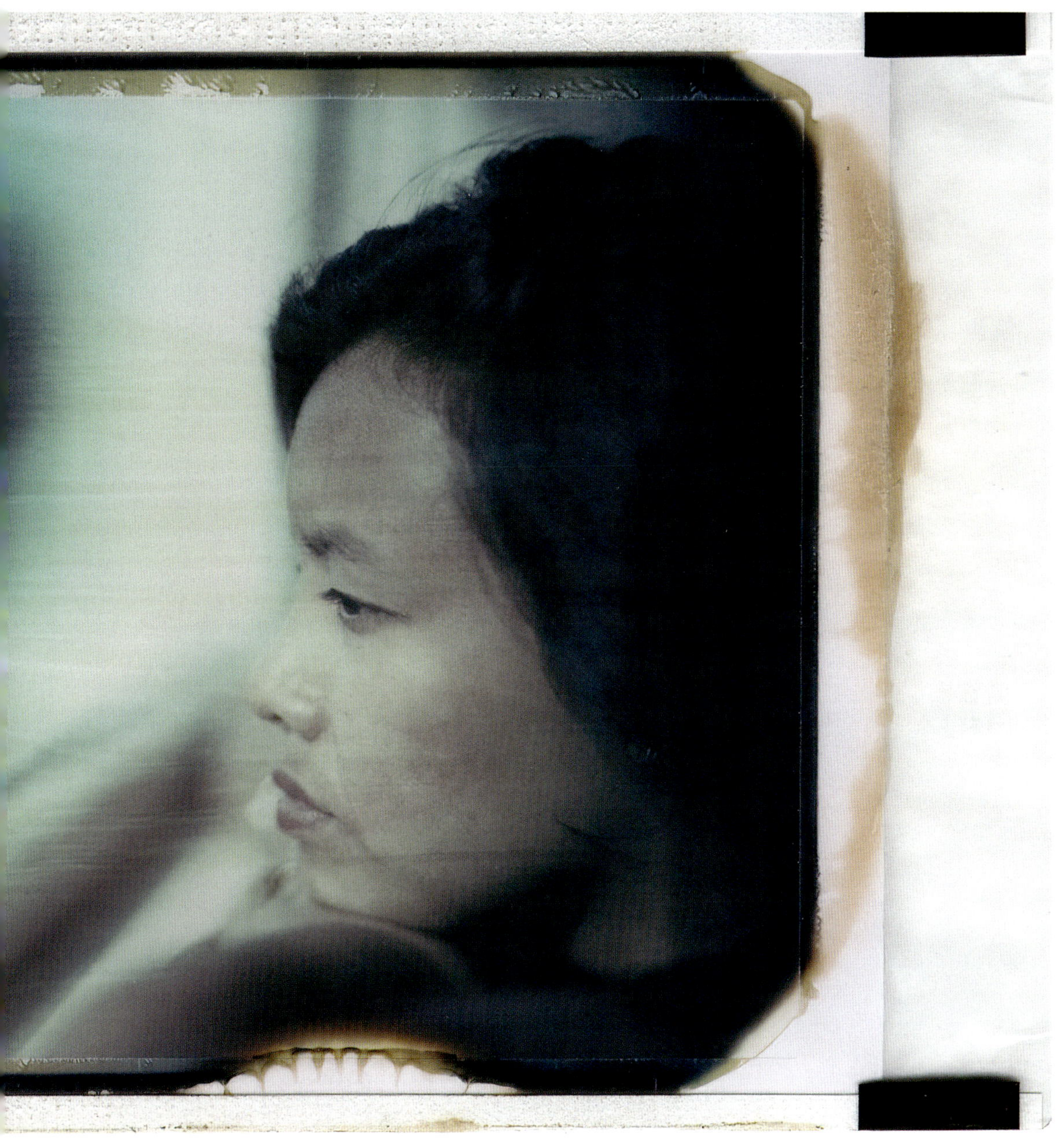

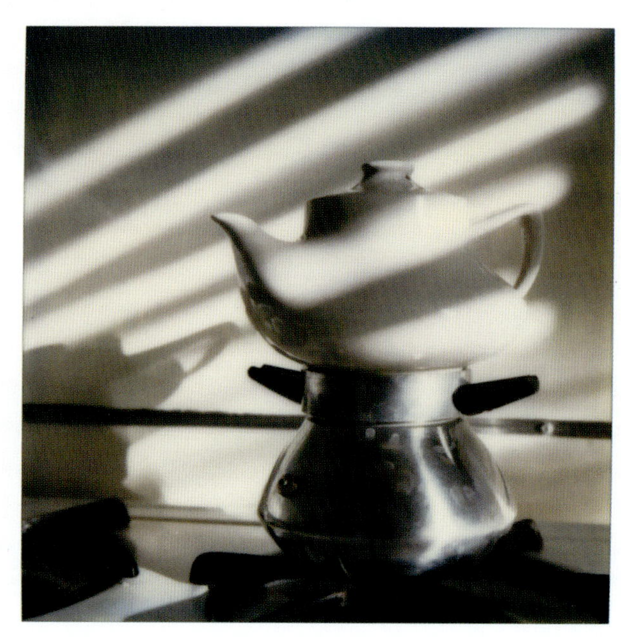

86   Robby Müller, *Kensington Motel*

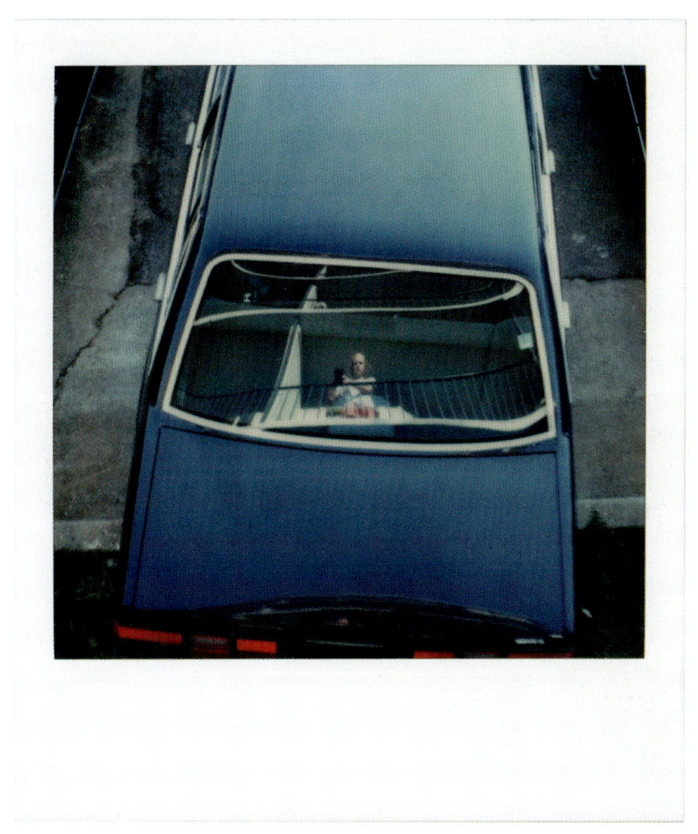

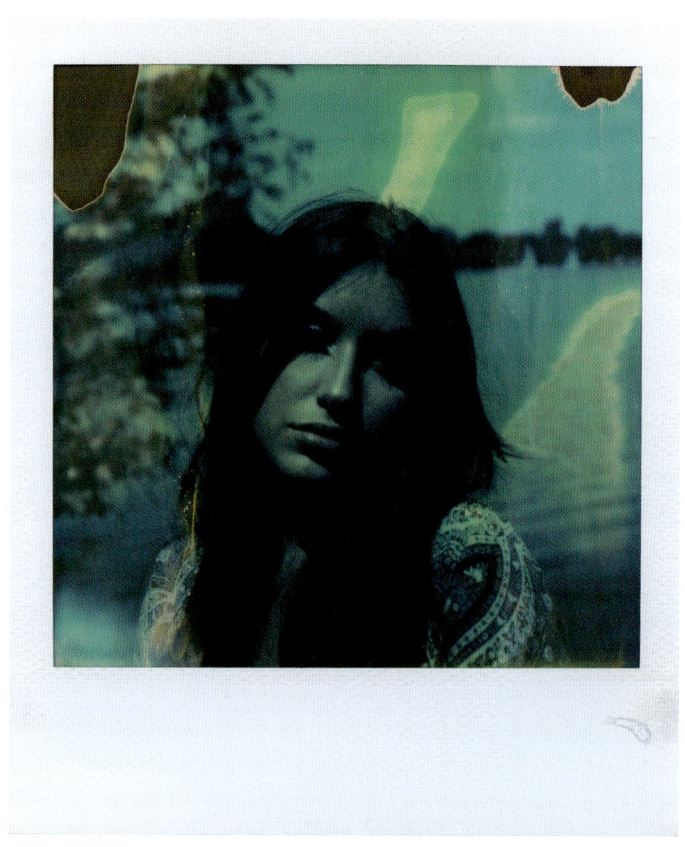

88   Julia Beyer, *Dreams (Like a heartbeat Drives You Mad)*

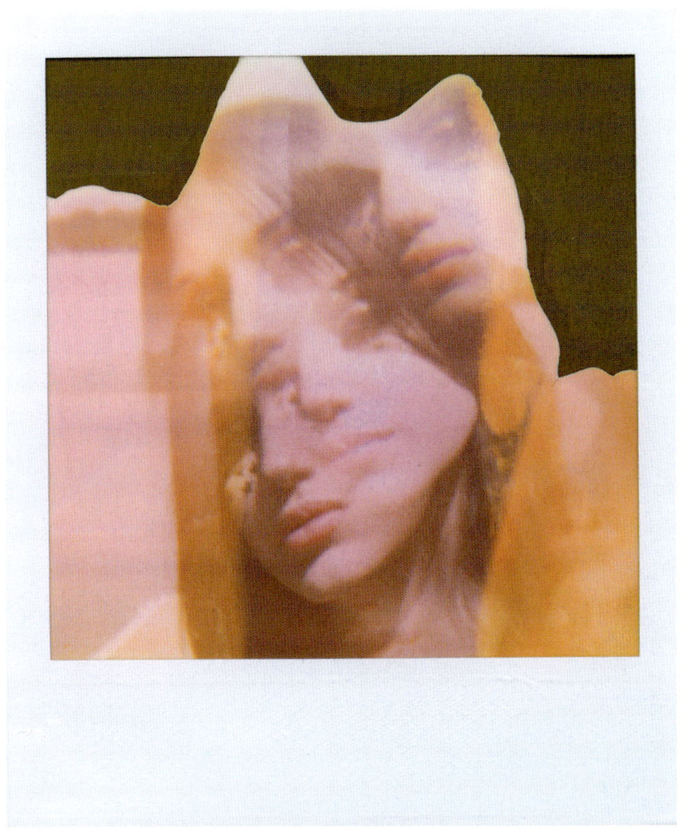

Julia Beyer, *Warm Ways*

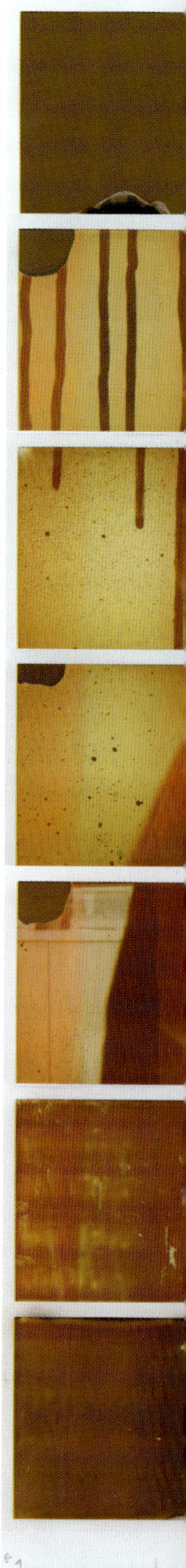

   Guillaume Nalin, *Narcisse*

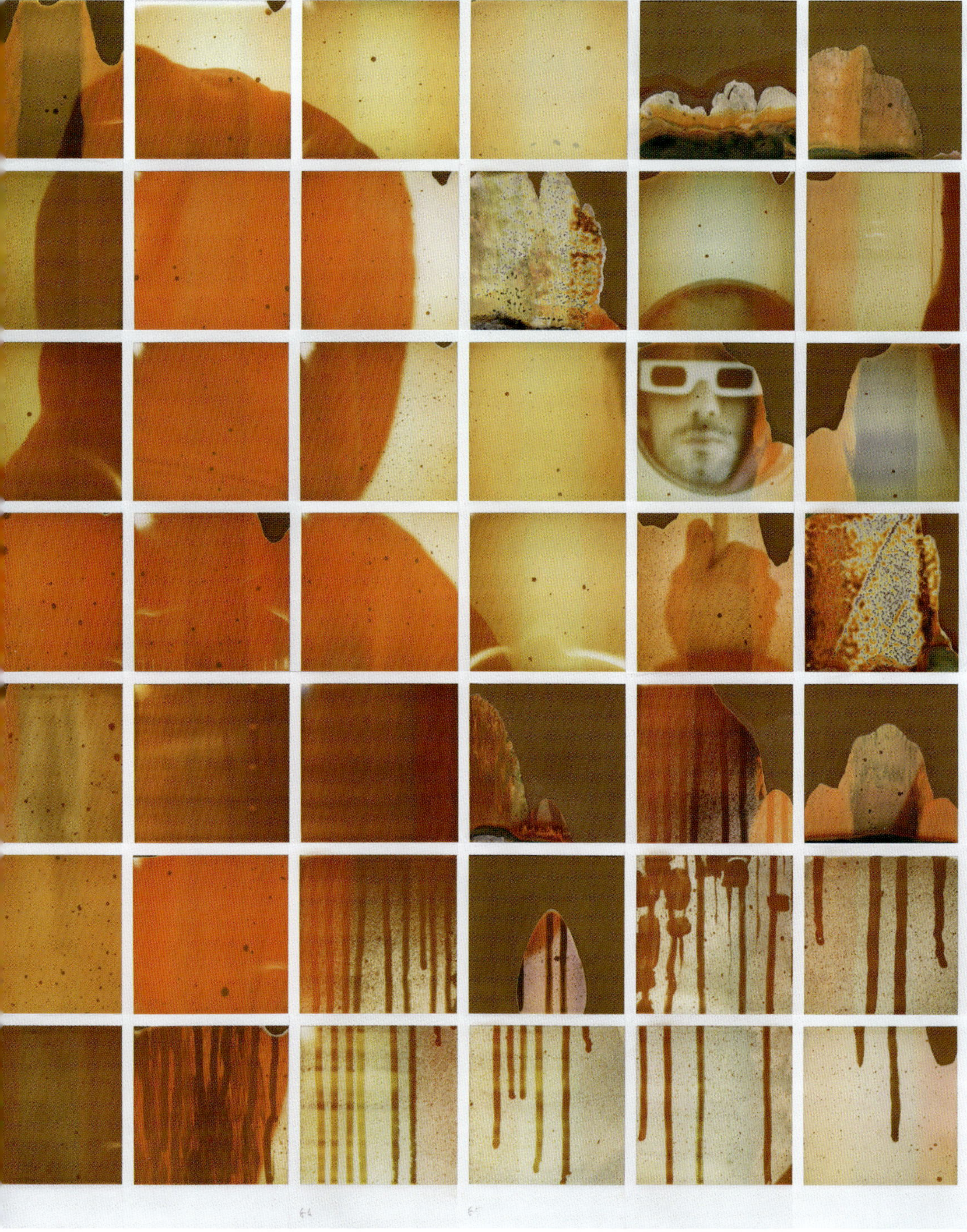

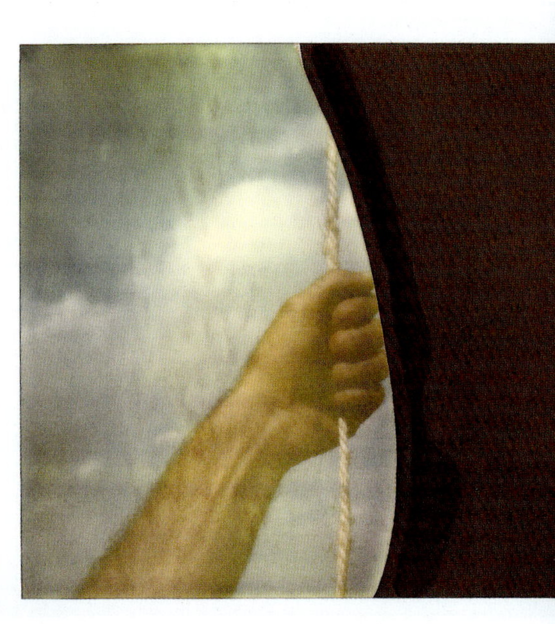

92 Stefano Questorio, *The Day I Tried to Climb the Sky*

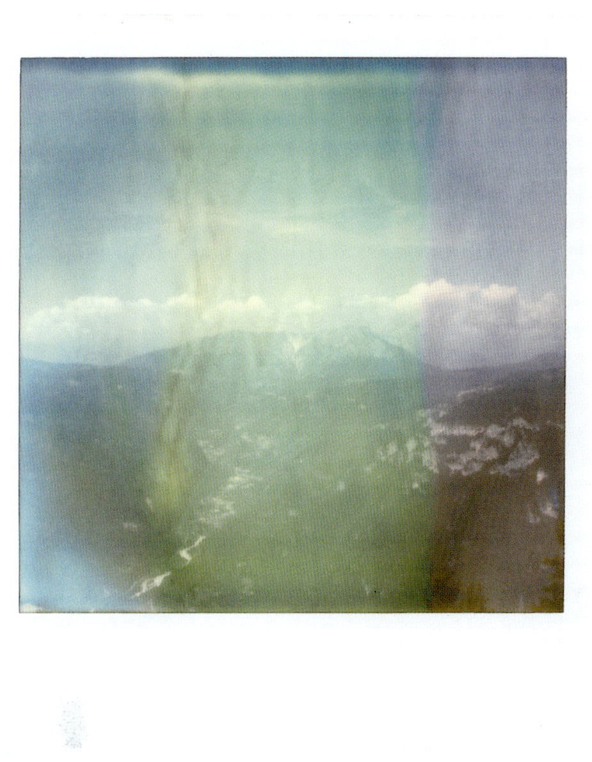

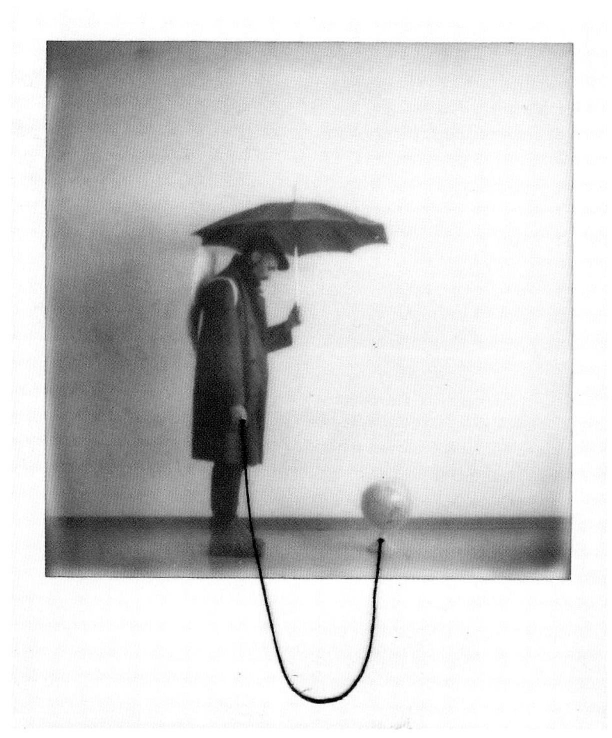

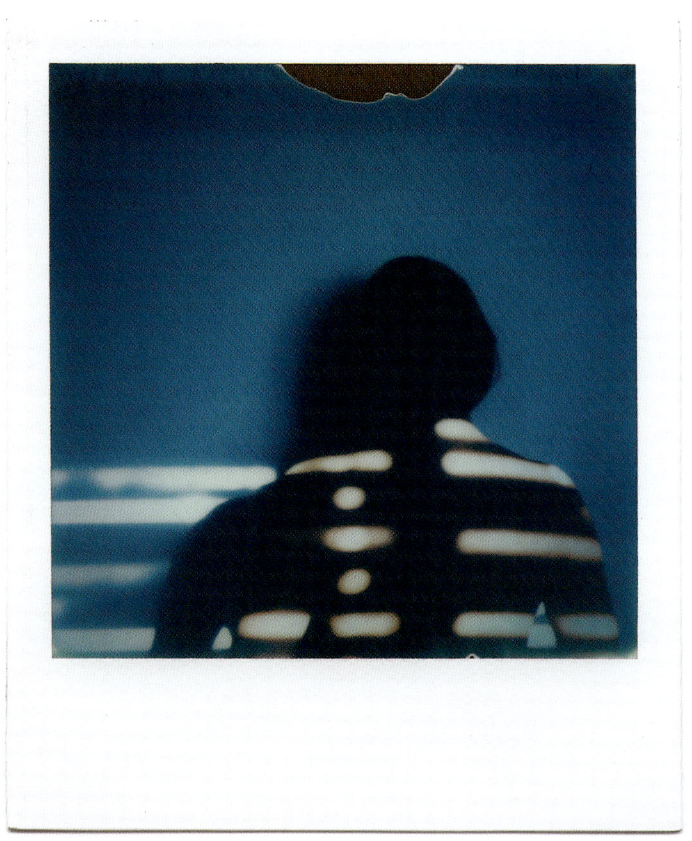

  Francesco Sambati, *Bonaccia series*

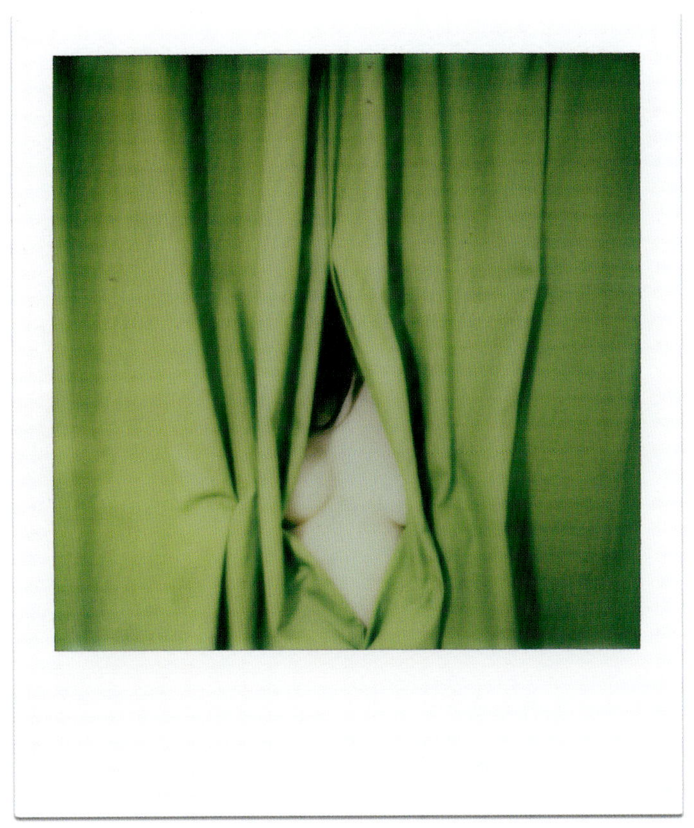

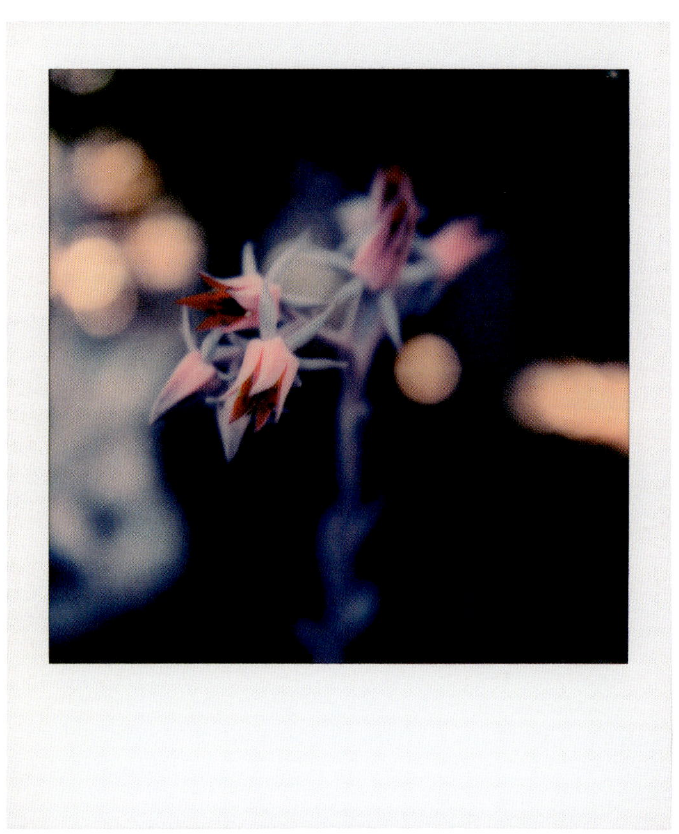

98   Toby Hancock, *Echeveria Laui*

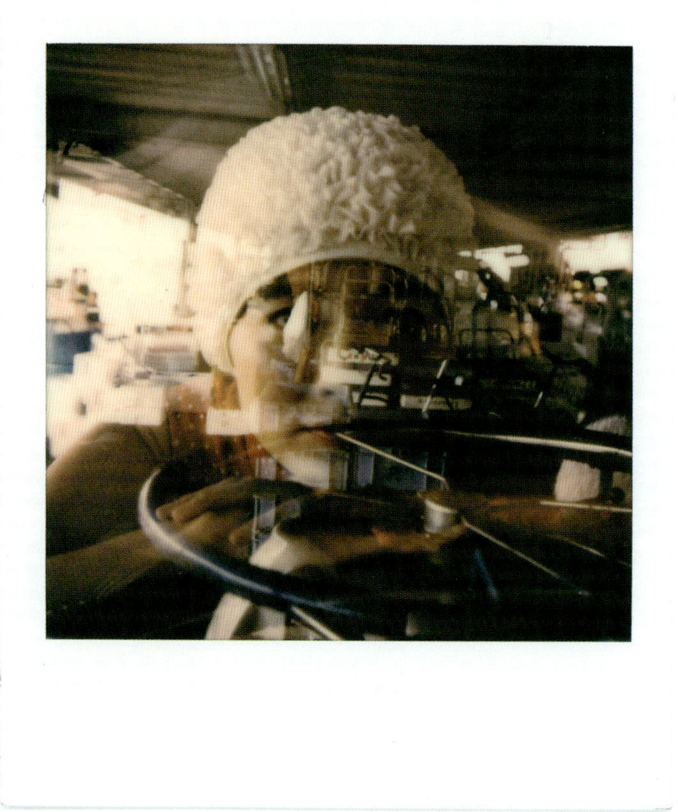

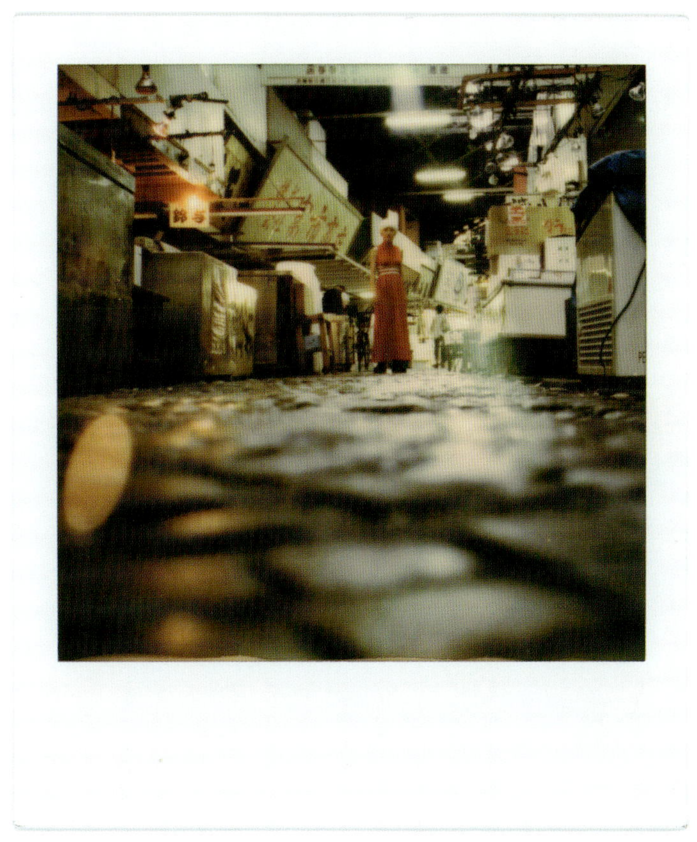

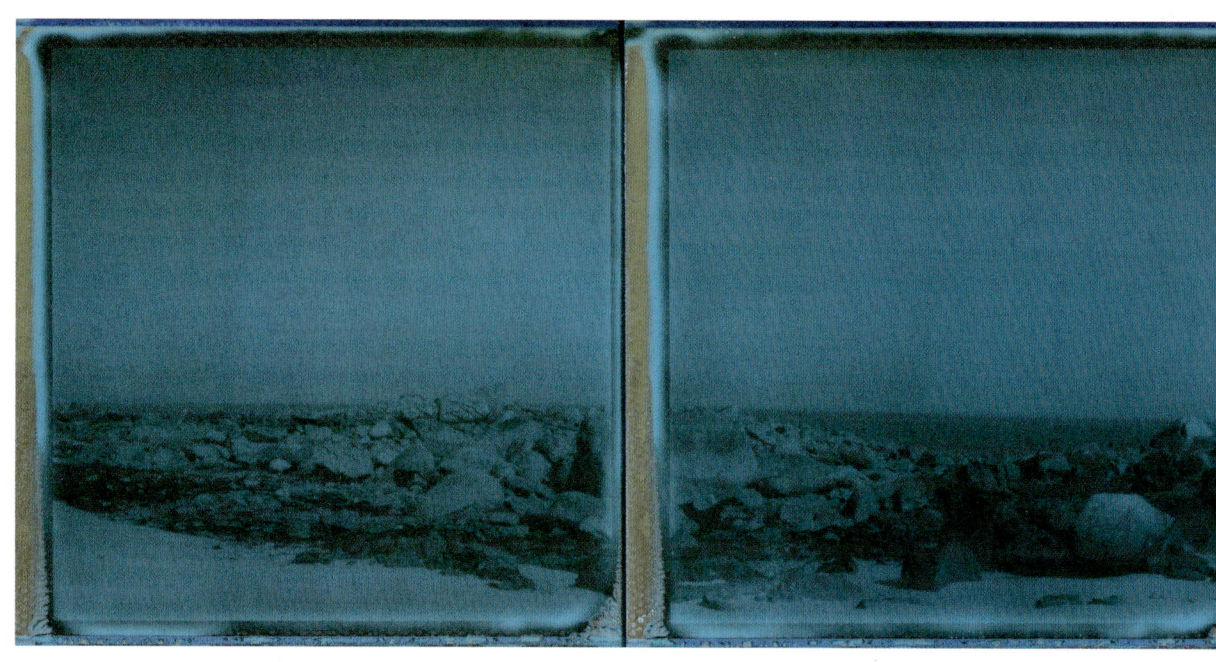

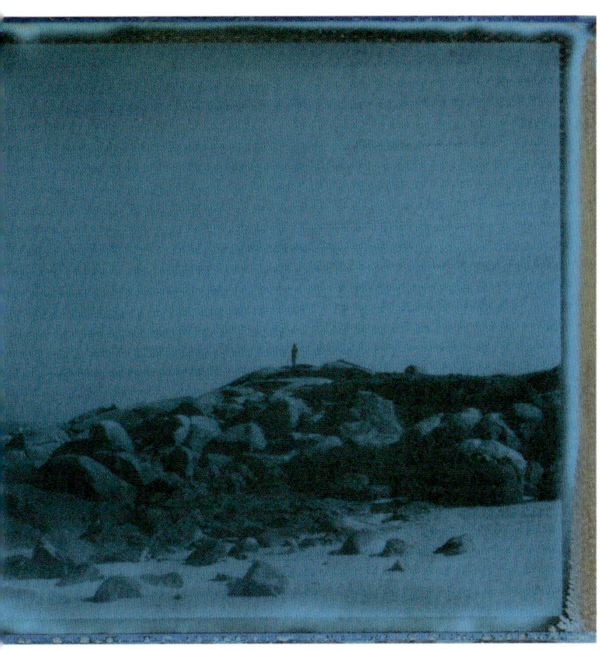

   Ruth Storey, *We're all going somewhere. I hope I'm going there with you*

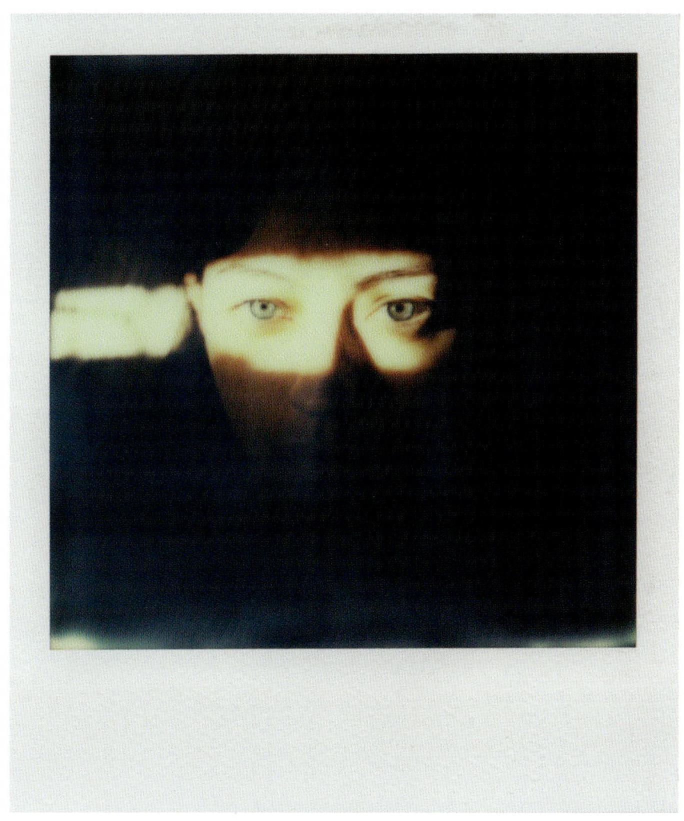

    Ina Echternach, *The Quiet Ripple of the Brook*

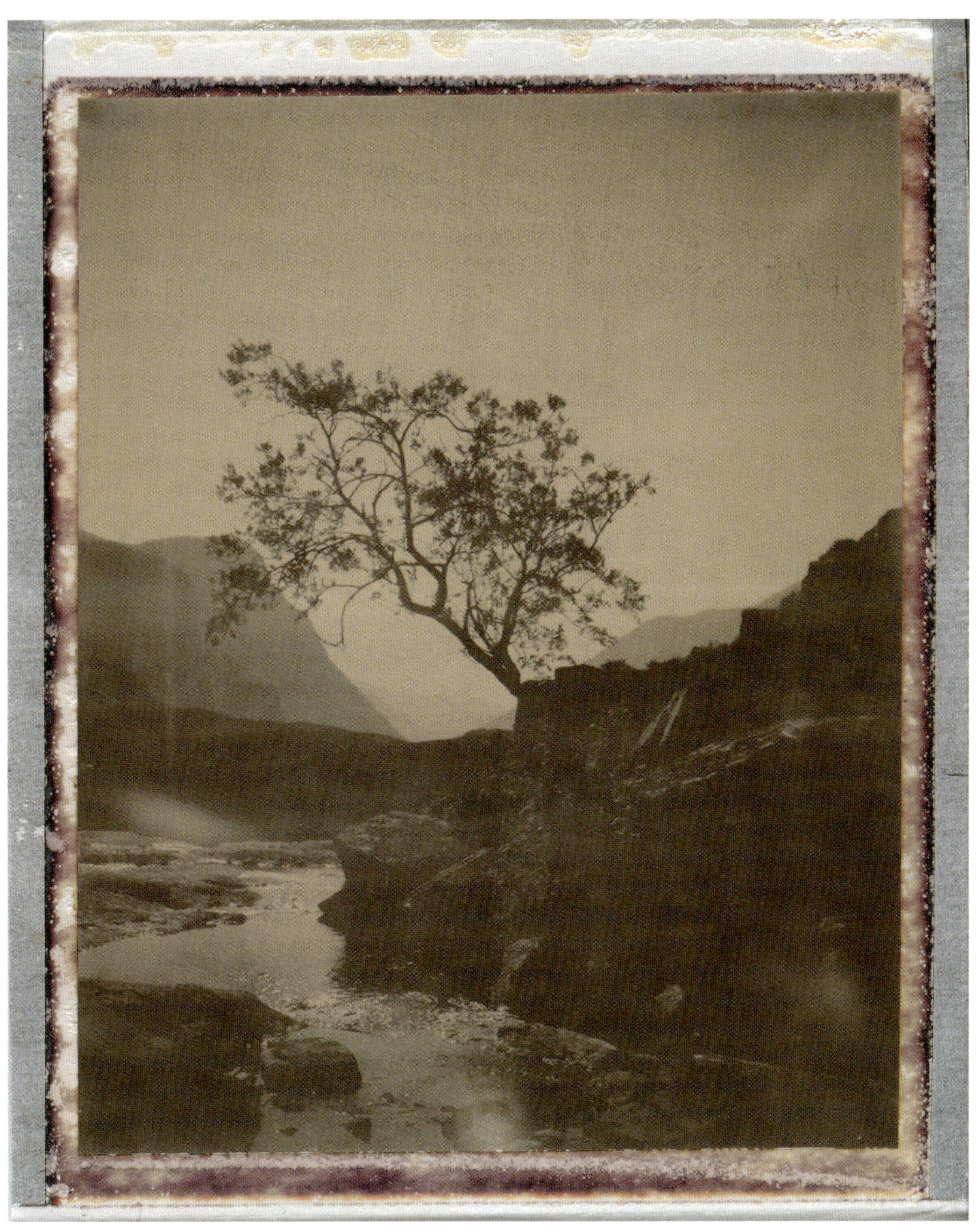

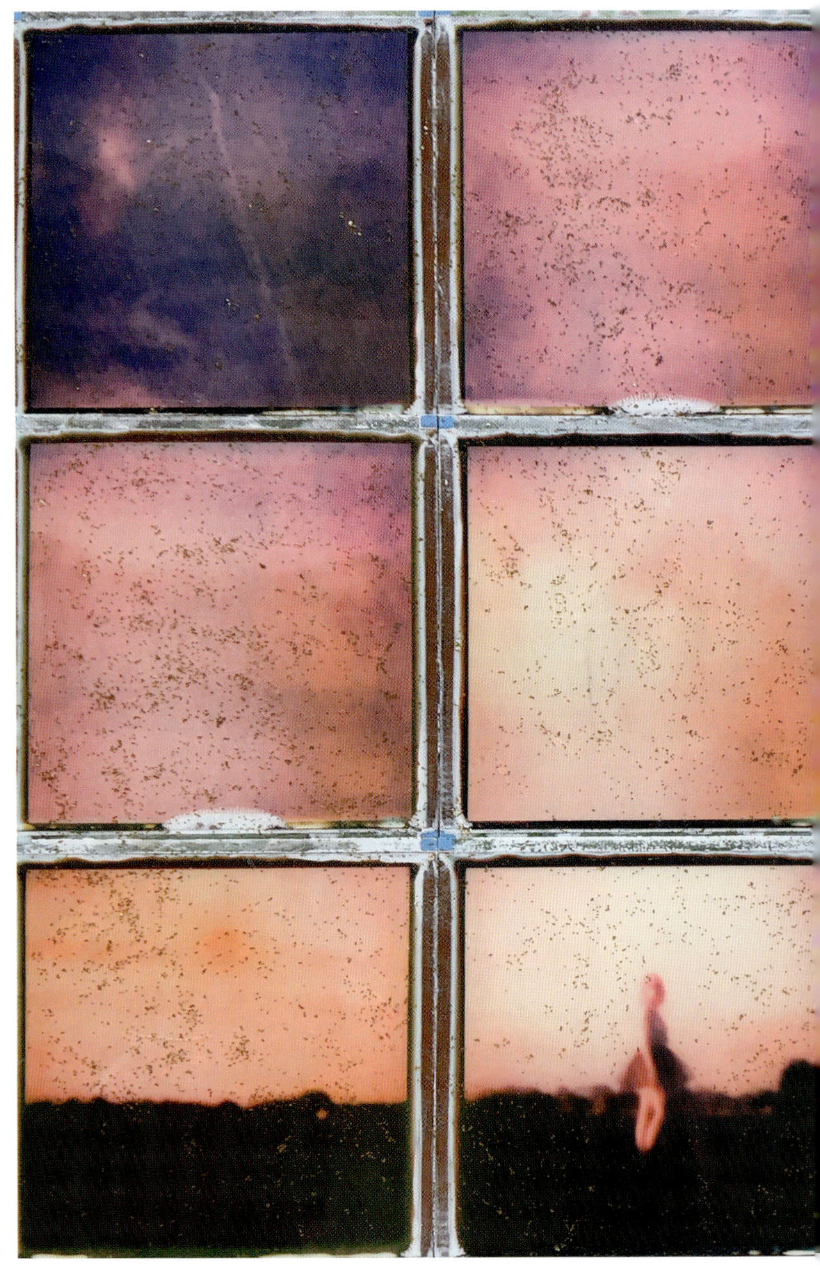

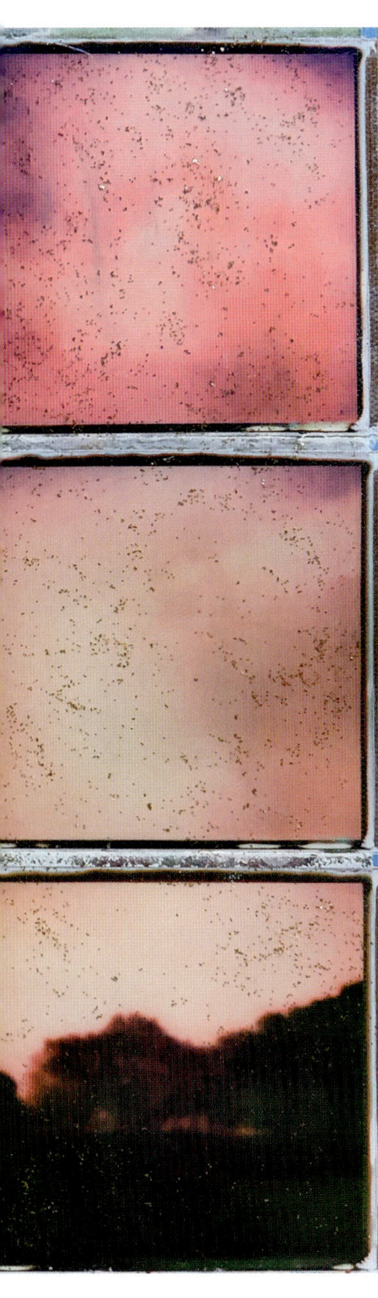

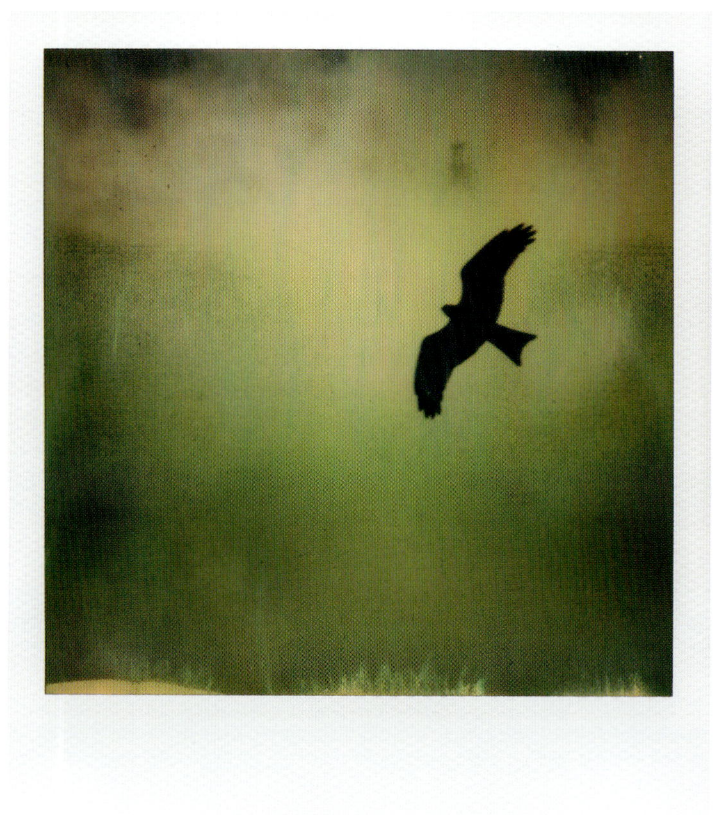

110   Kirsten Thys Van Den Audenaerde, *Come Fly With Me*

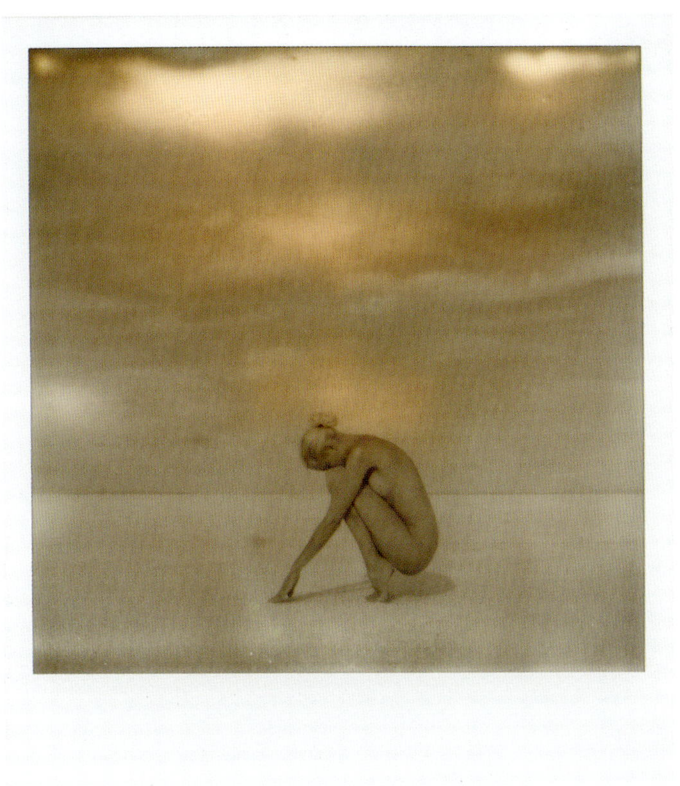

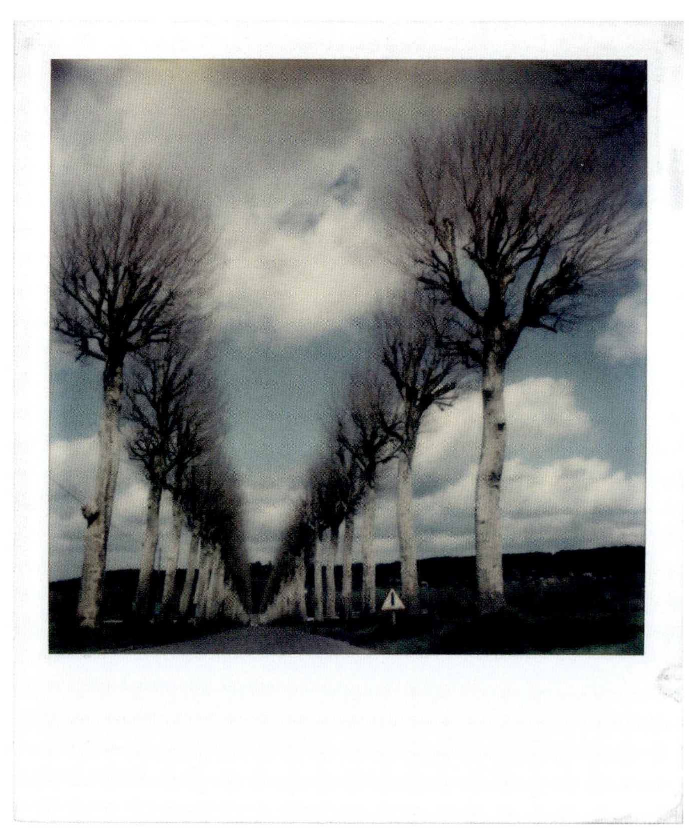

112   Robby Müller, *Winter Trees*

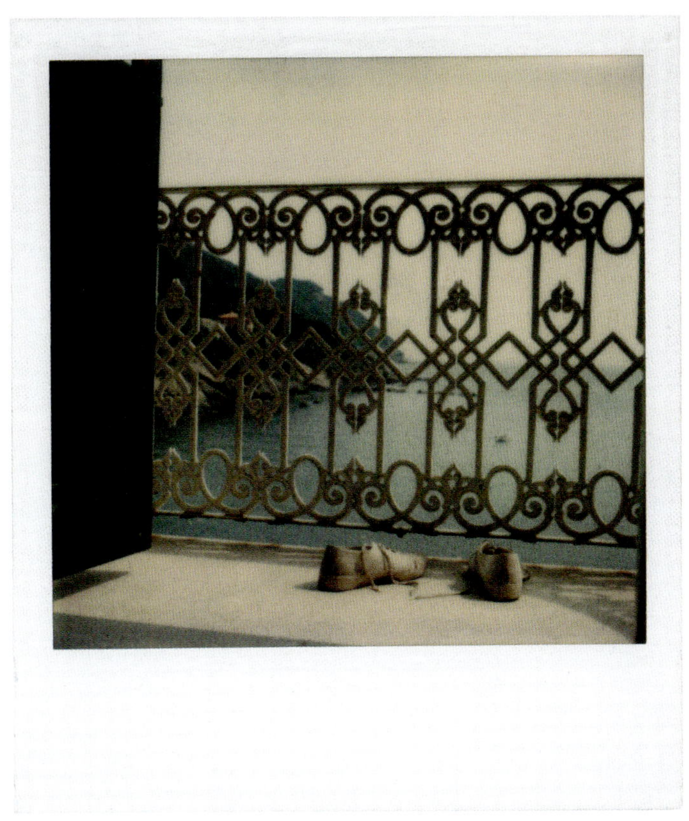

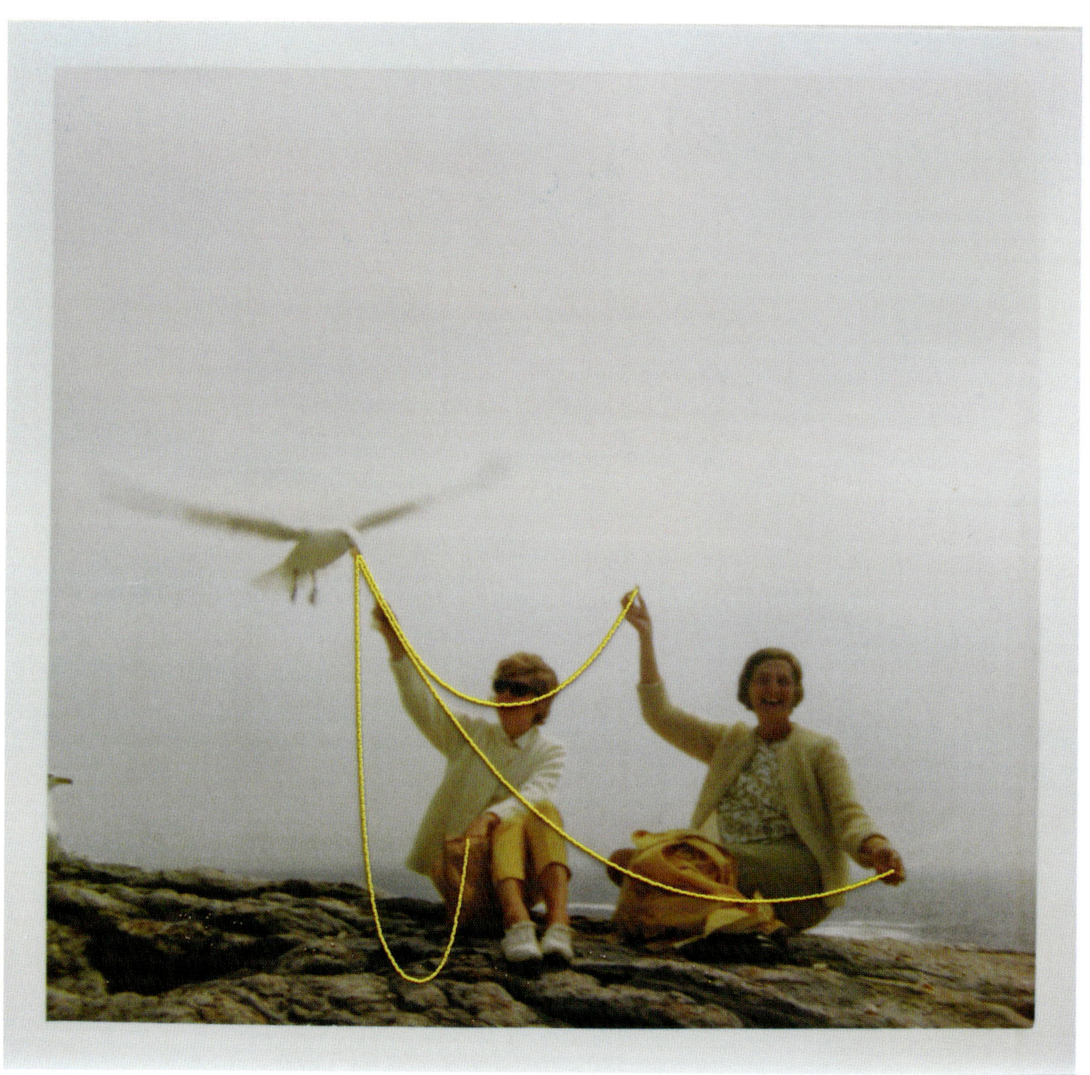

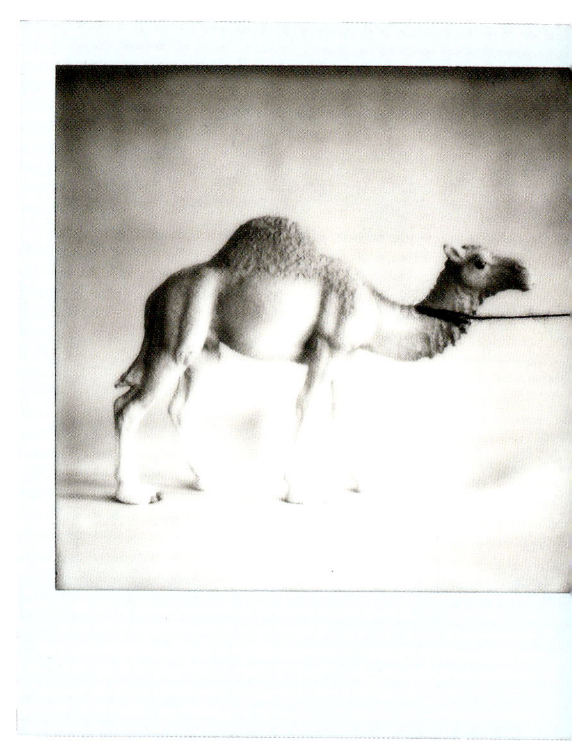

116   Stefano Questorio, *The Philosophy of Mr. Q / Optimism*

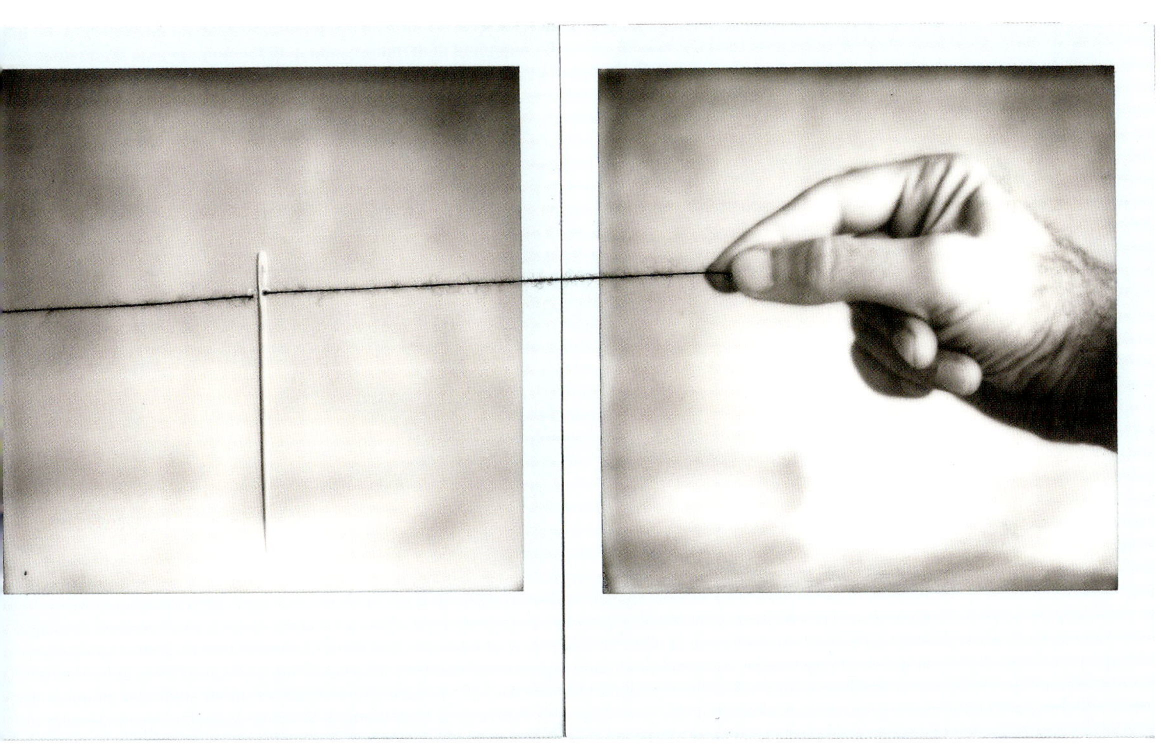

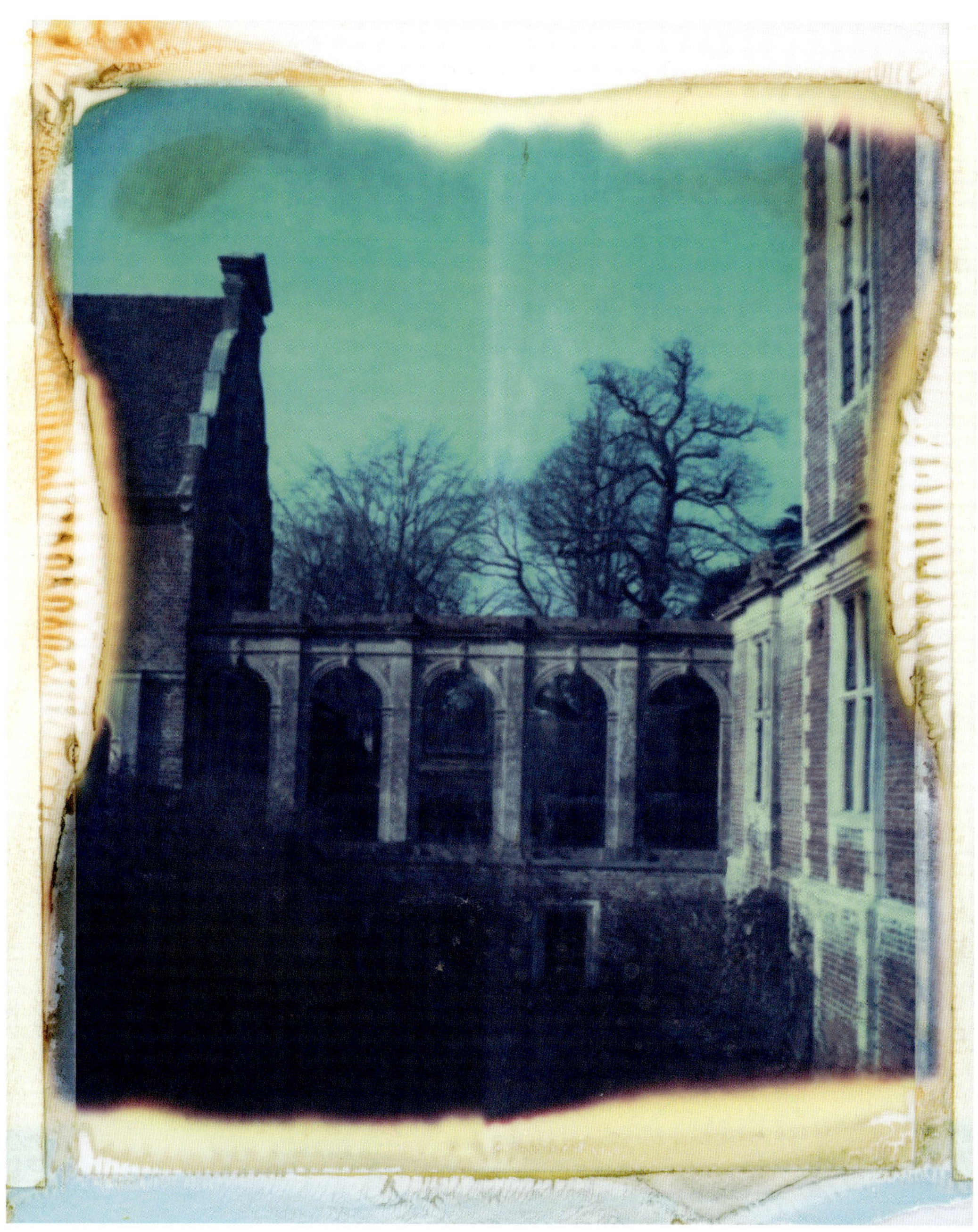

    Meredith Wilson, *Untitled*

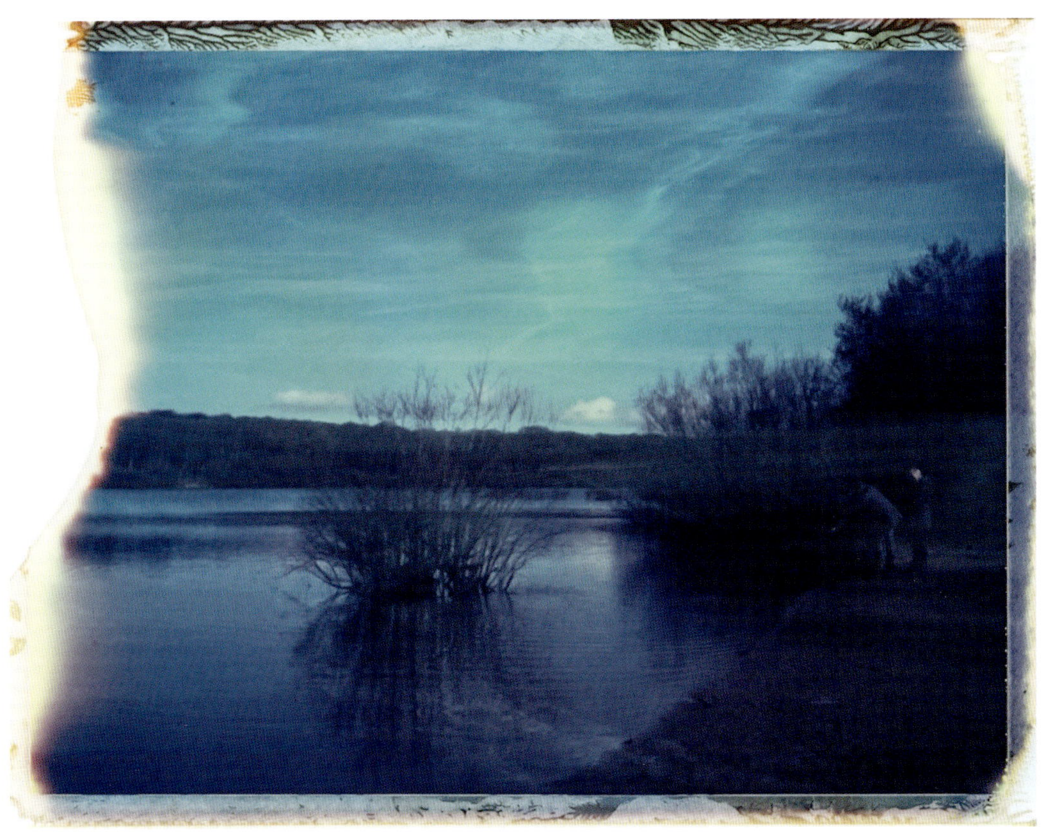

Meredith Wilson, *Dog Beach*   119

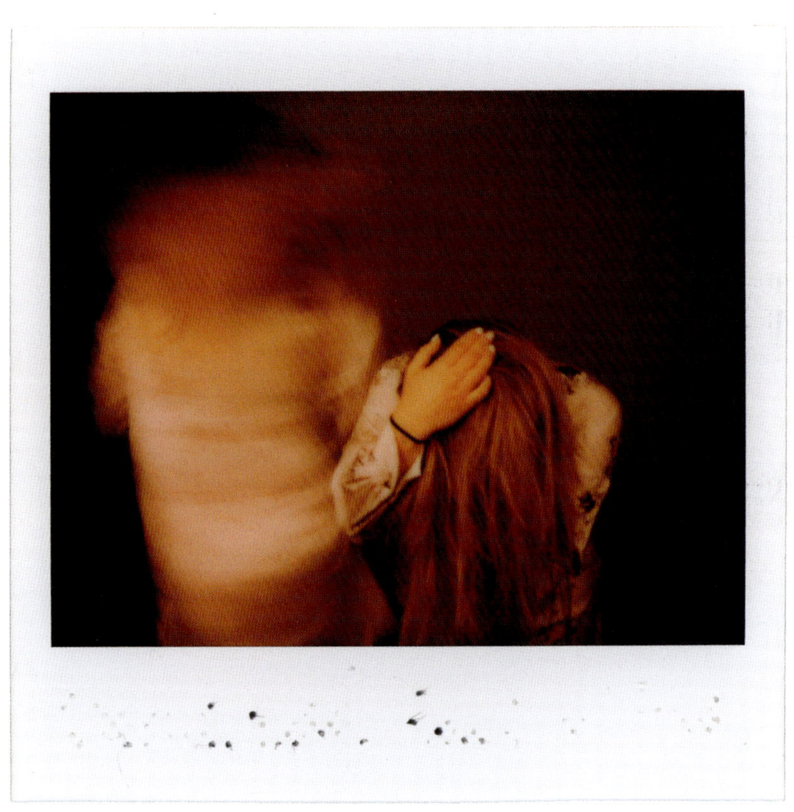

120   Noah Zyla, *Twins of Leda I and II*

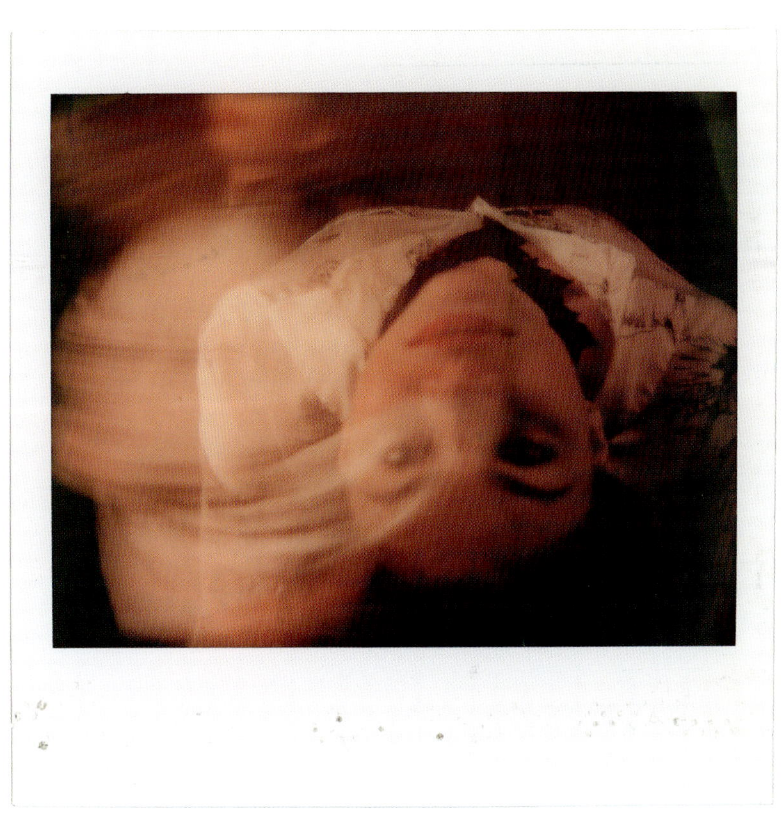

   Nadia Lee Cohen with Charlie Denis, *Nadia Vogue Italia*

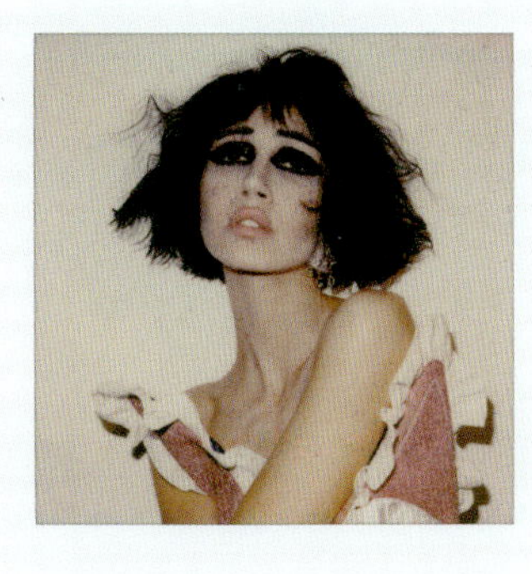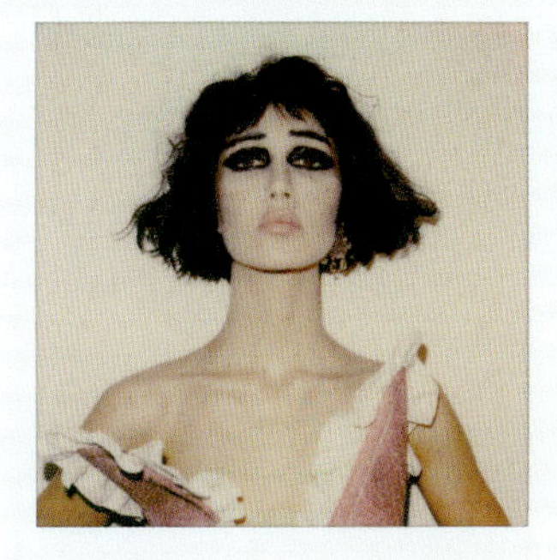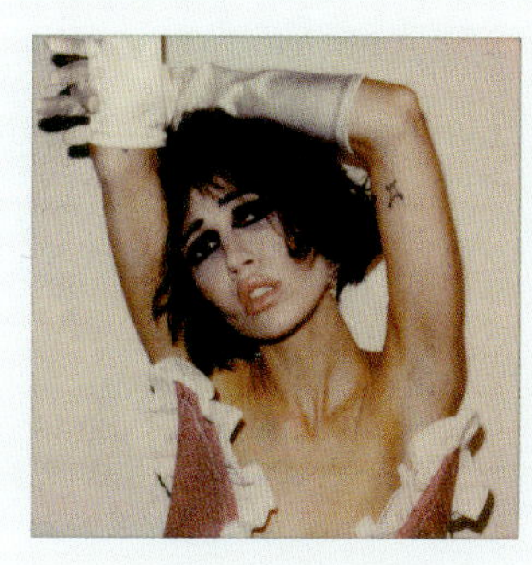
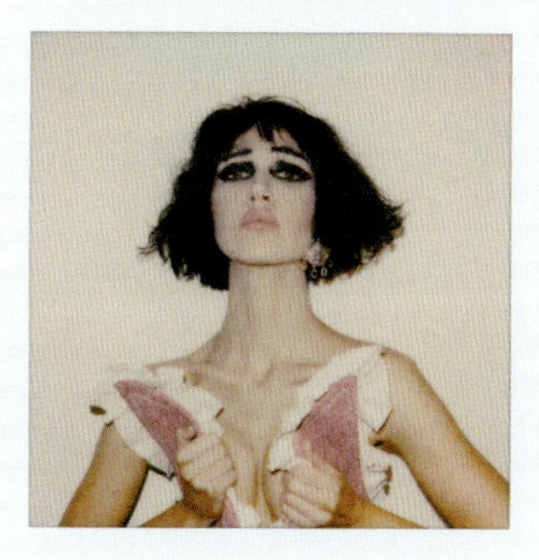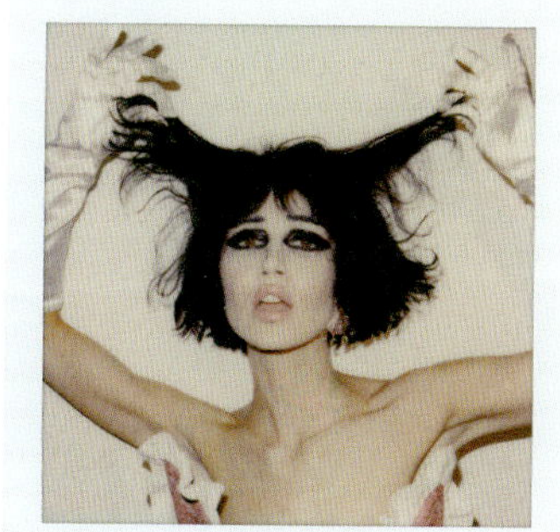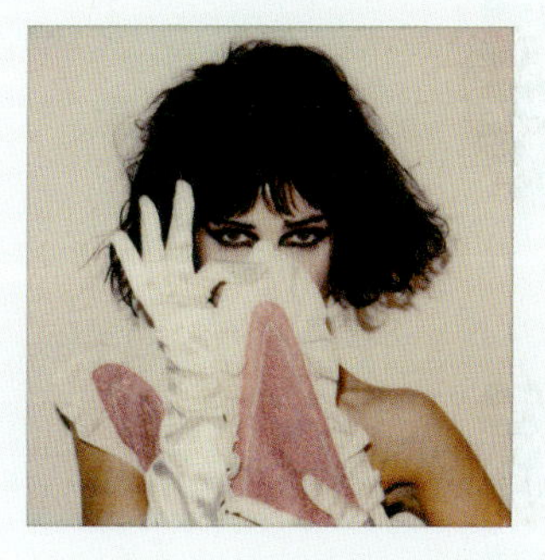
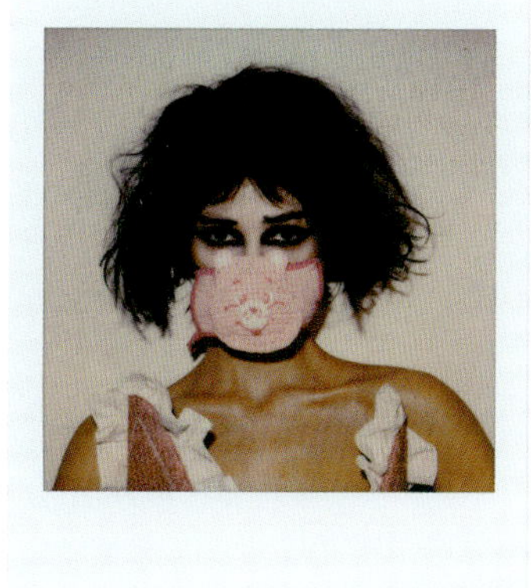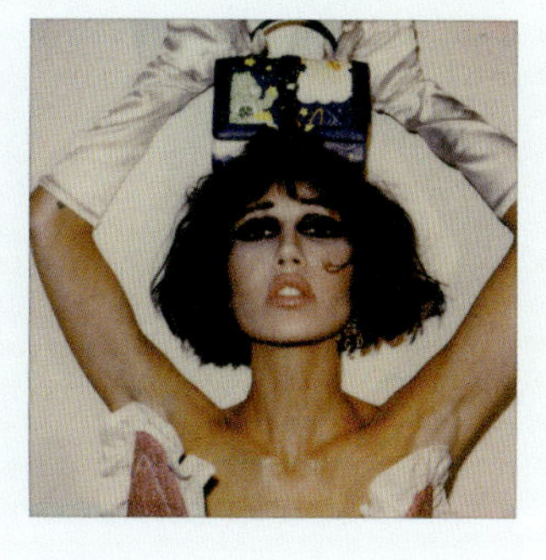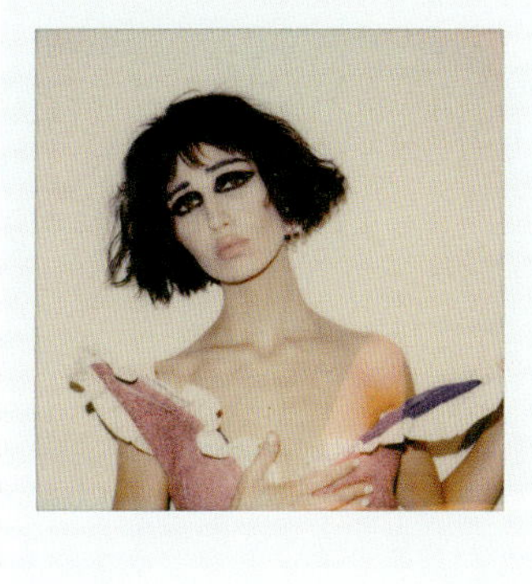

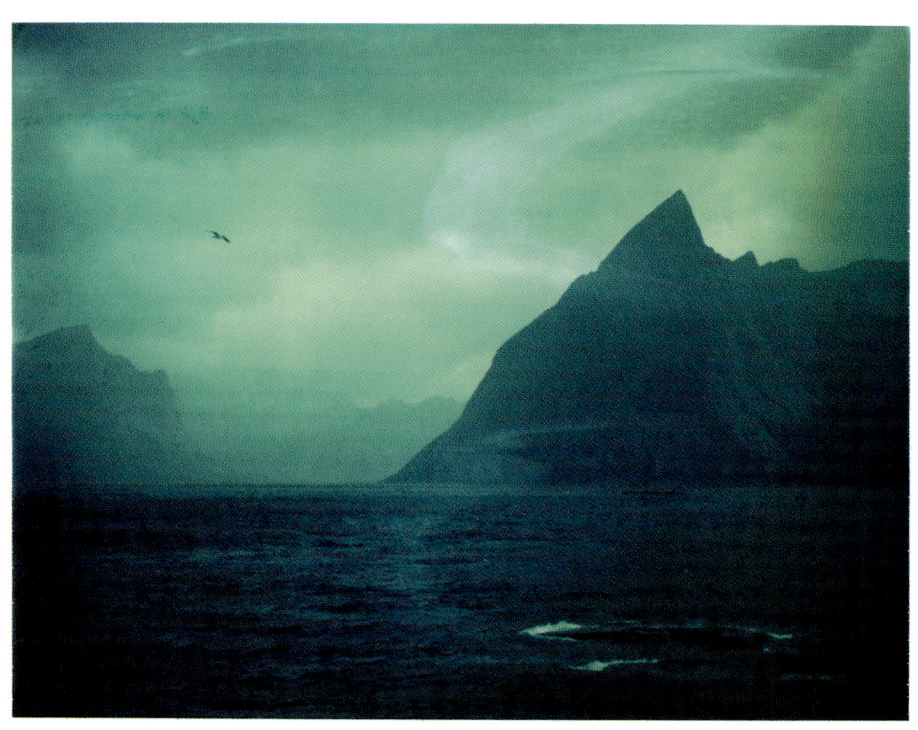

124   Alex Conu, *Lofoten*

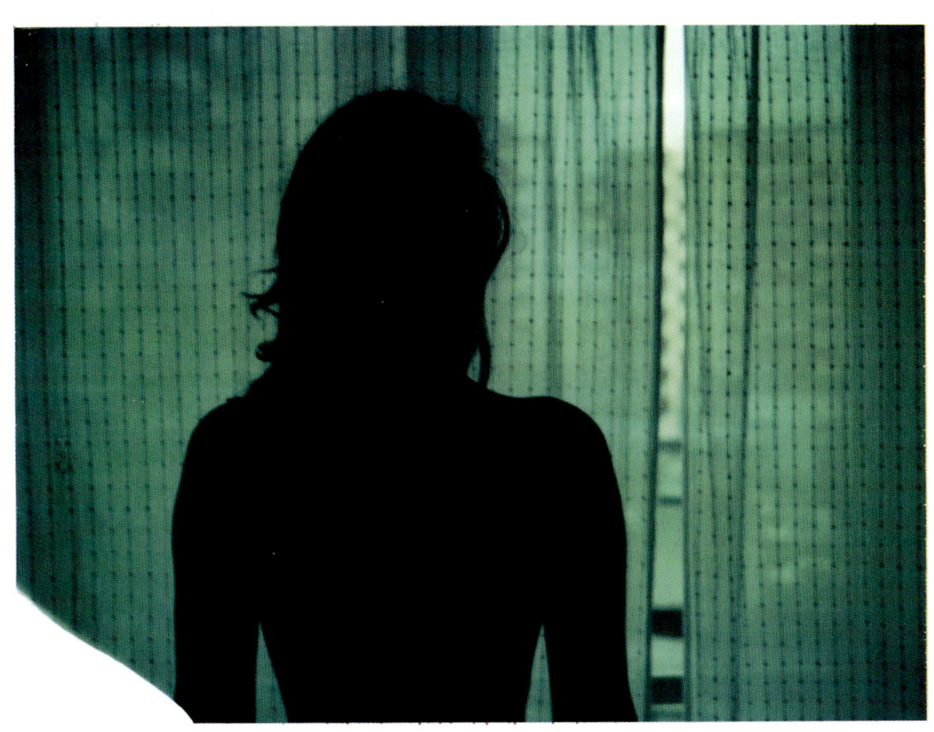

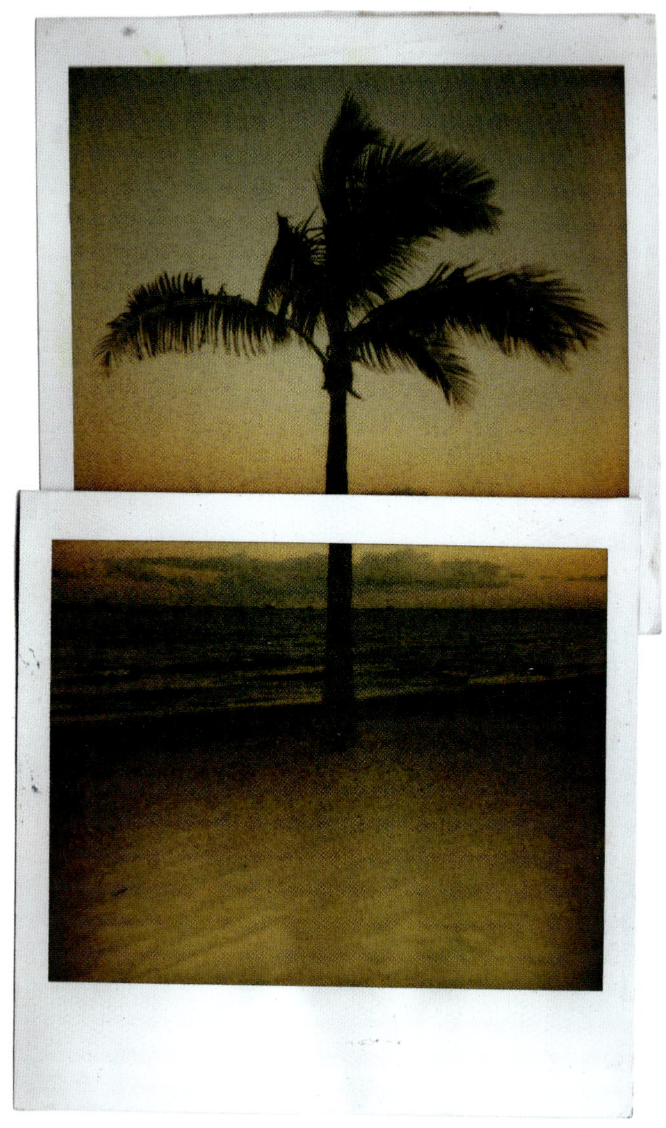

  Brian Downey, *Palm Tree*

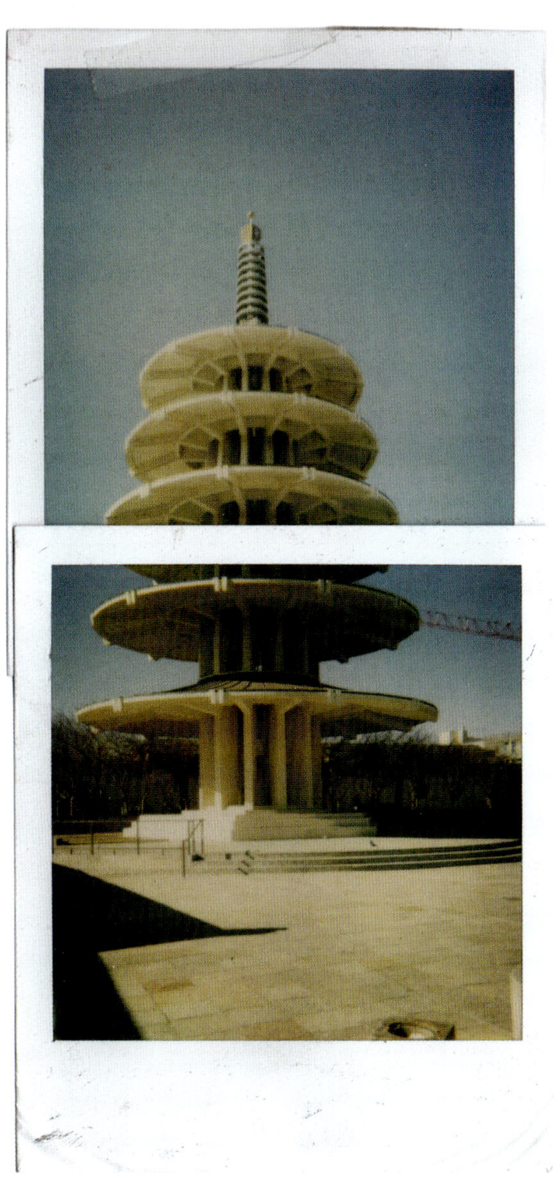

  Francesco Sambati, *Bonaccia series*

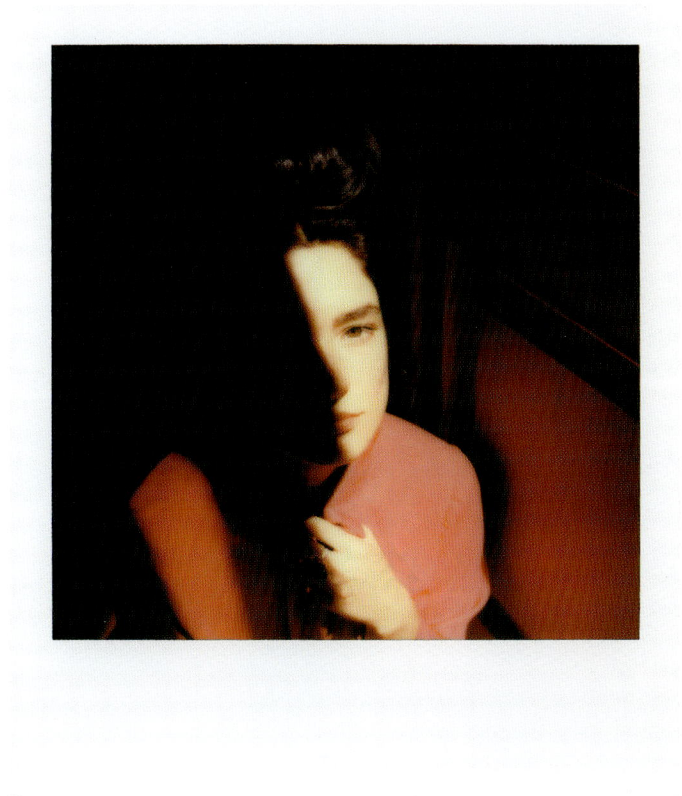

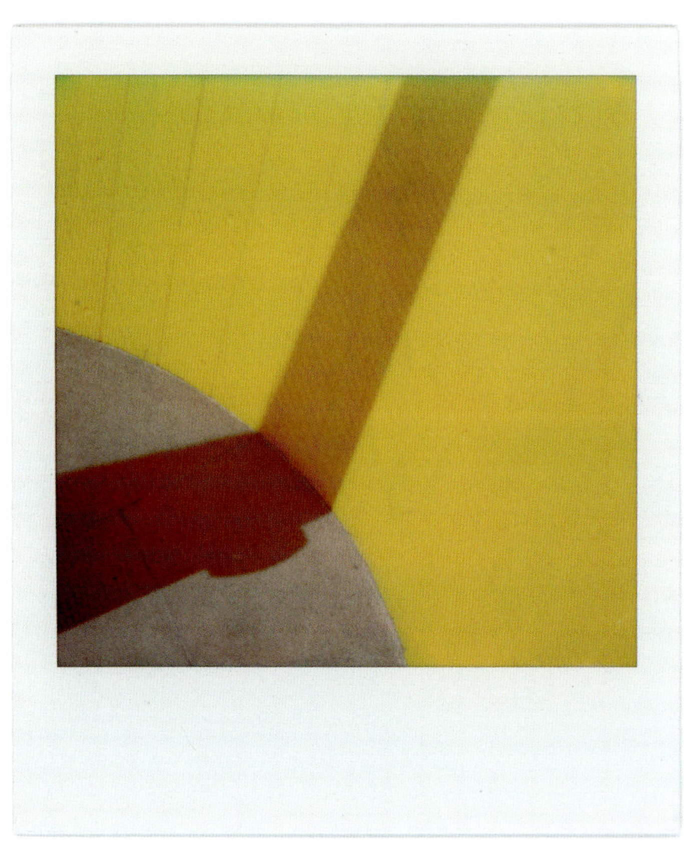

  Steven Meyer-Rassow, *Study in Yellow, Part 1*

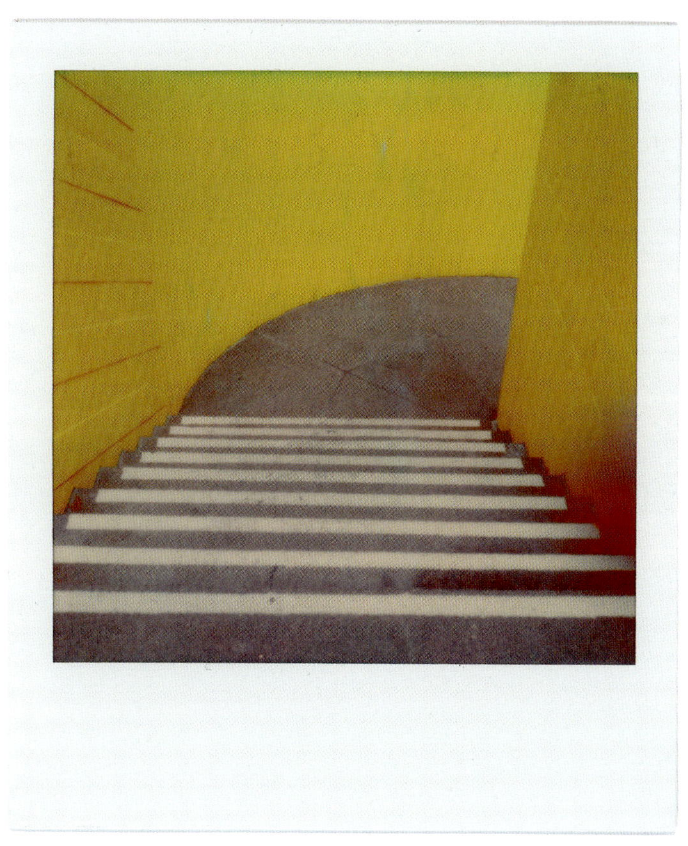

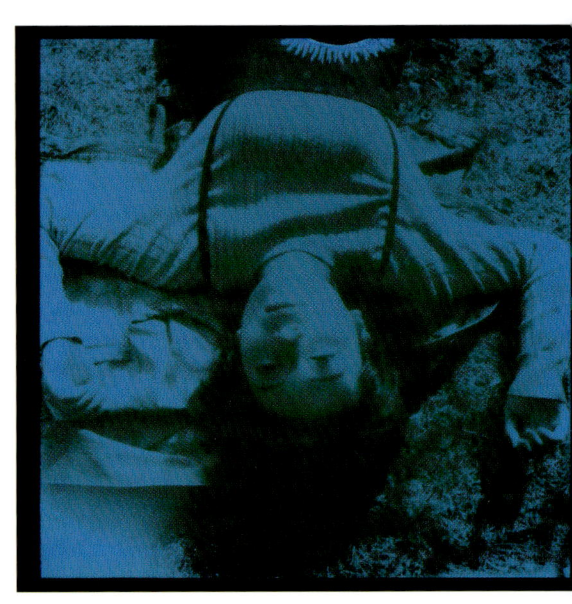

132   Akio Nakai, *Blue the Sleepy, no.1, 2, and 3*

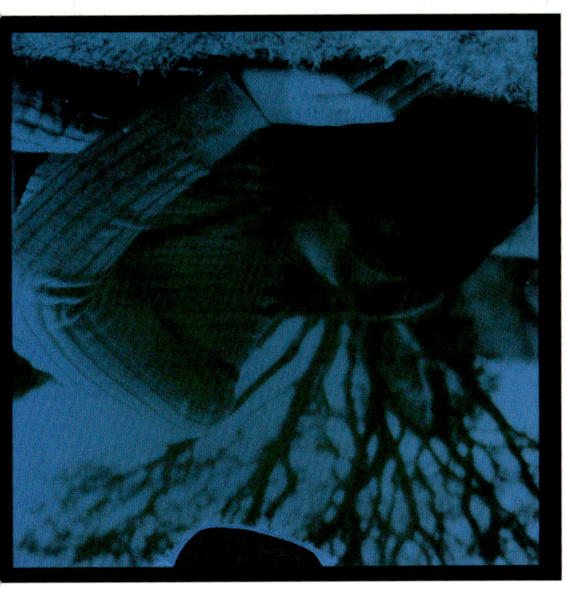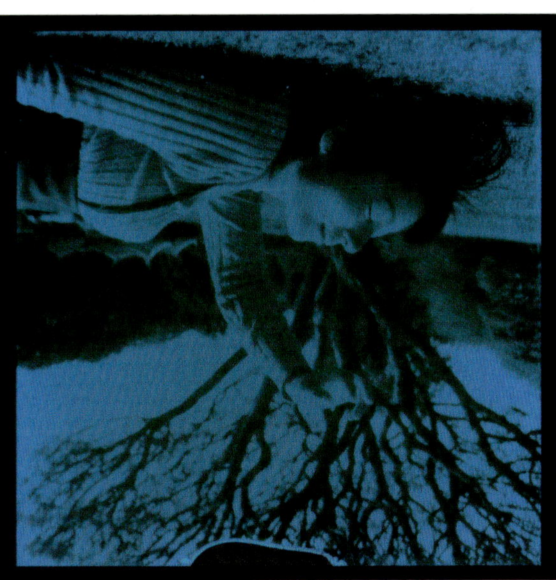

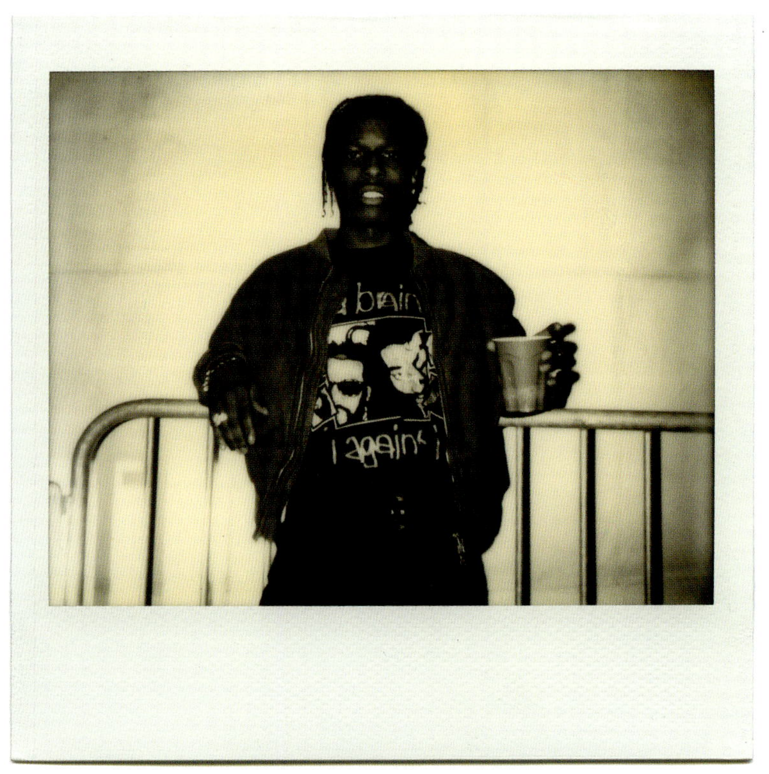

134   Brock Fetch, *ASAP Rocky*

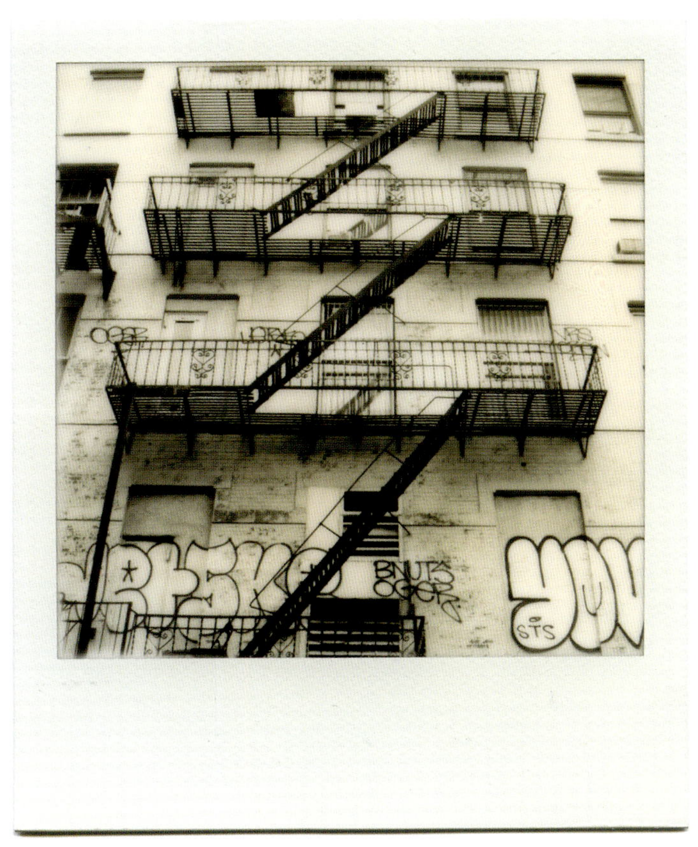

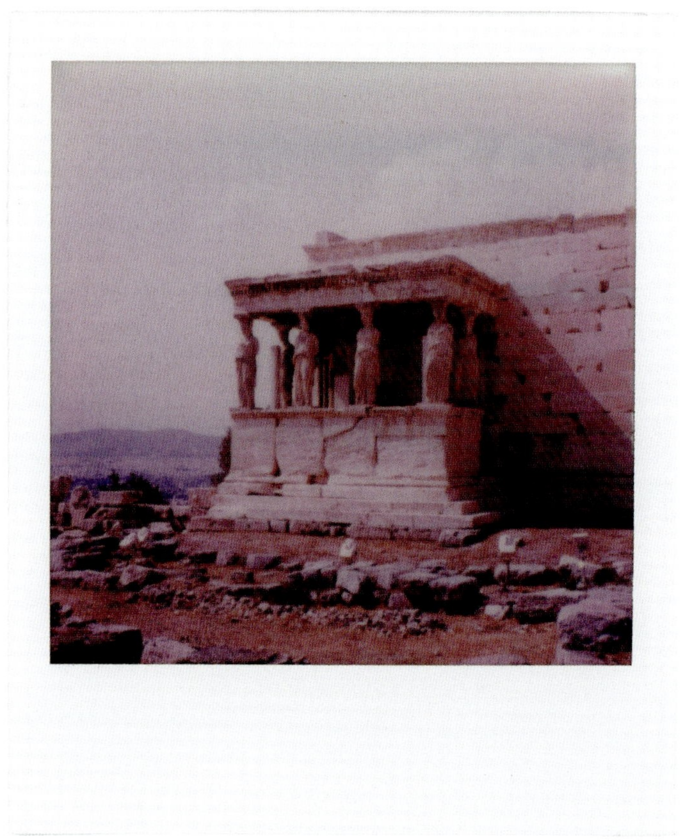

136   Sebastien Duval, *Untitled*

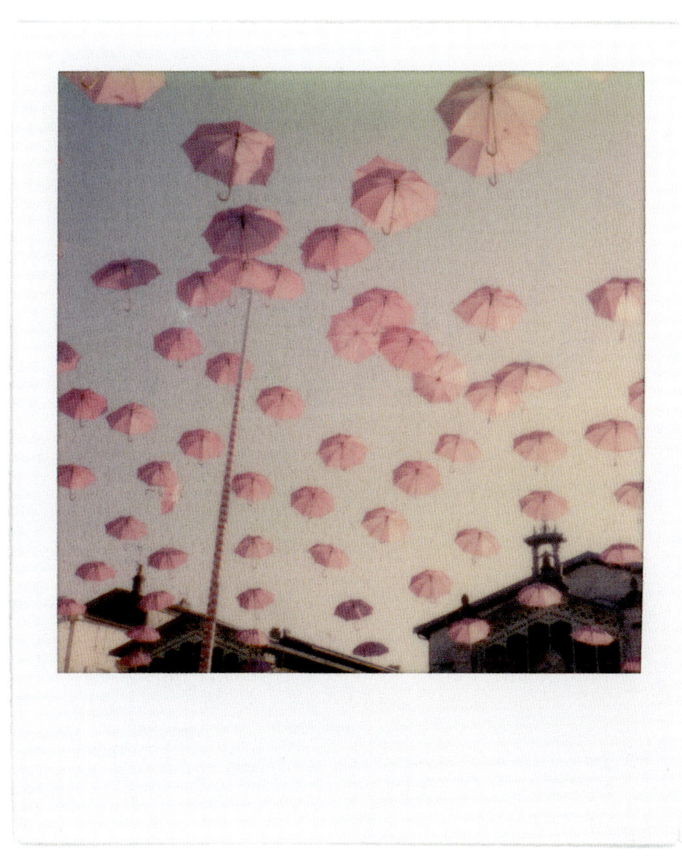

Sebastien Duval, *Untitled*   137

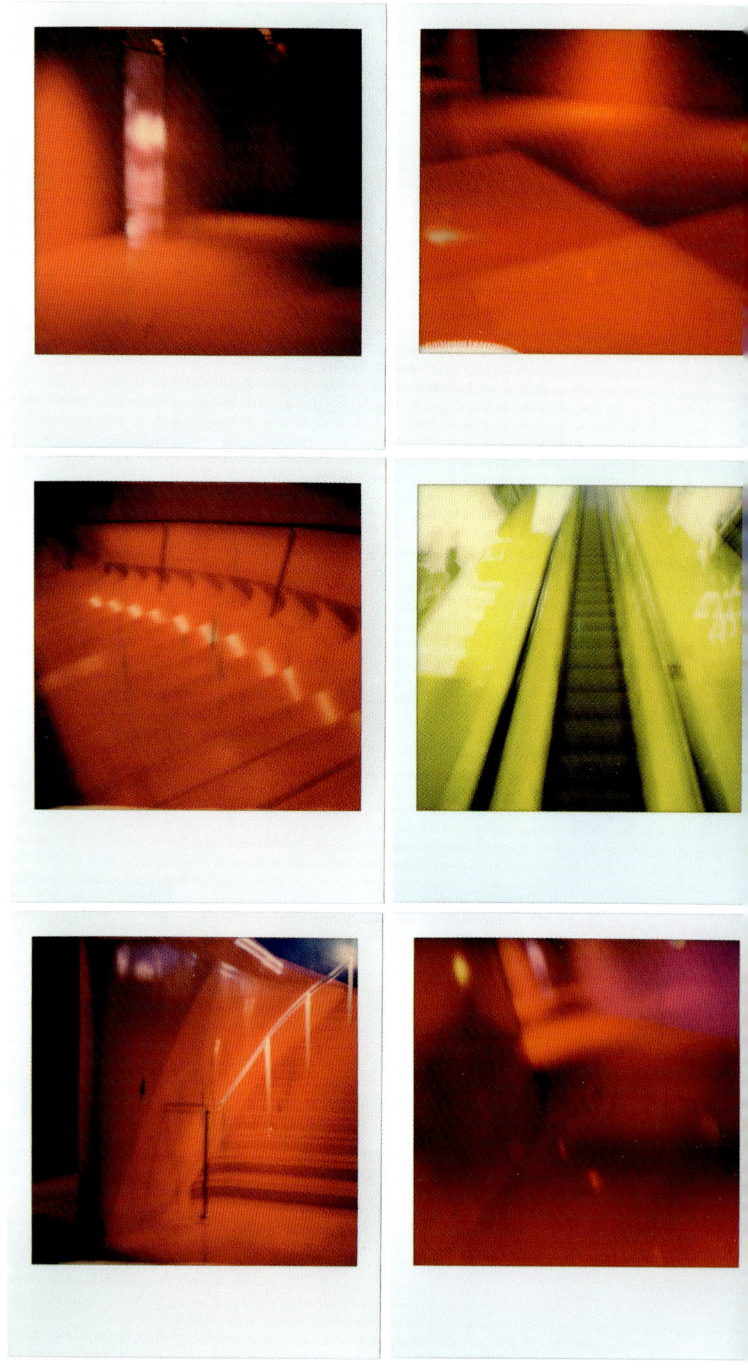

    Terry Karboski, *Untitled*

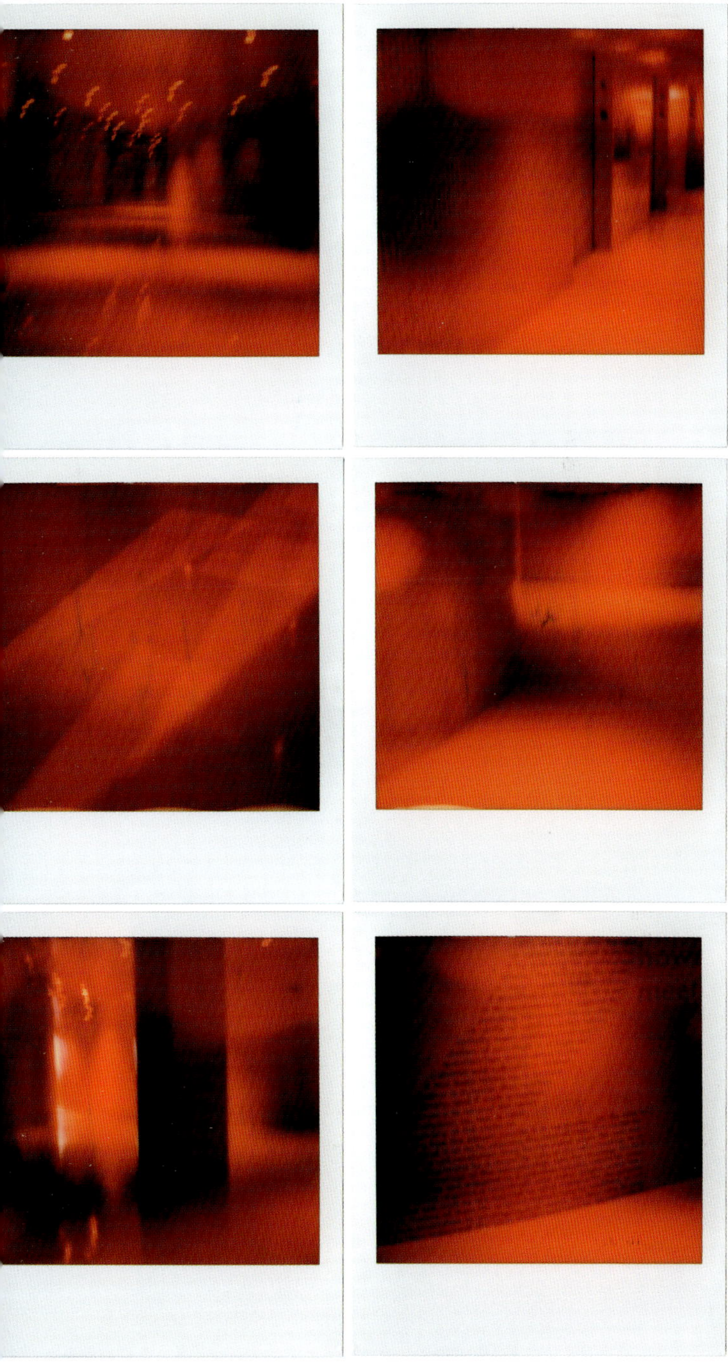

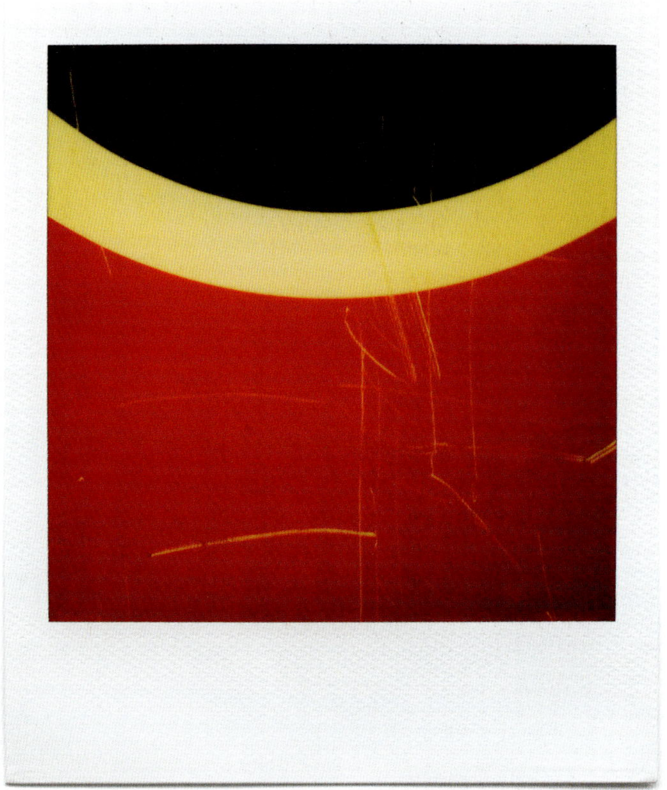

140   Grant Hamilton, *Smile*

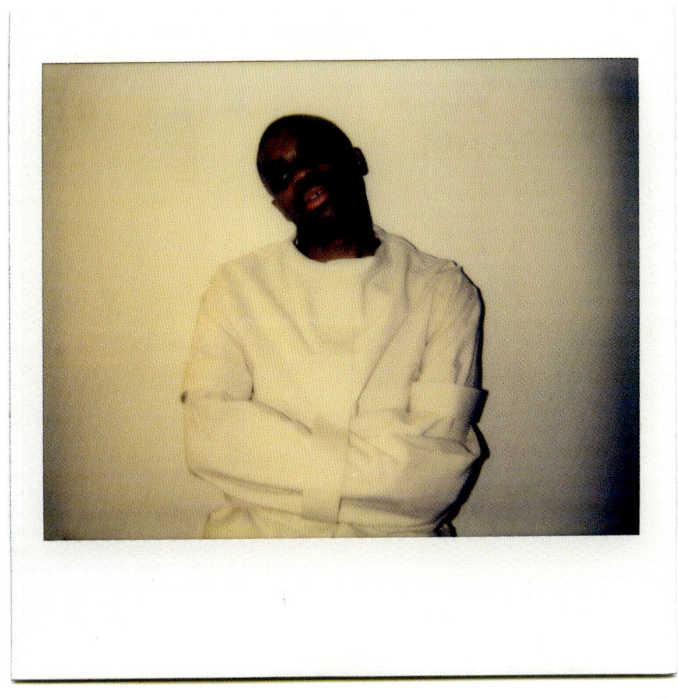

    Paolo Ferruzzi, *Windows*

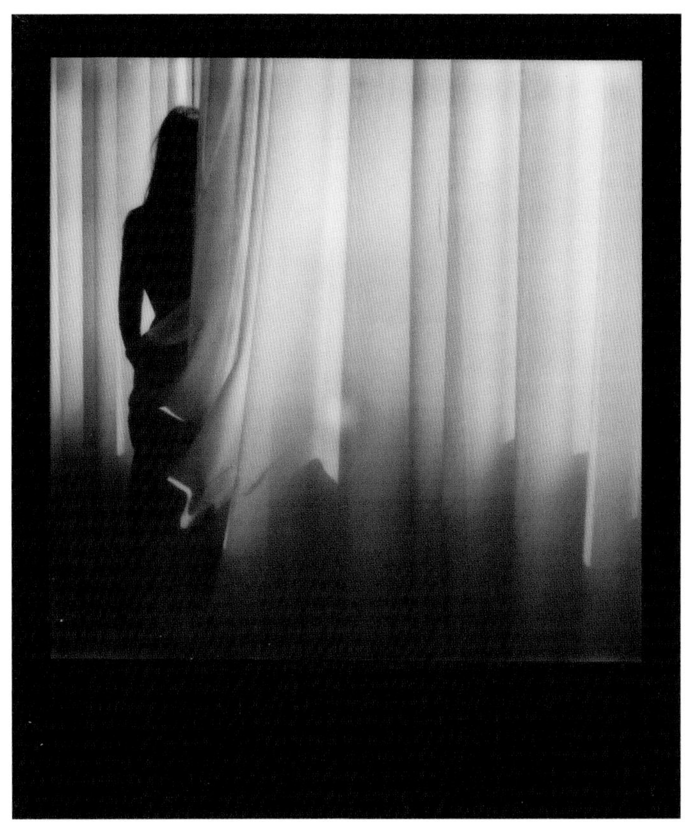

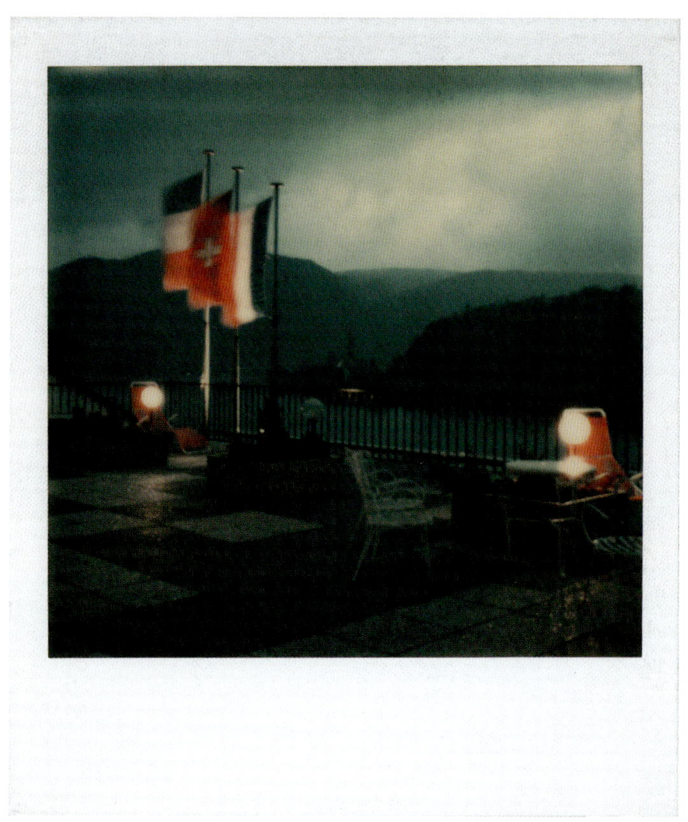

144   Robby Müller, *While shooting Falsche Bewegung*

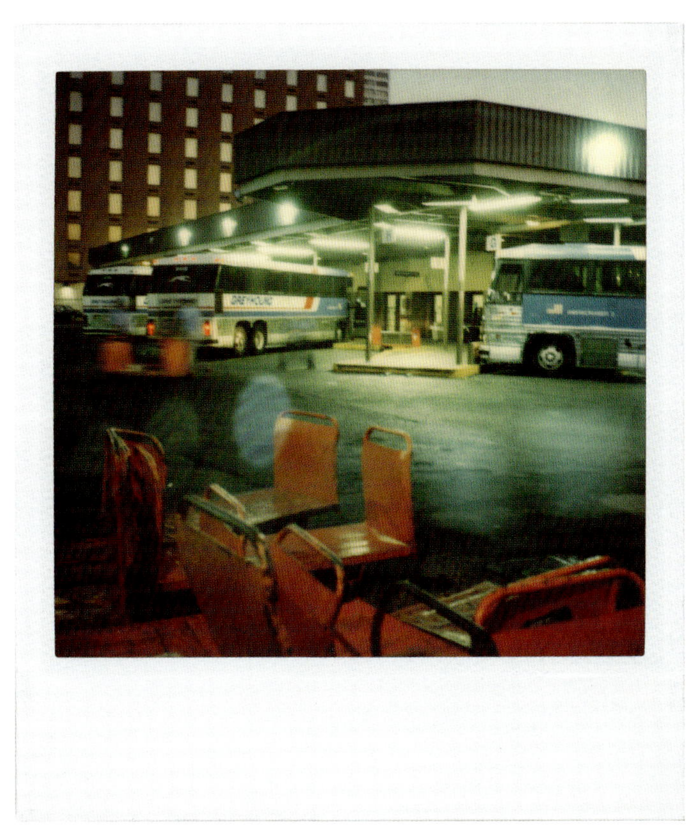

Robby Müller, *While shooting Honeysuckle Rose*   145

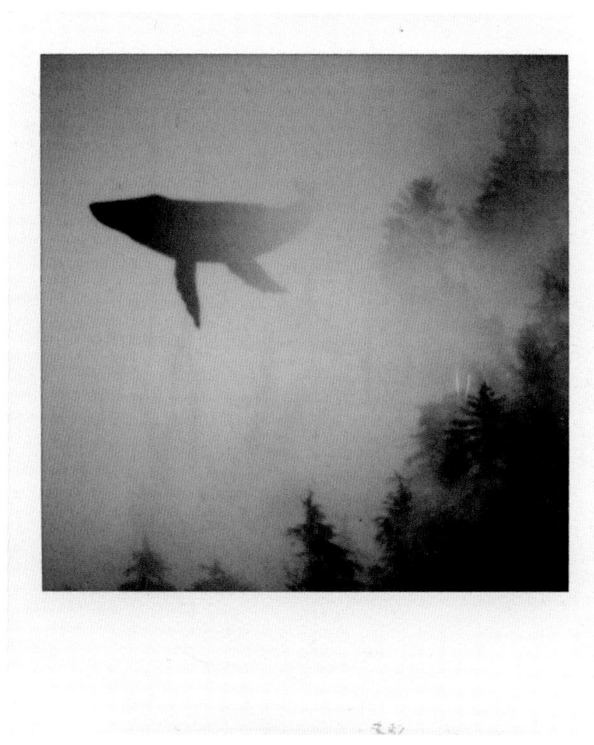

146   Alan Marcheselli, *My Dreams are Heavy*

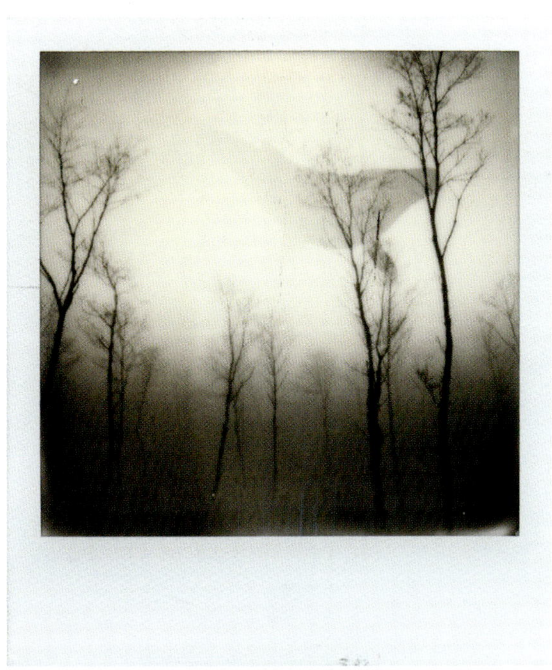 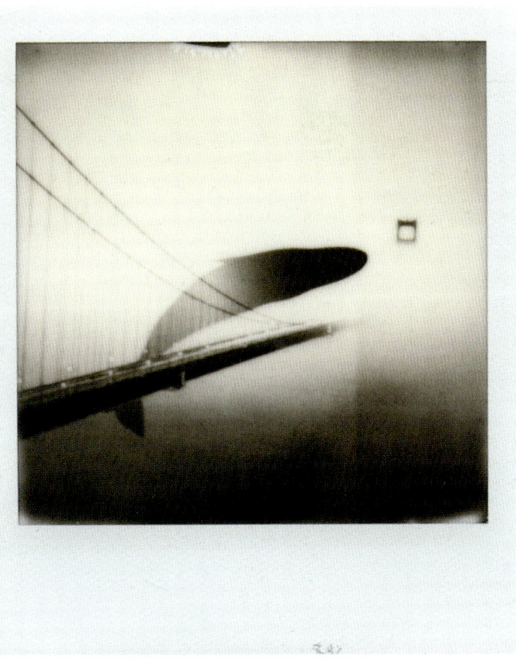

    Brady Flores, *Untitled*

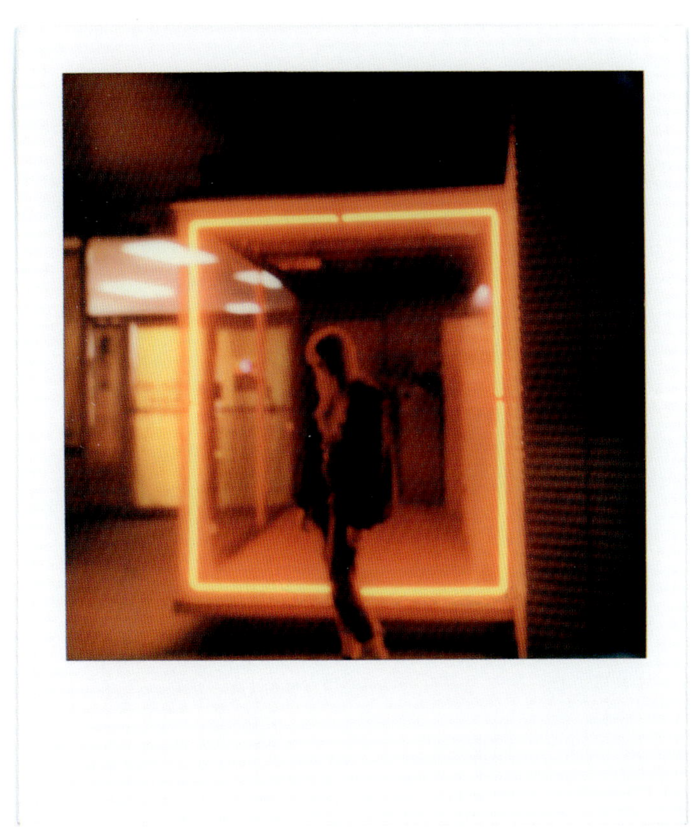

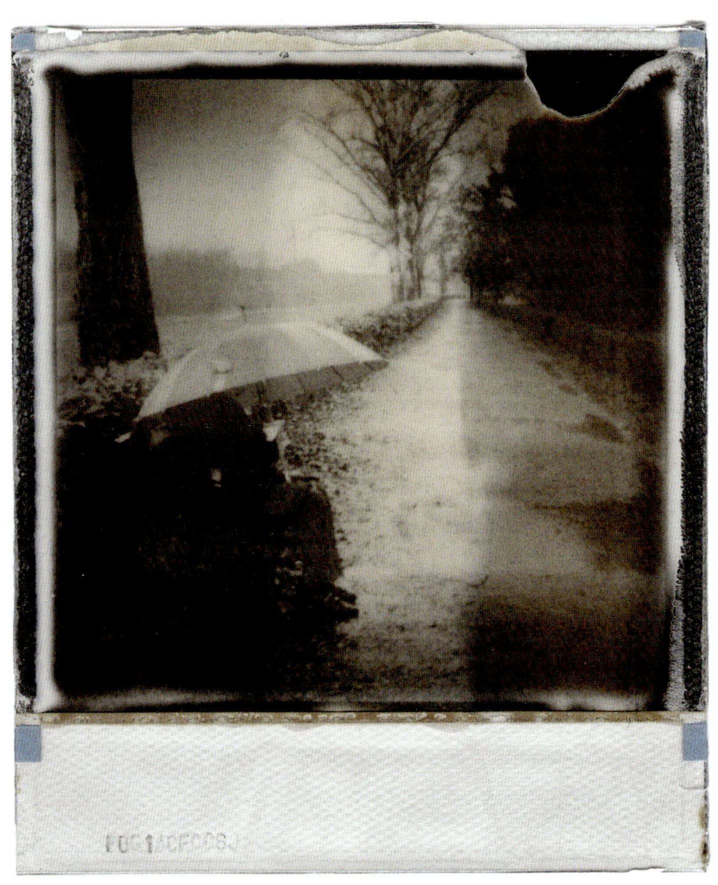

150   Amedeo Fontani, *Tardus Pluvia*

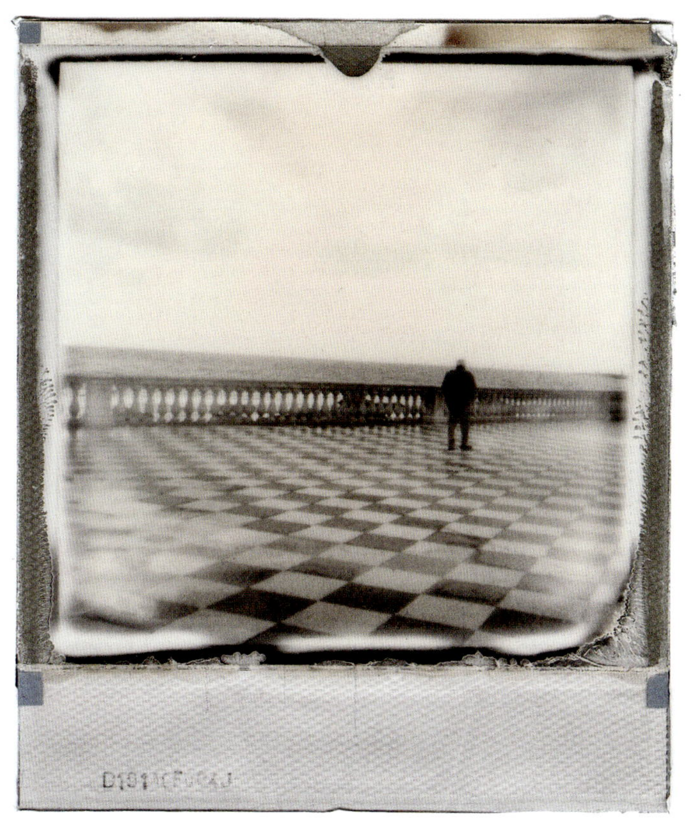

Amedeo Fontani, *Under The Shutter*   151

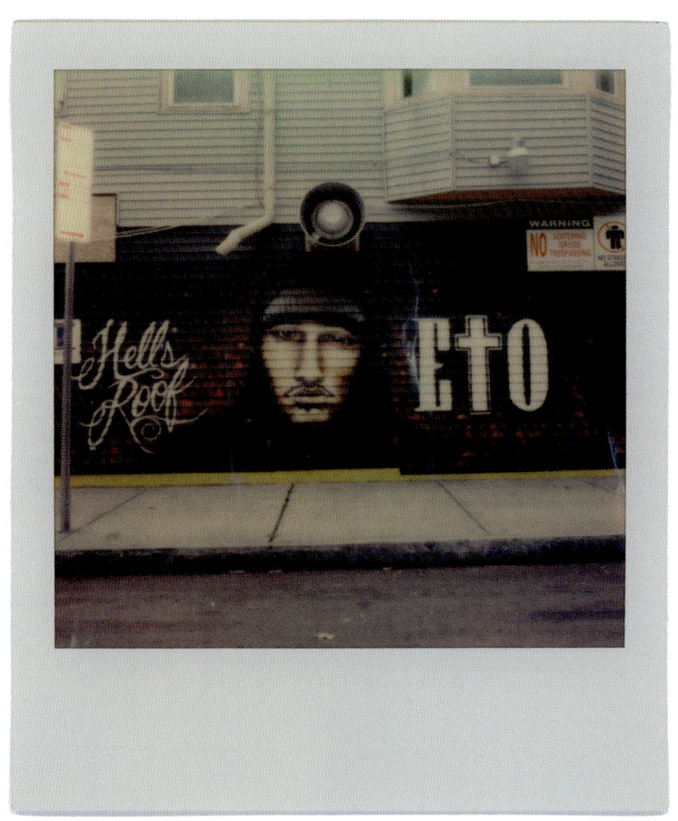

152   Ramon Lazo, *HELL'S ROOF*

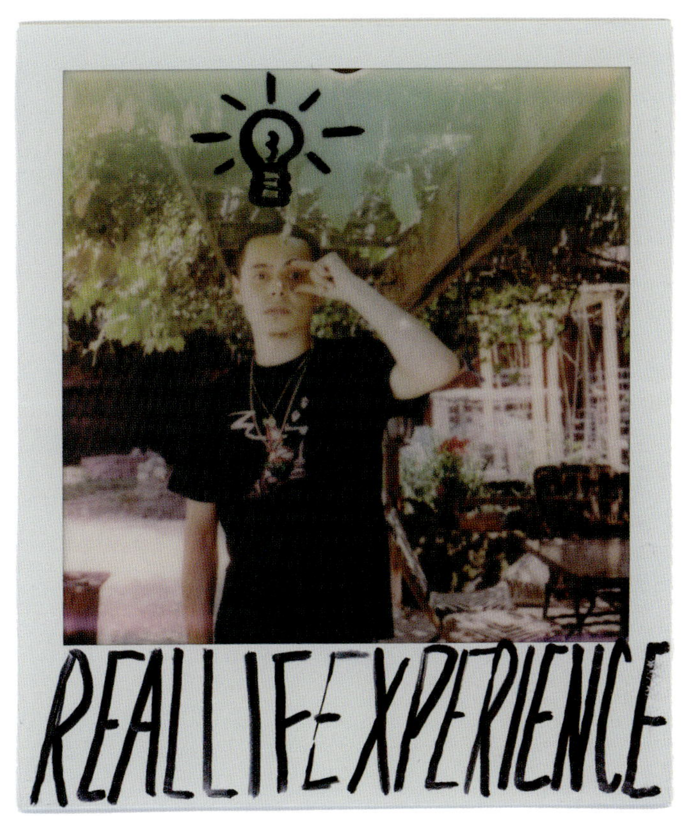
REALLIFEXPERIENCE

    Urizen Freaza, *Georg's mask*

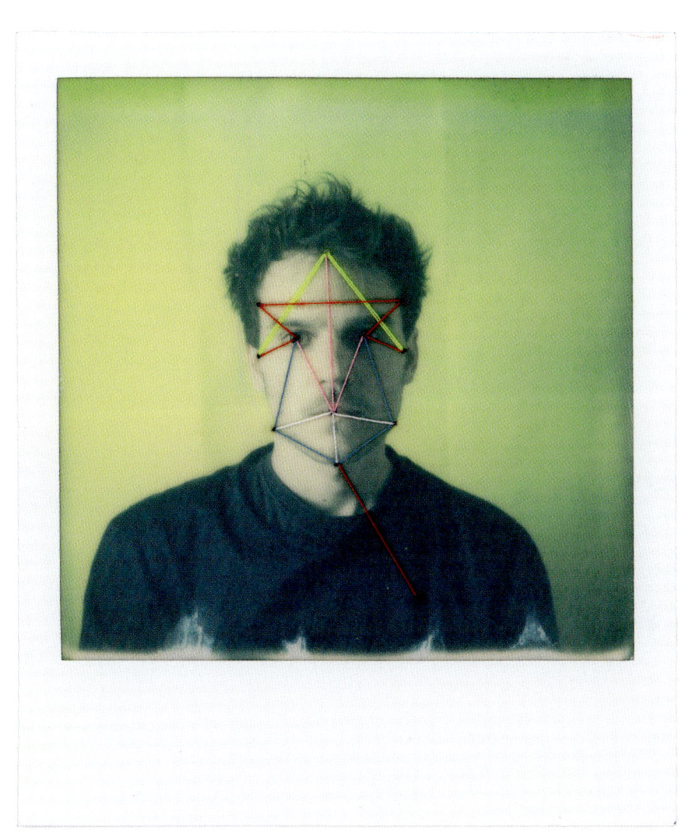

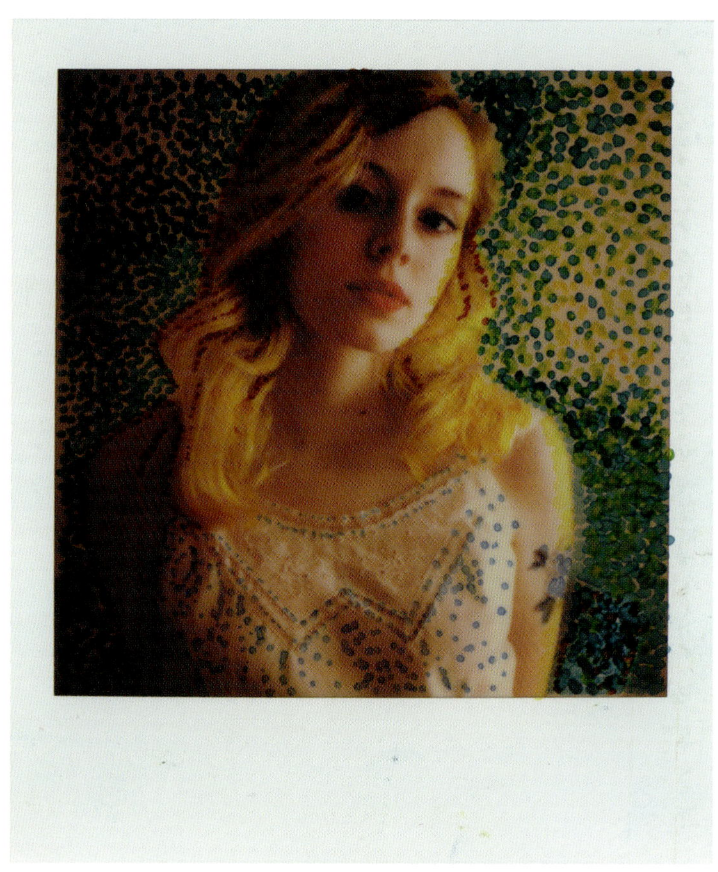

156   Penny Felts, *Emily*

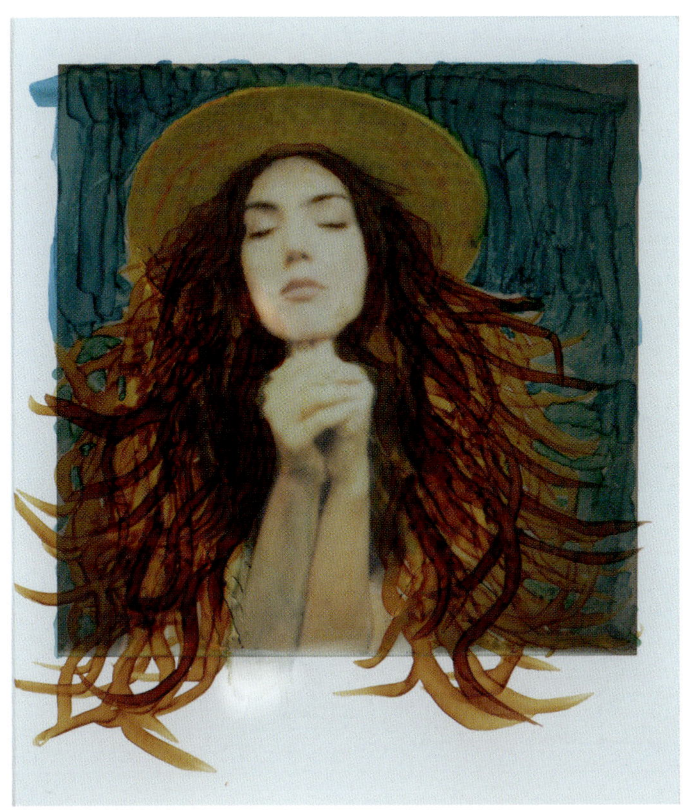

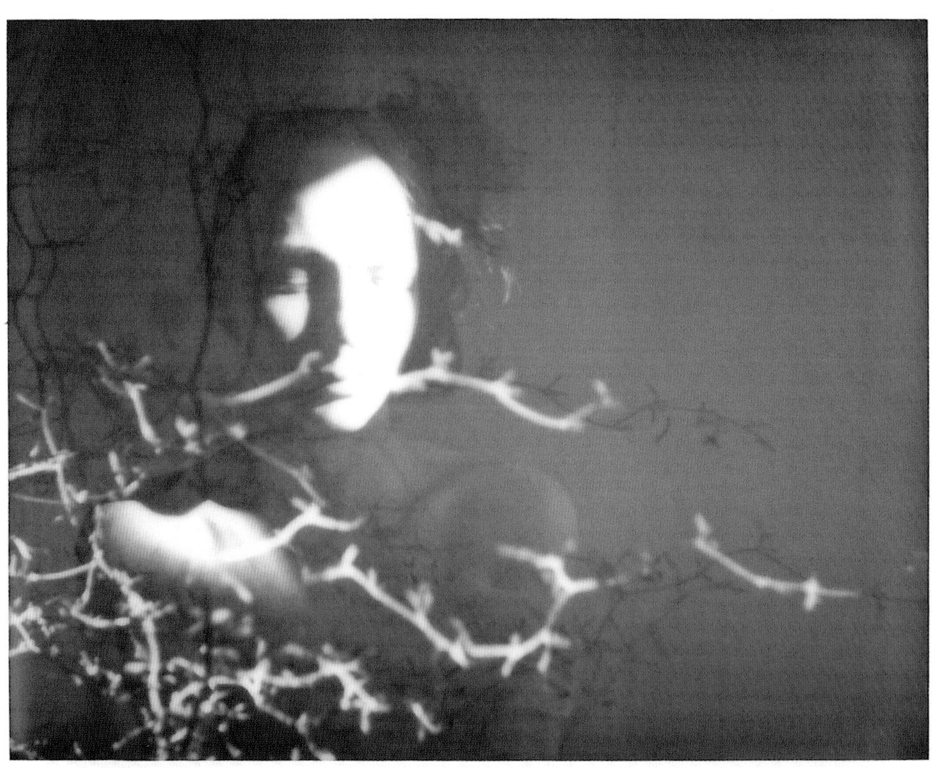

158   Alex Conu, *Untitled*

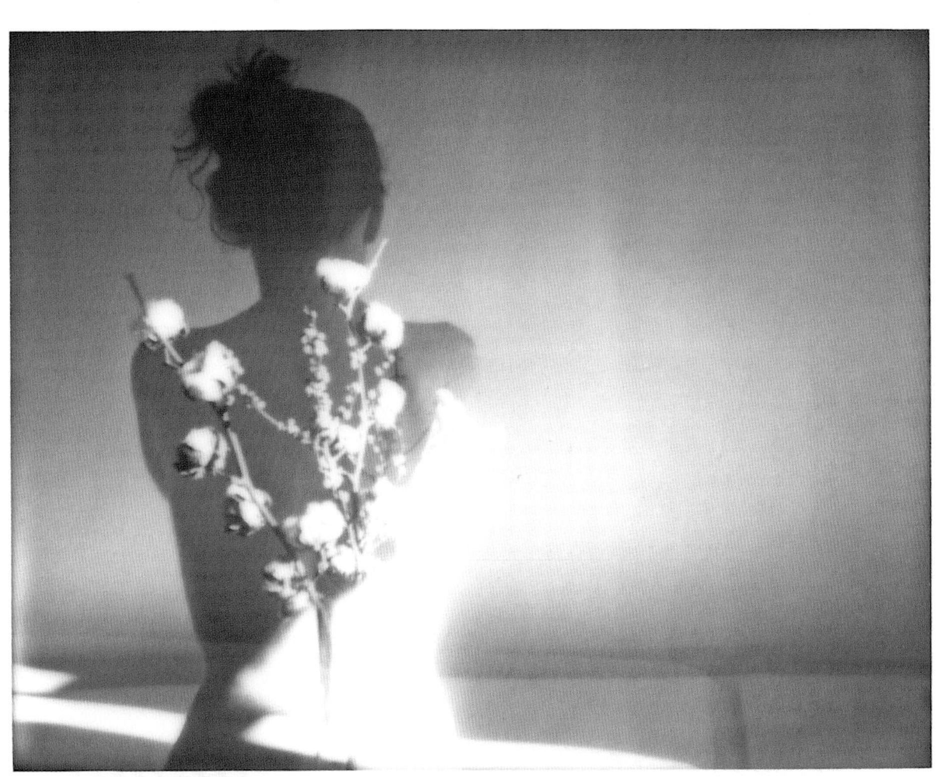

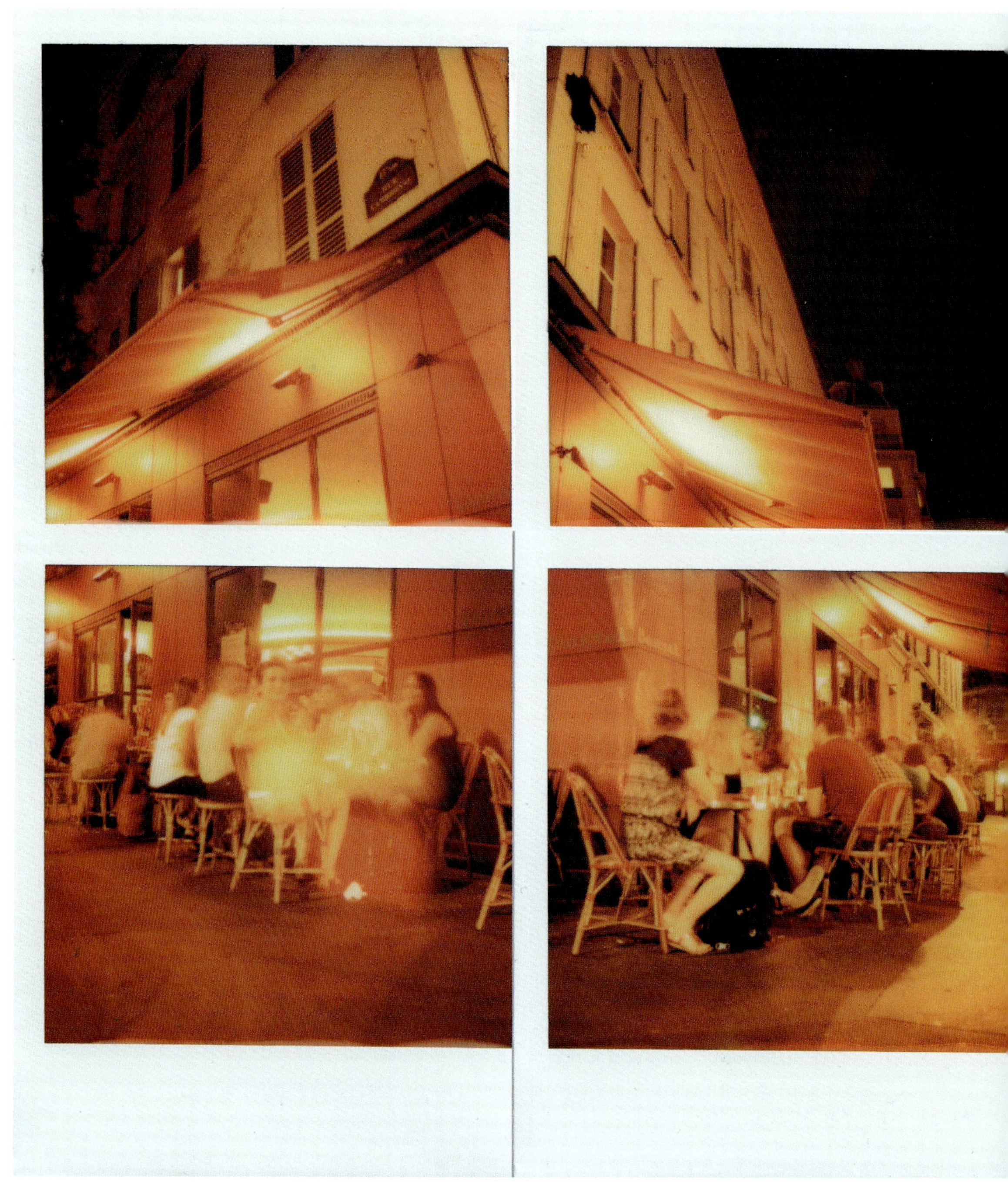

160 Clément Grosjean, *Aux 4 Coins - La Nuit*

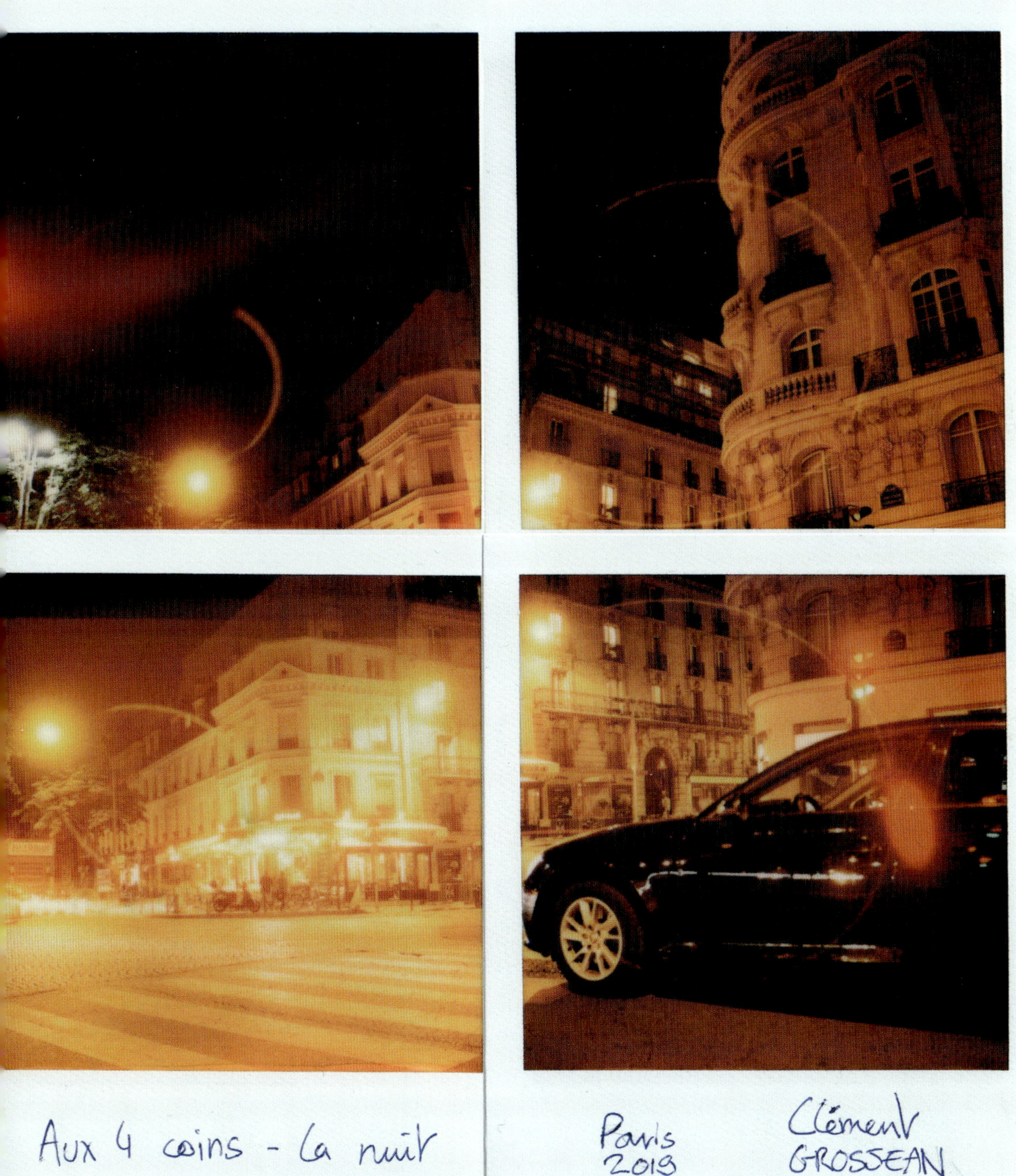

Aux 4 coins - La nuit
Paris
2019
Clément
GROSSEAN

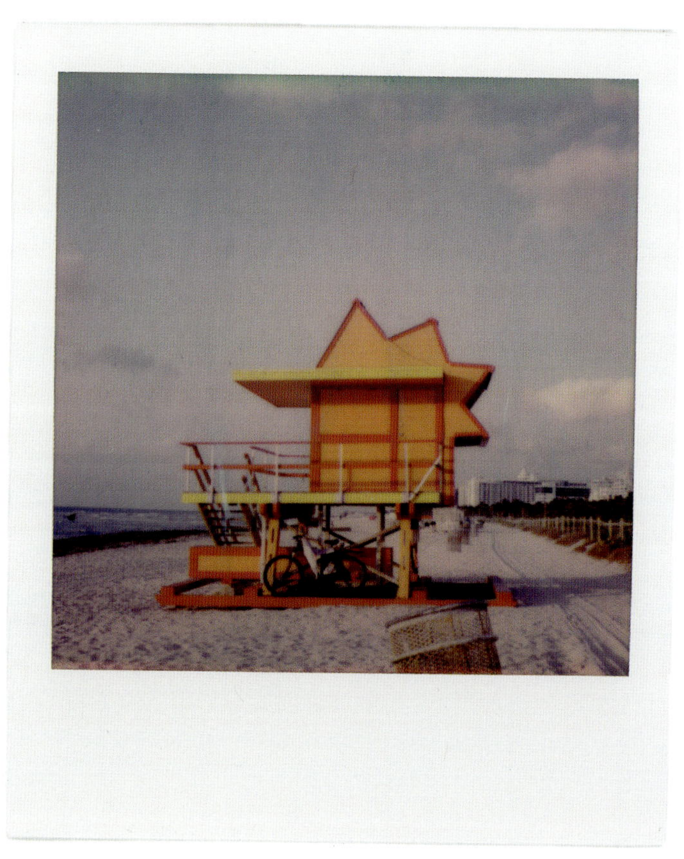

162   Sebastien Duval, *Untitled*

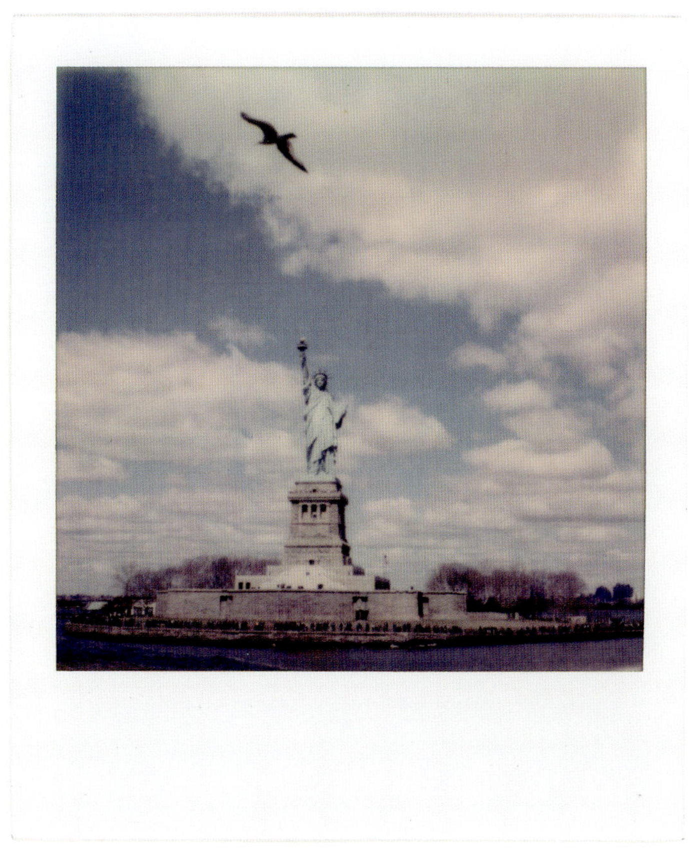

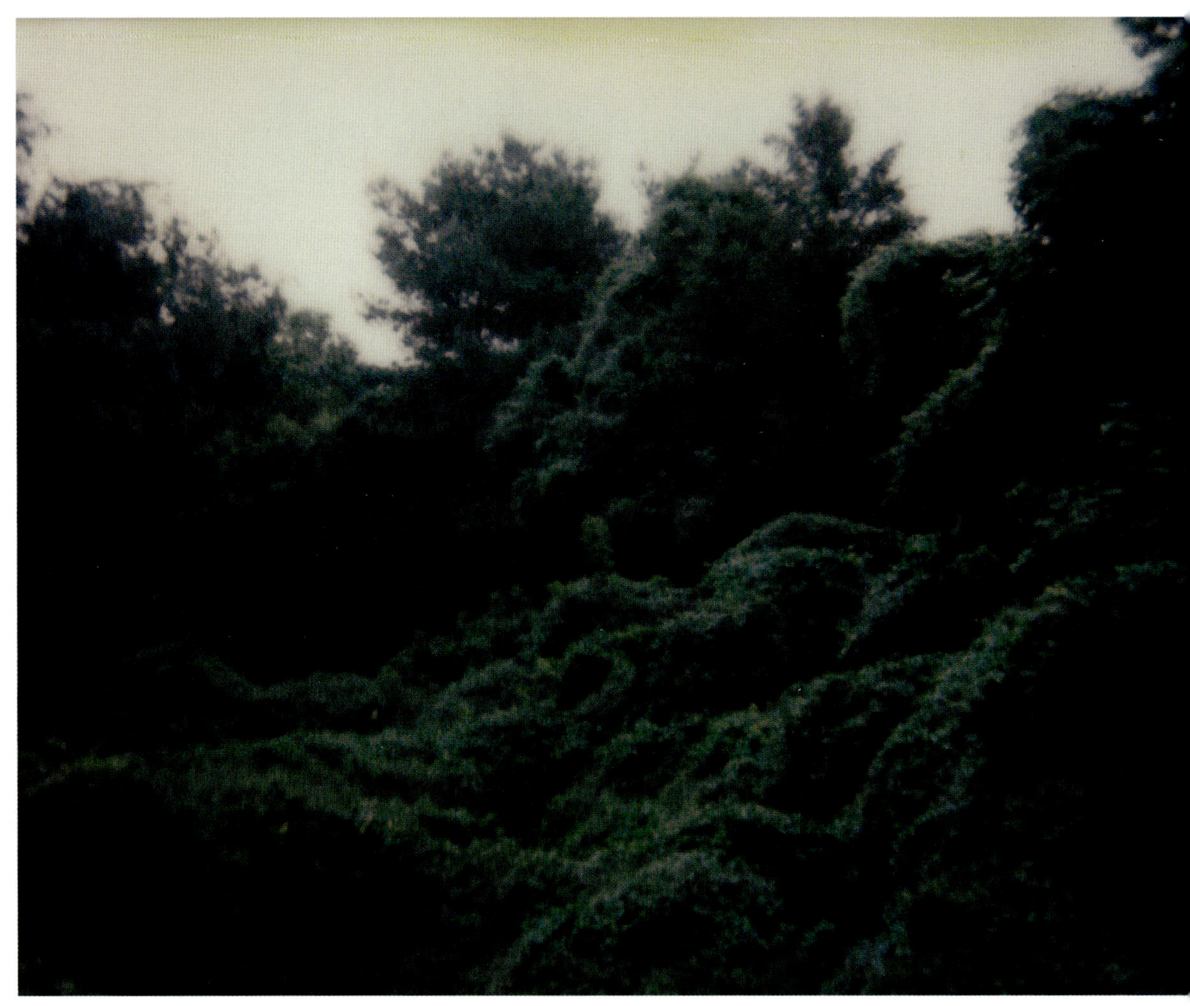

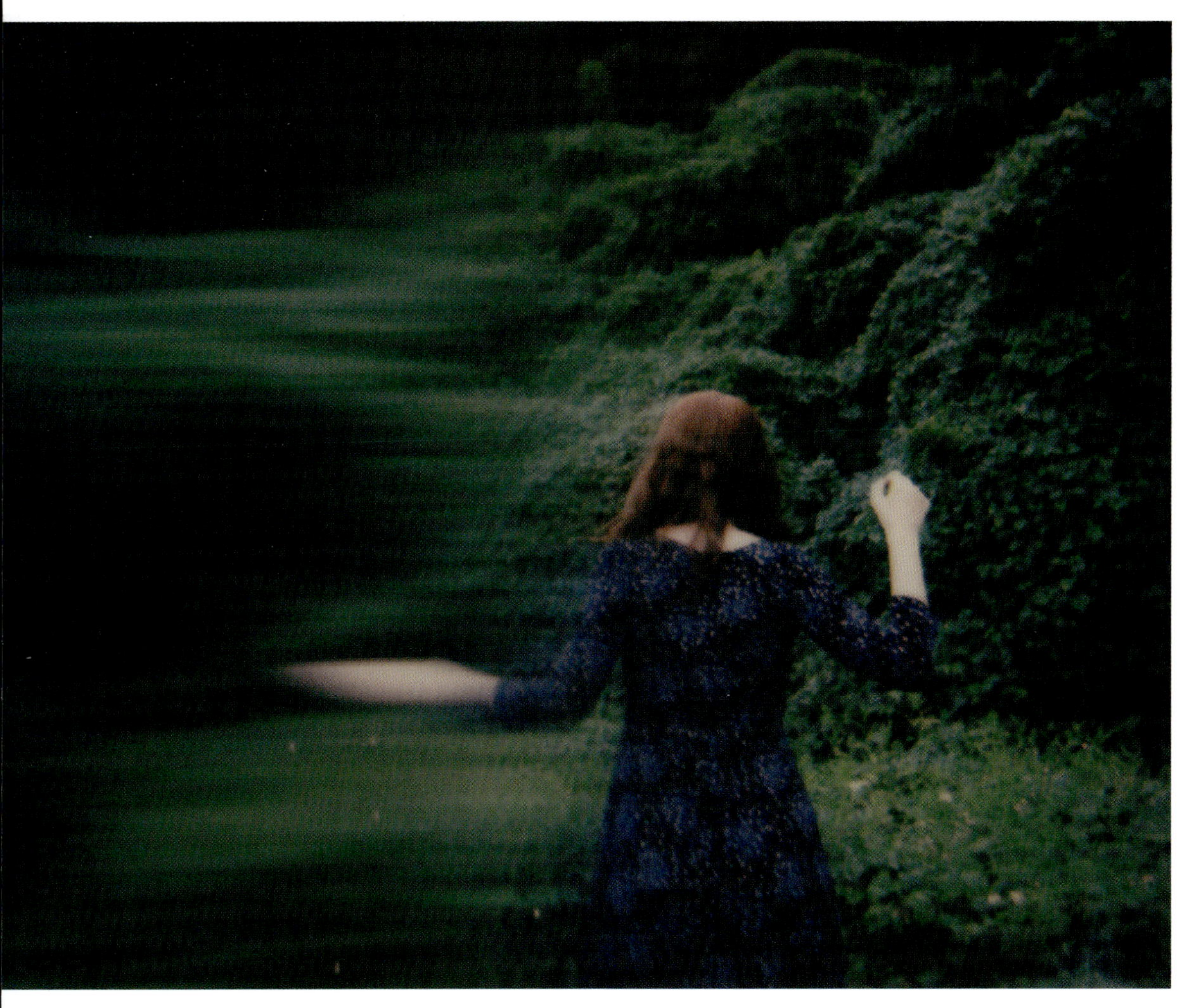

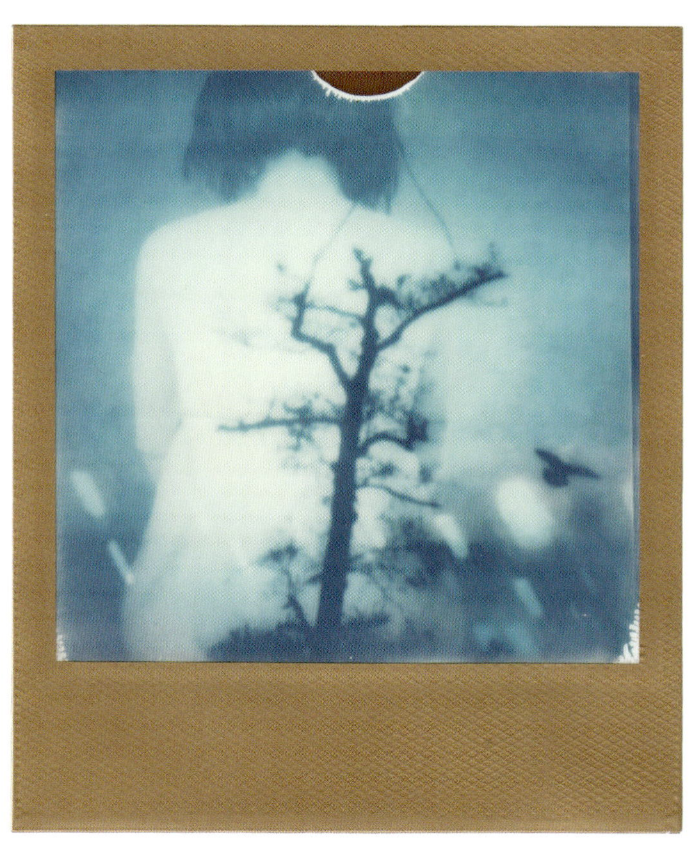

166   Lela Gruen, *My Connection*

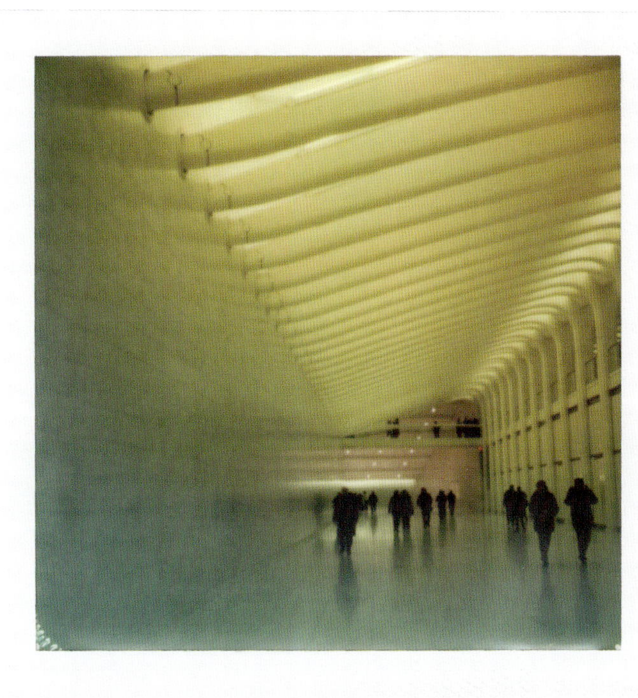

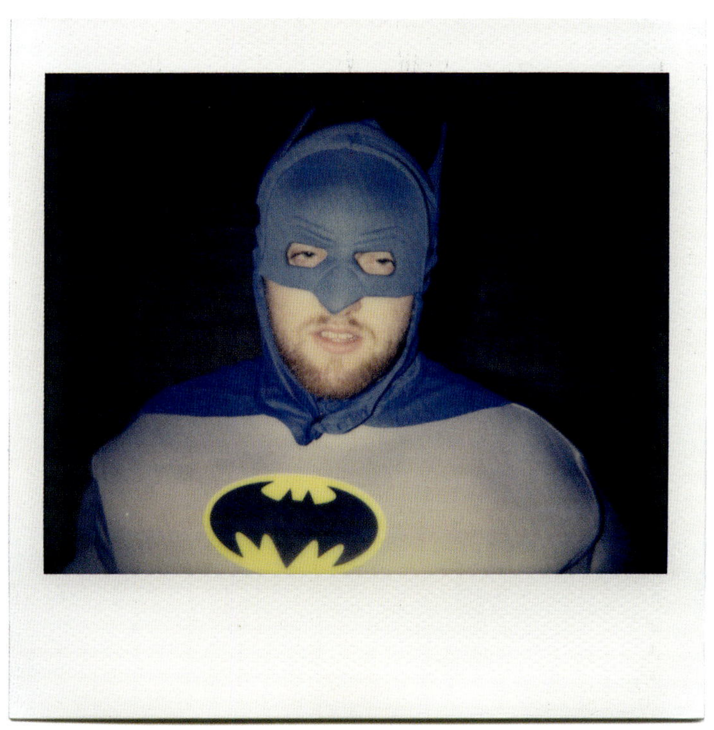

168   Brock Fetch, *Mac Miller*

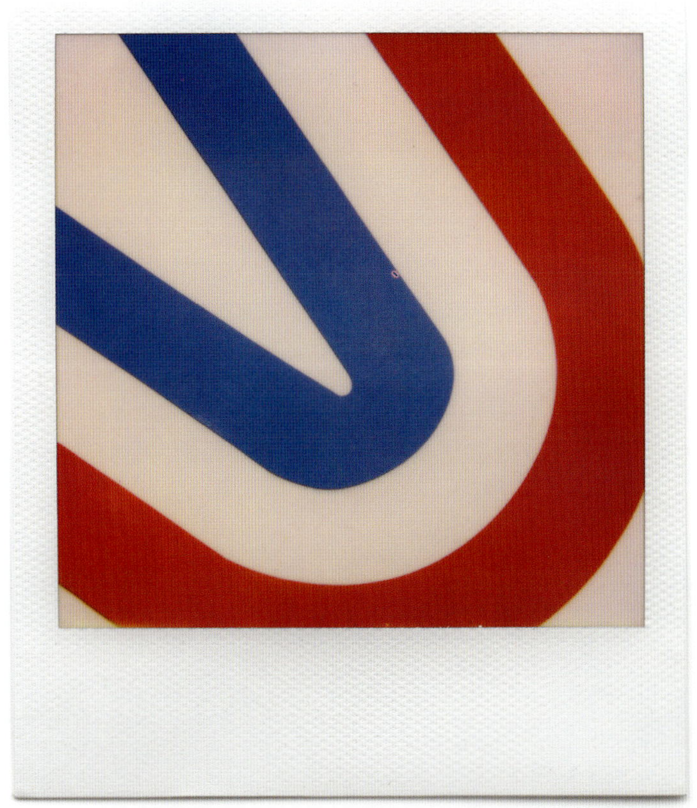

Grant Hamilton, *Spirit of '76*   169

 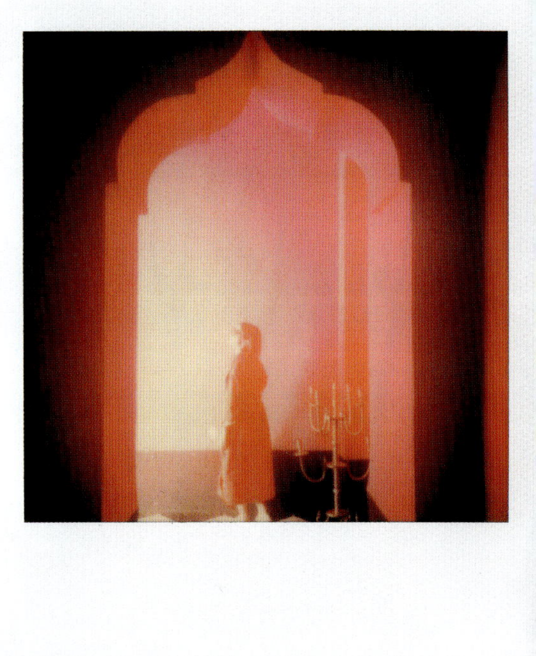

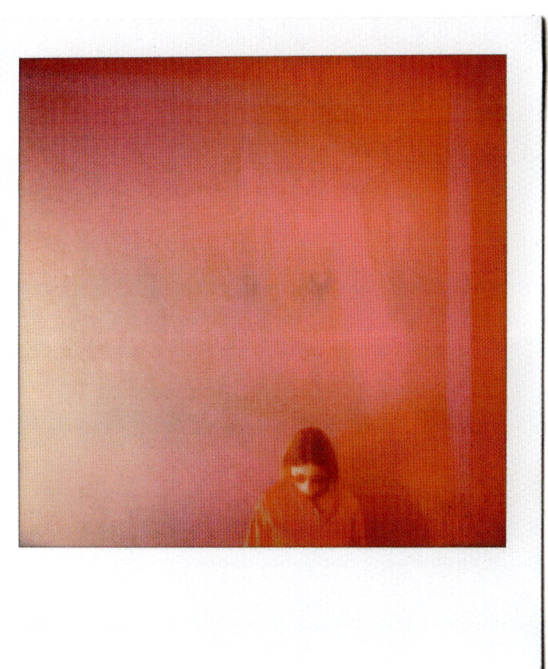

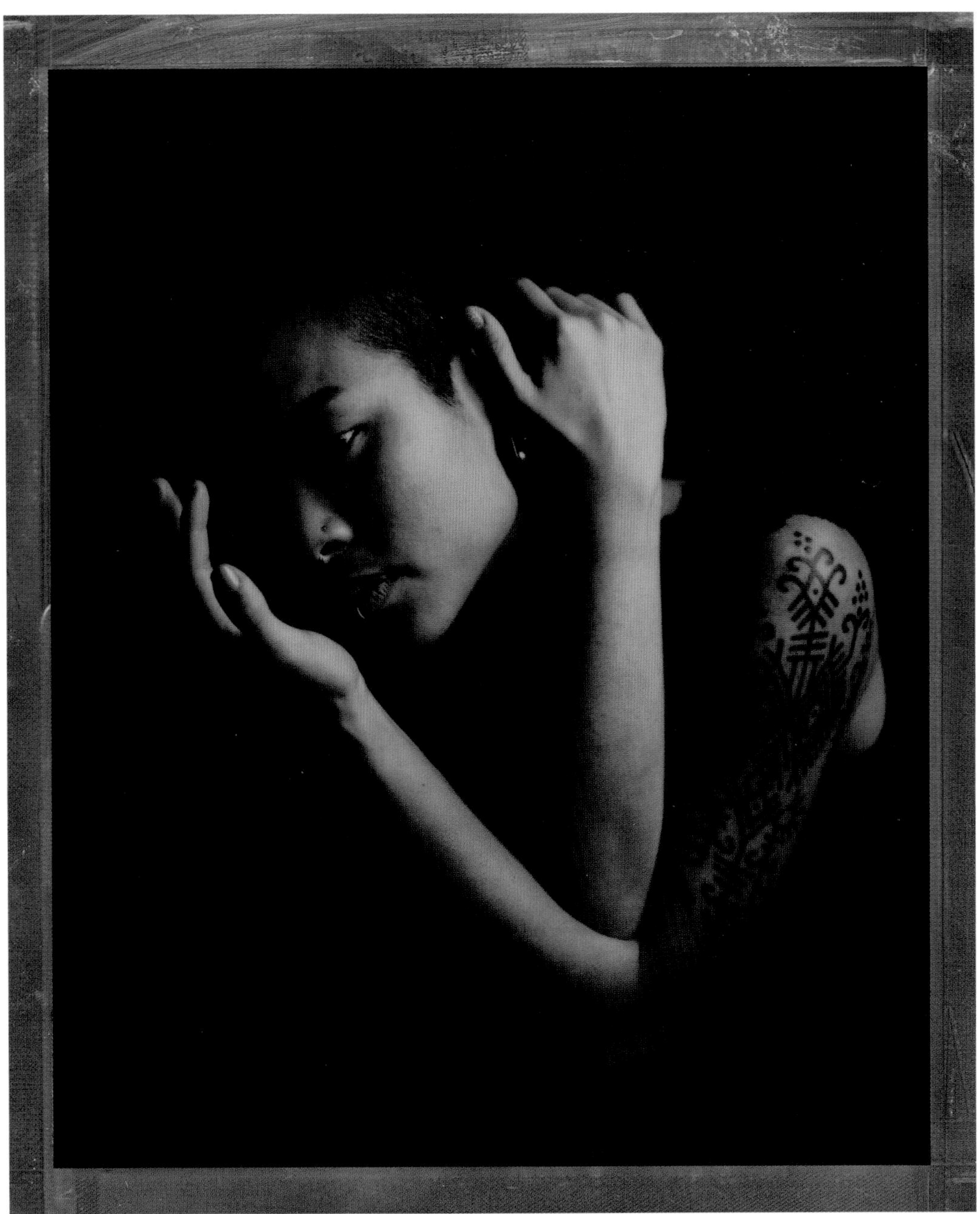

172   Harriet Browse, *Untitled*

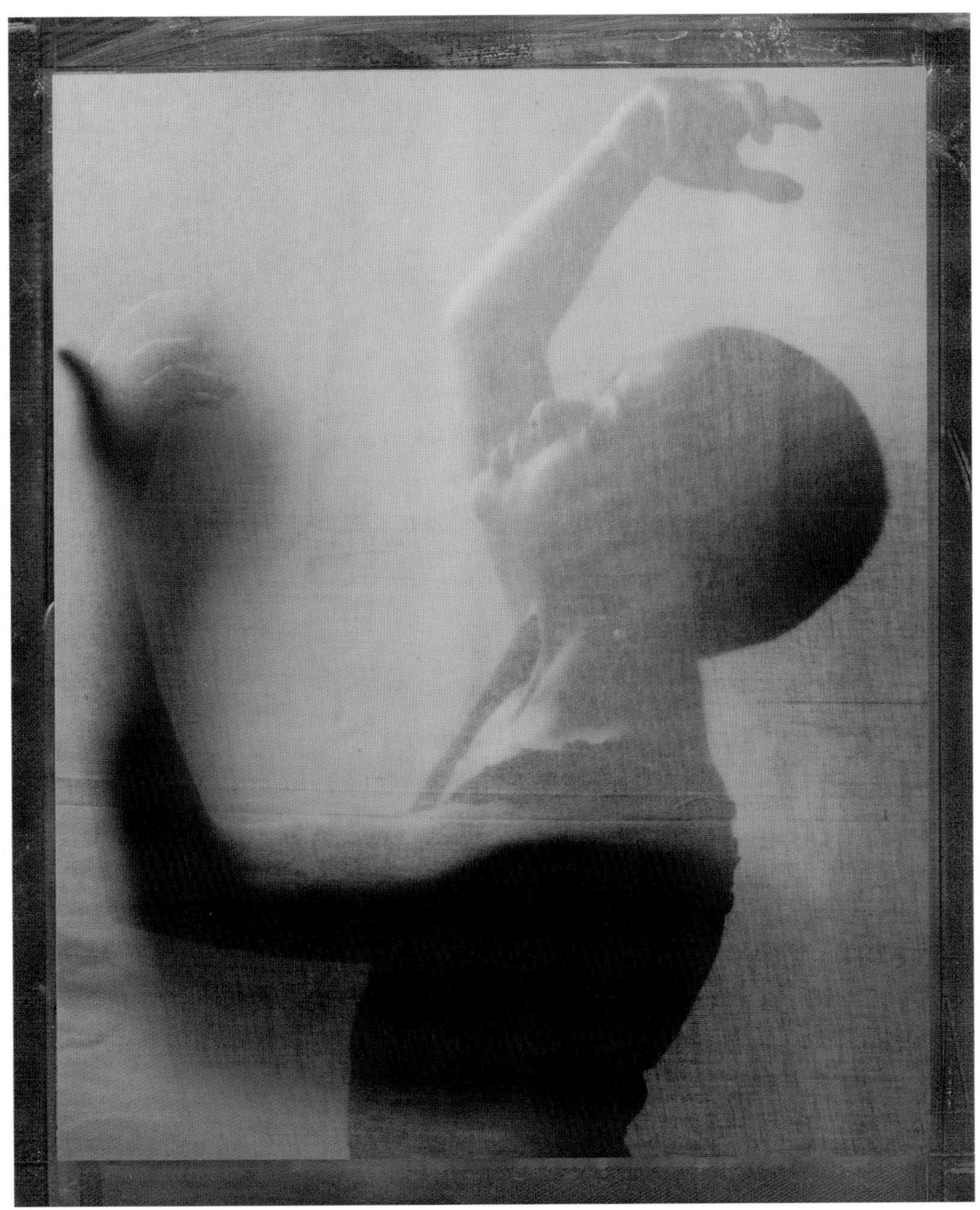

Harriet Browse, *Untitled*   173

 Lilian Wildeboer, *Swan of the Lake*

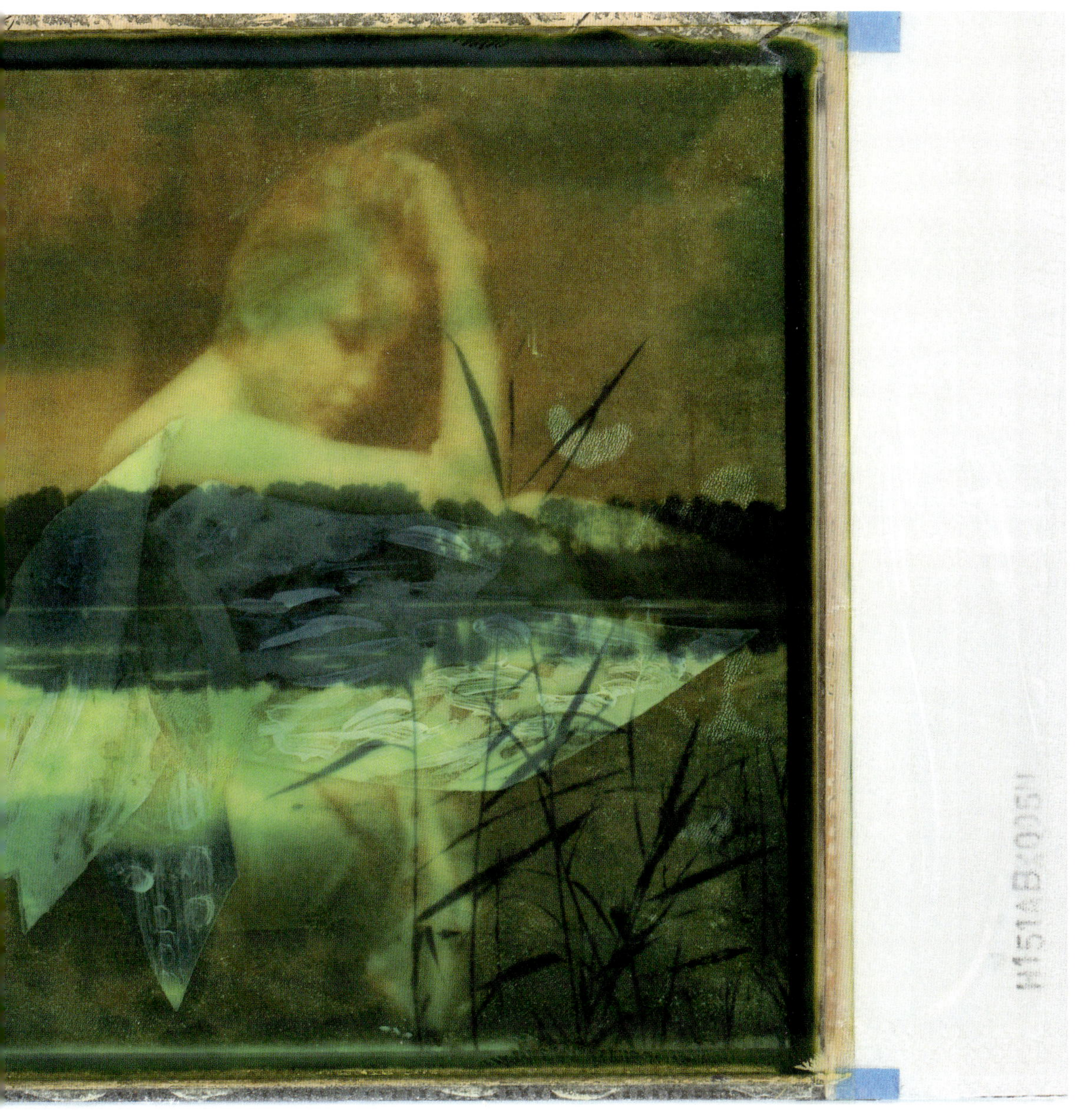
"151AB'035"

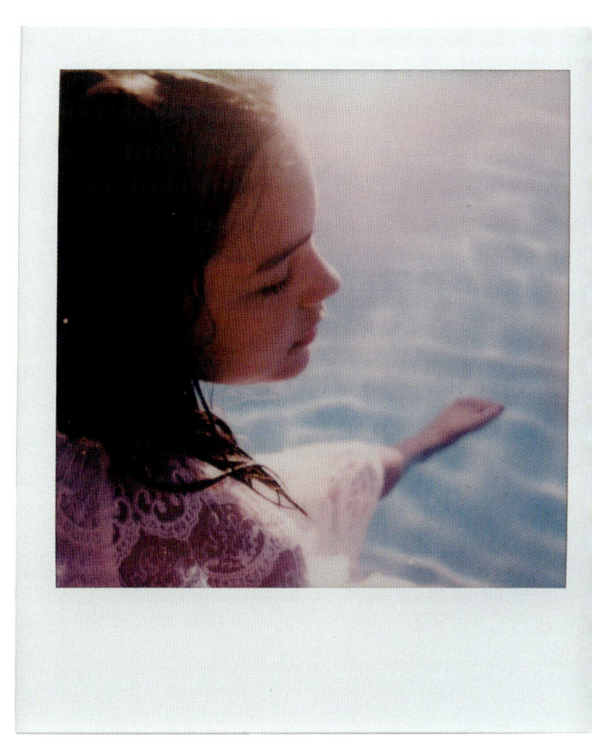

    Noemi Heidel, *A Pool Fairytale*

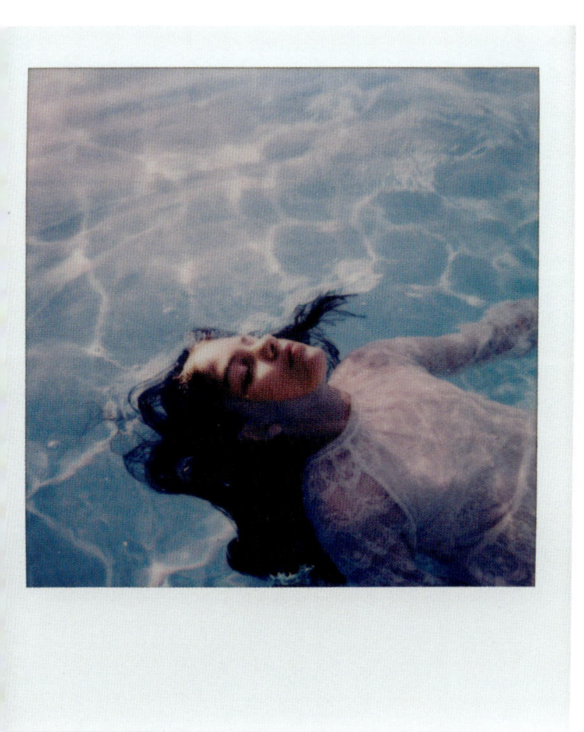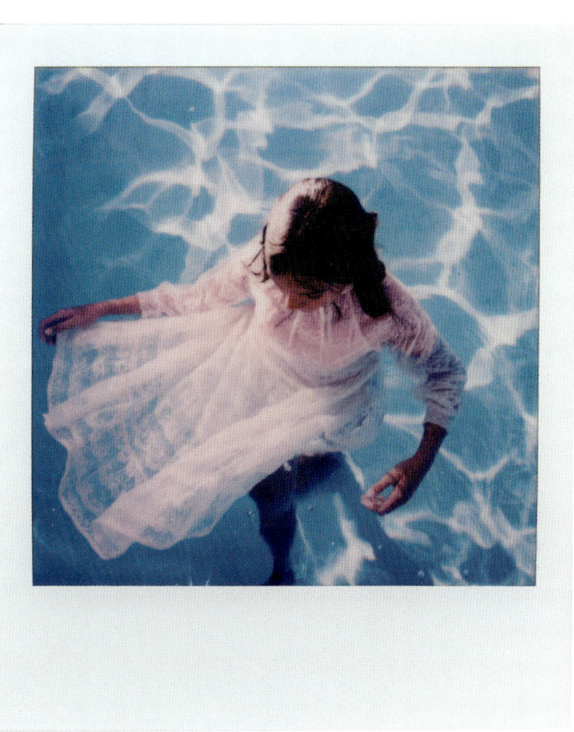

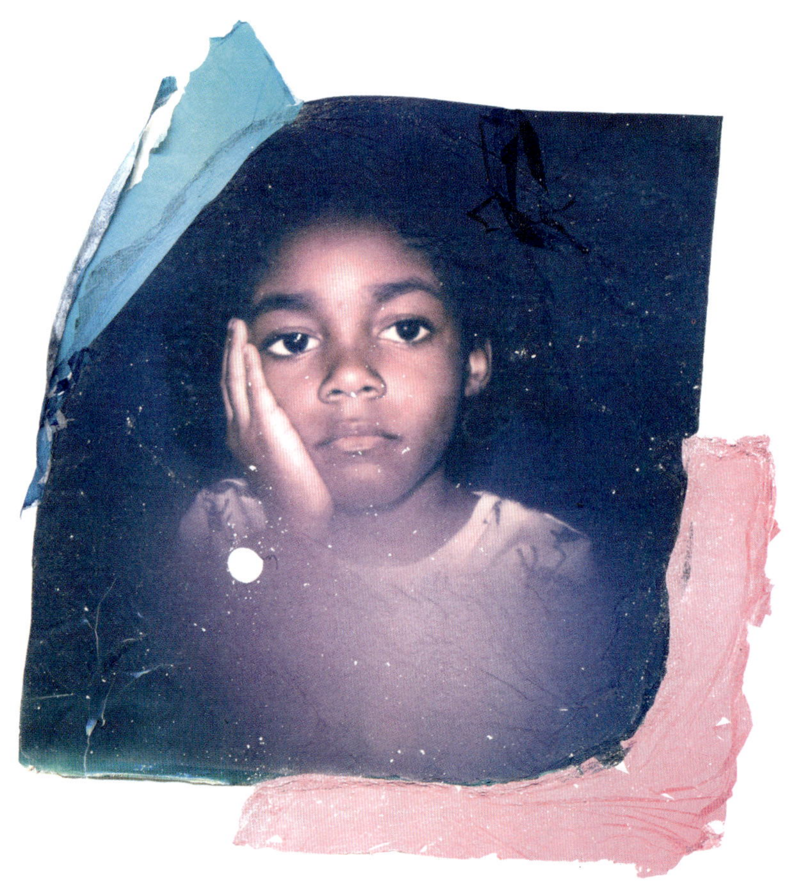

    Jerome Freeman, *Isabella*

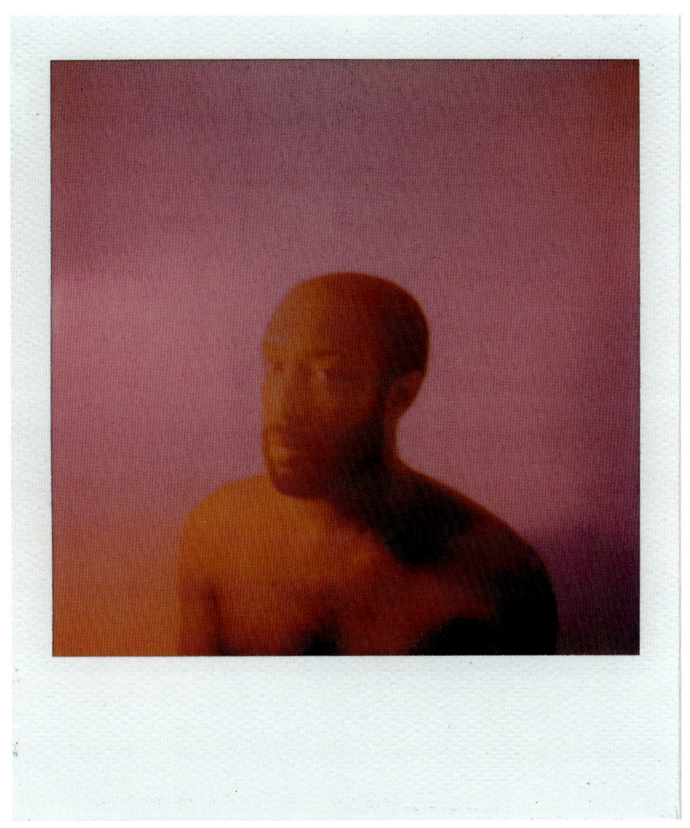

Jerome Freeman, *Untitled*   179

   Grant Hamilton, *Poolside*

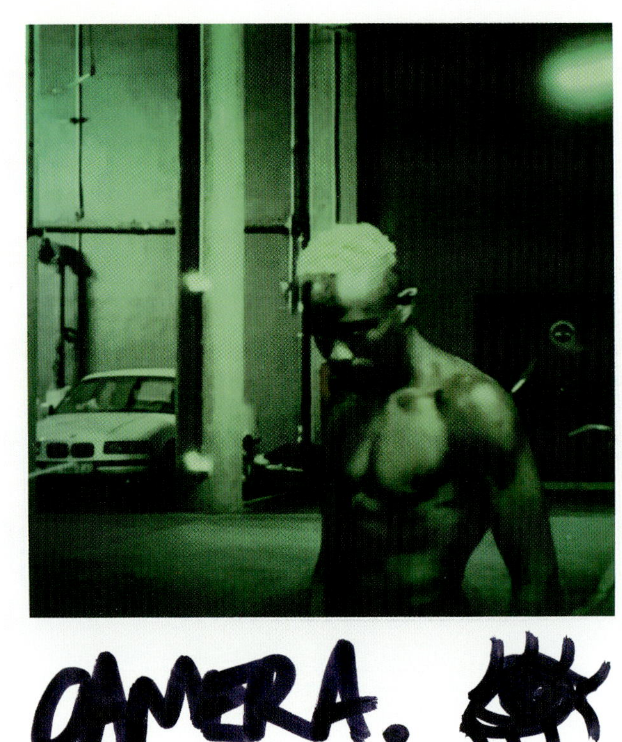

   Rayan Nohra, *Camera*

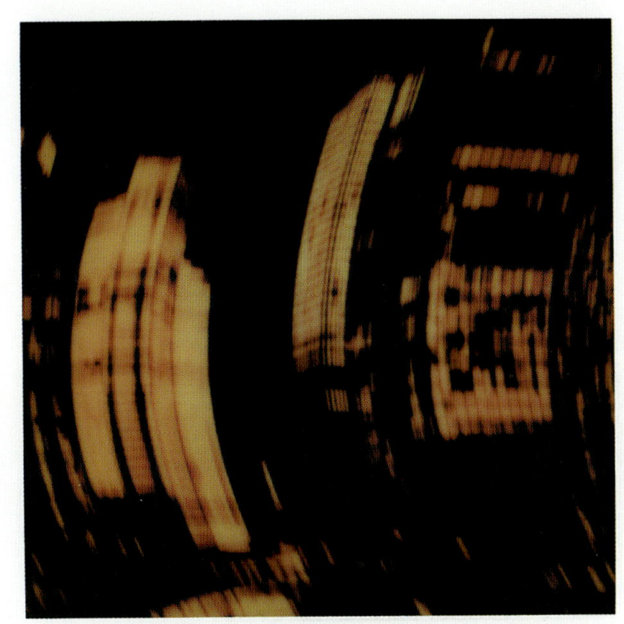
DISTORTION WITH A GLASS
(PARIS , NIGHT TIME)

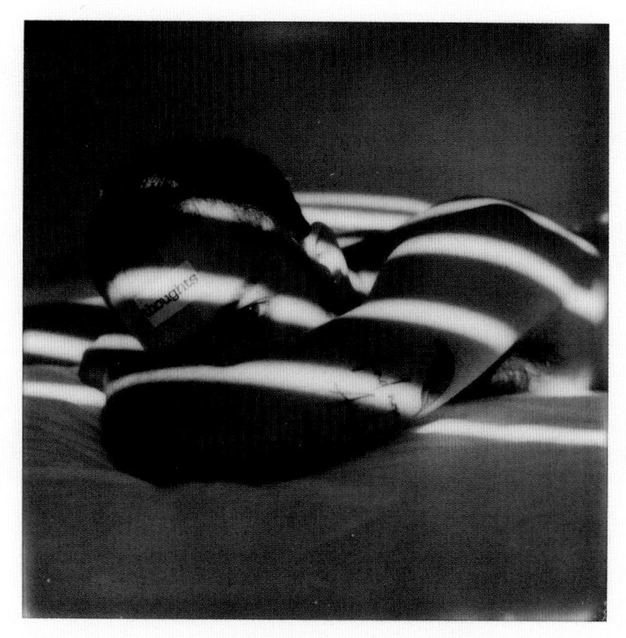

  Ariel Shelleg, *Idle Hands & Busy Minds* / self portrait

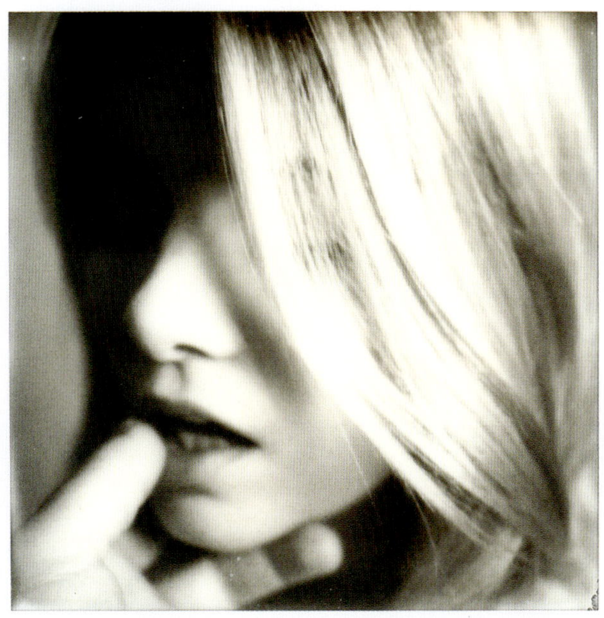

Ariel Shelleg, *Luxuria* / self portrait with Pauli   185

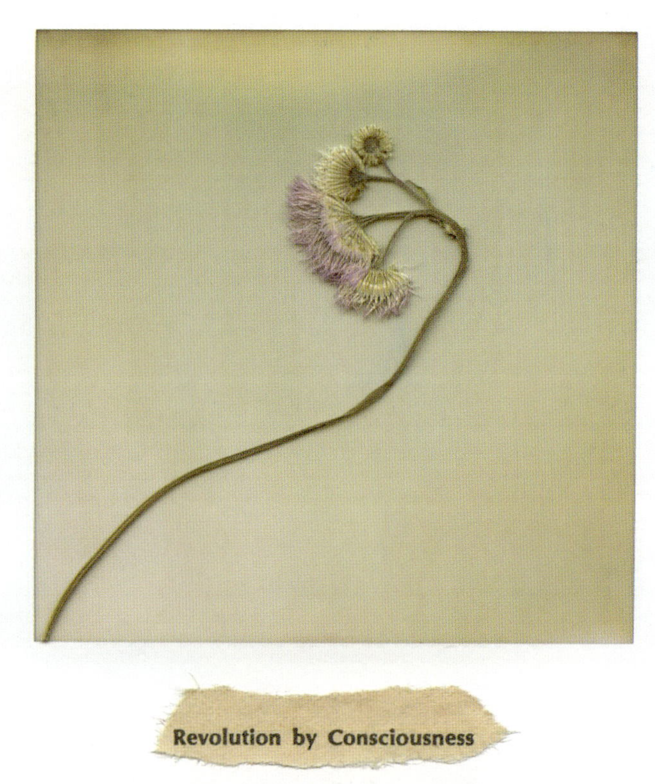

186   Nikita Gross, *Revolutions by Consciousness*

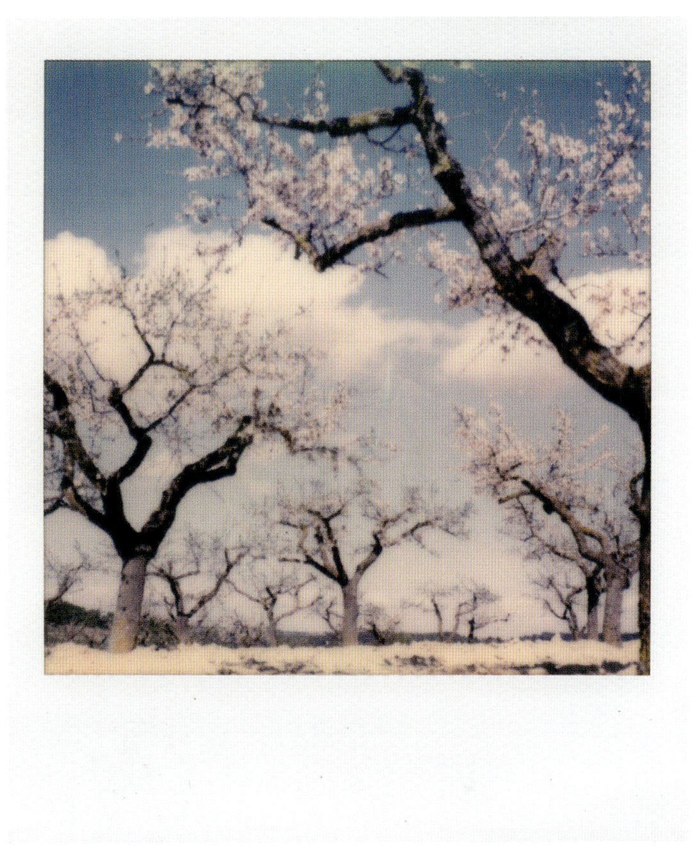

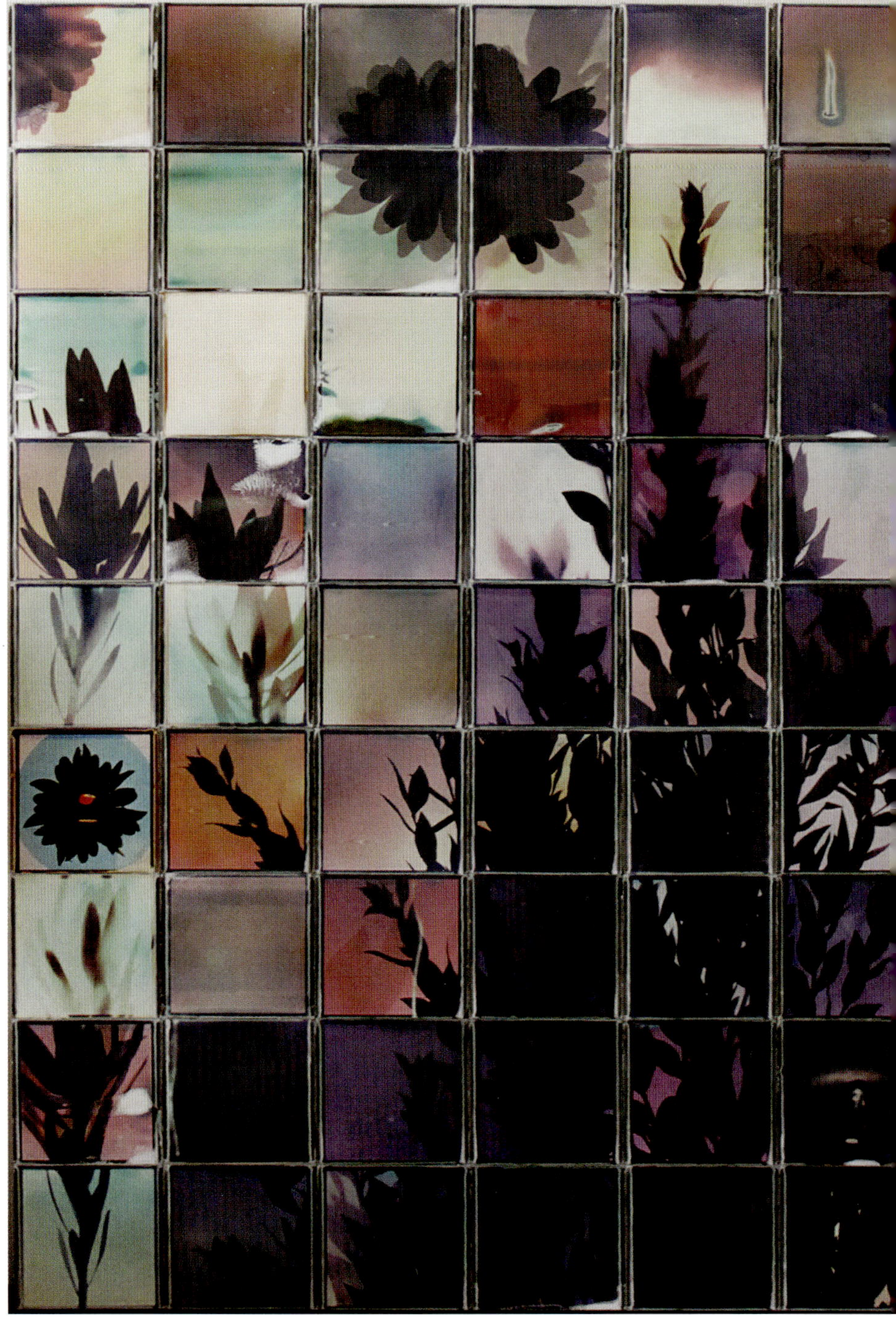

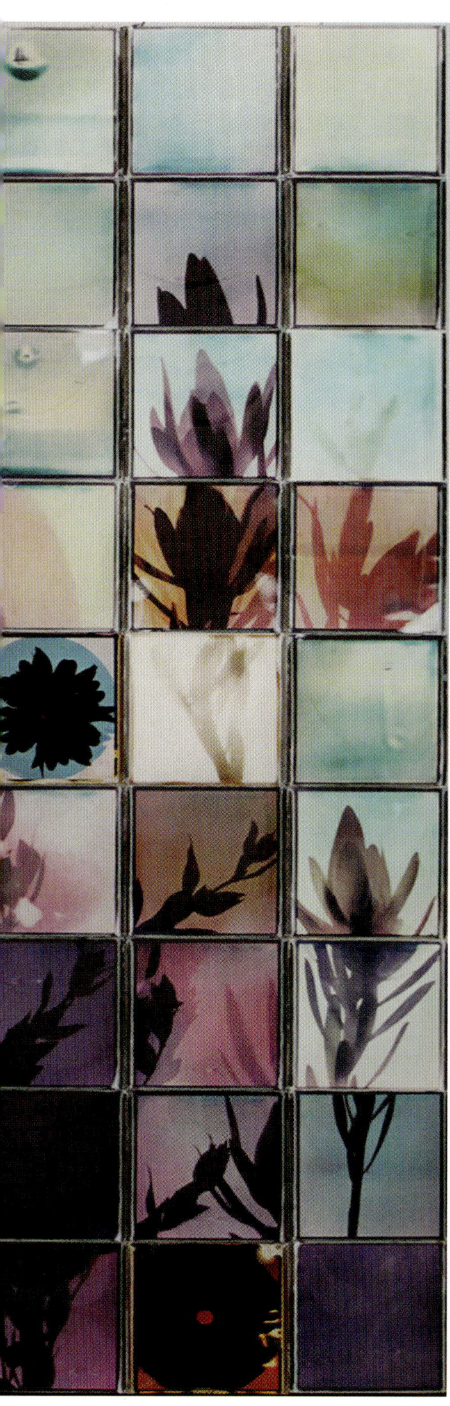

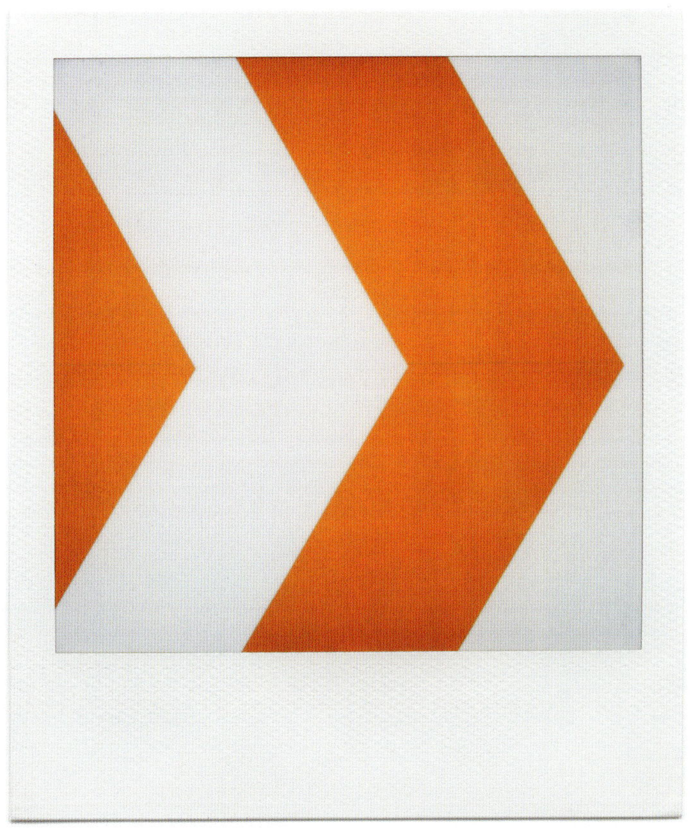

  Grant Hamilton, *Faster*

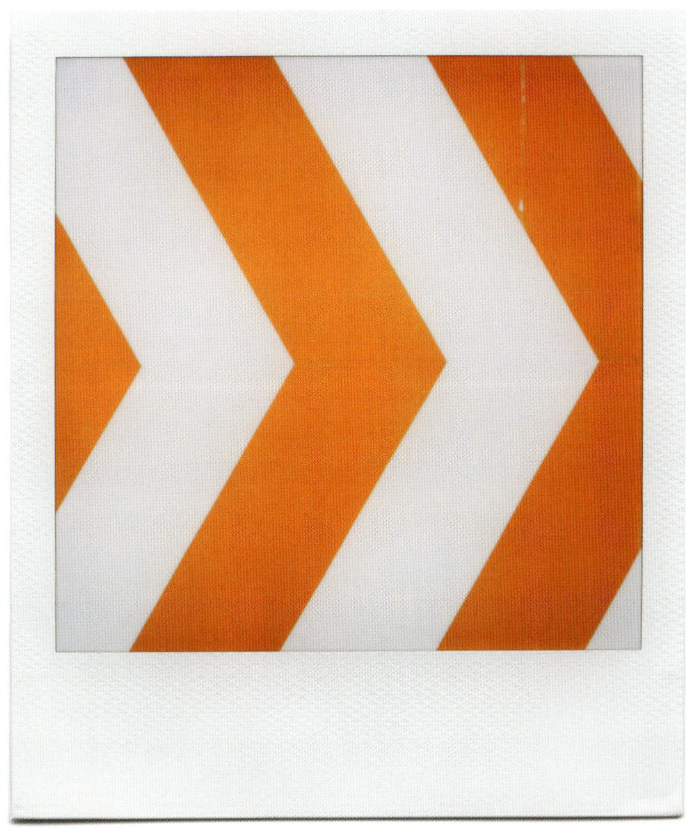

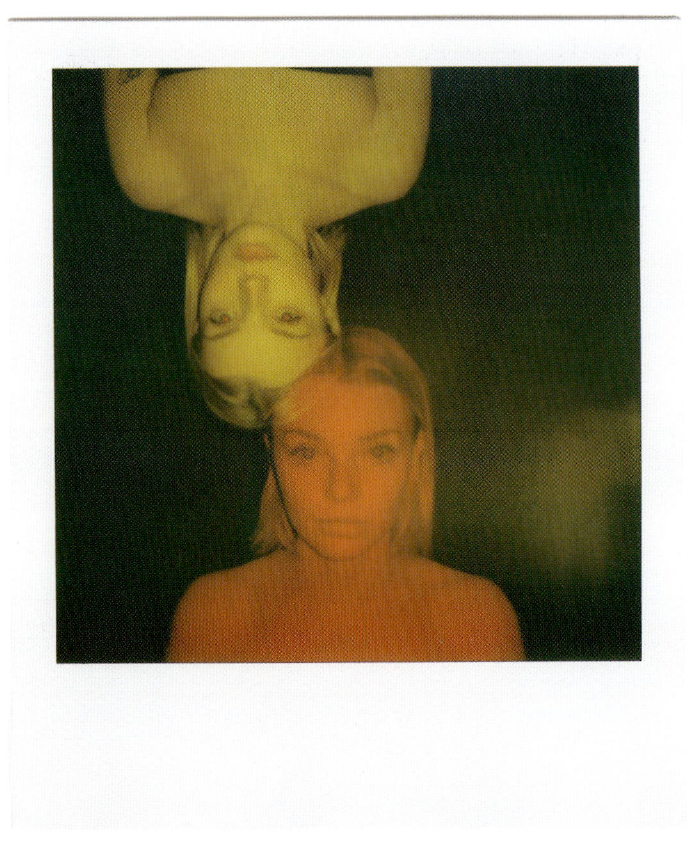

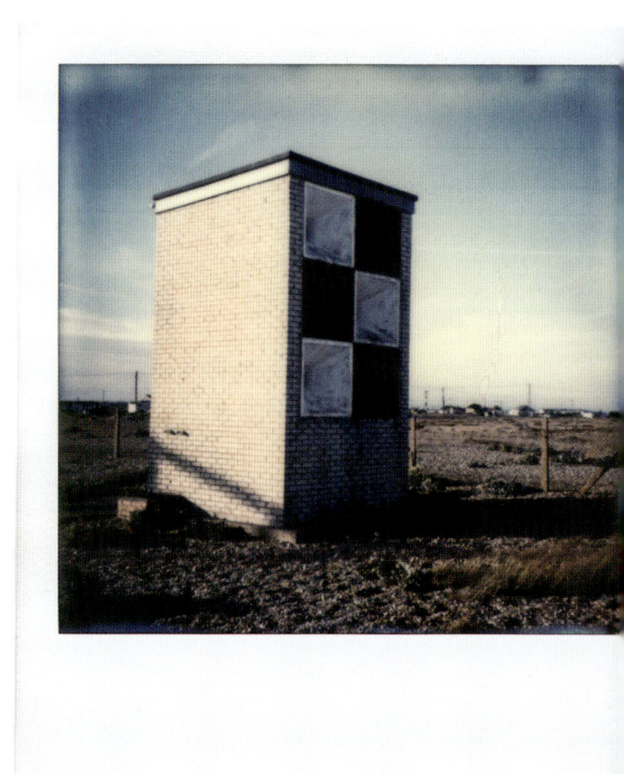

    Peter Knight, *Dungeness Triptych*

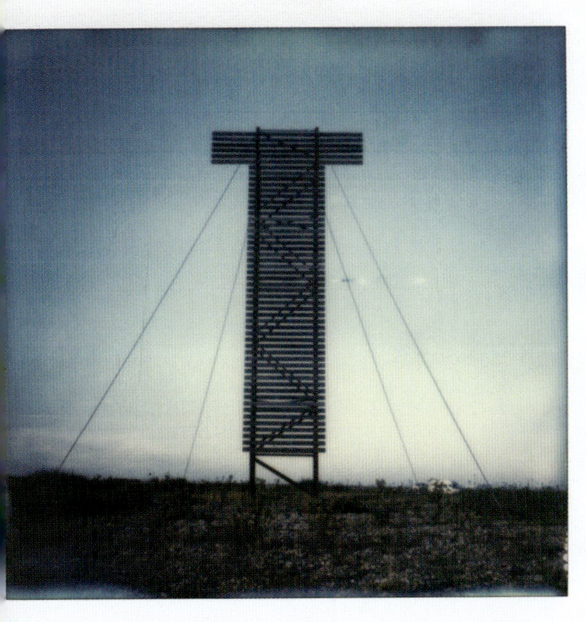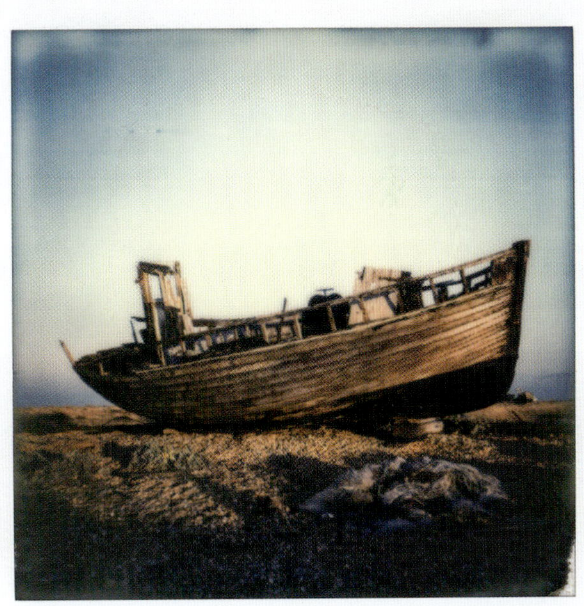

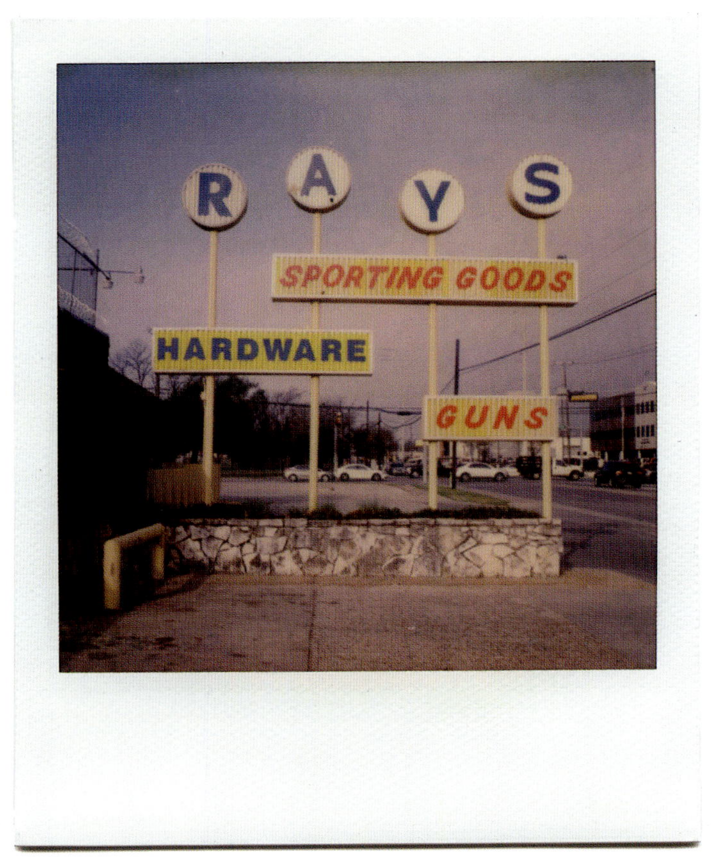

     Brock Fetch, *Rays Dallas*

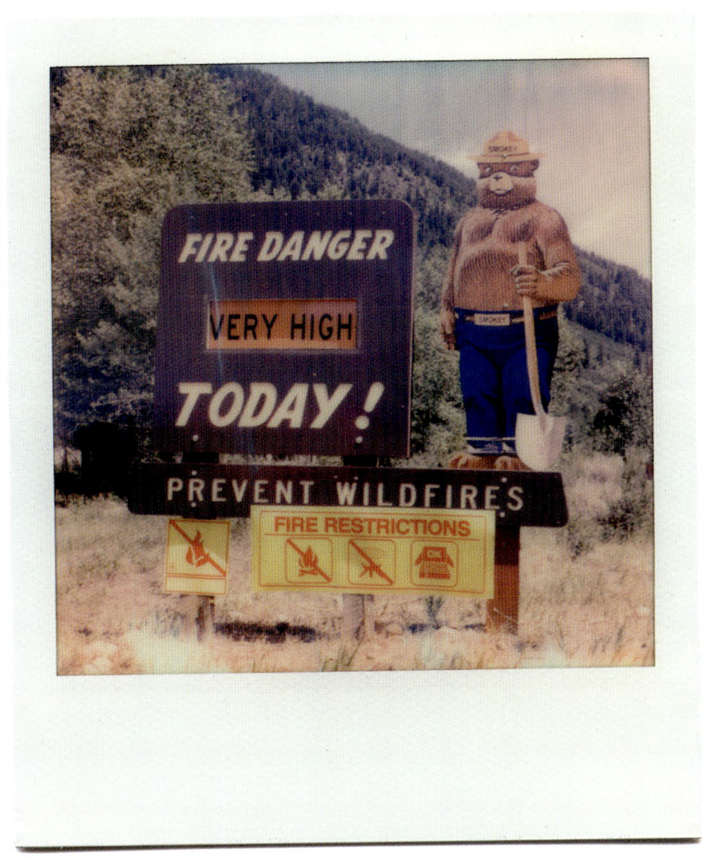

FIRE DANGER
VERY HIGH
TODAY !
PREVENT WILDFIRES
FIRE RESTRICTIONS
SMOKEY

  Anne Locquen, *Pink Time*

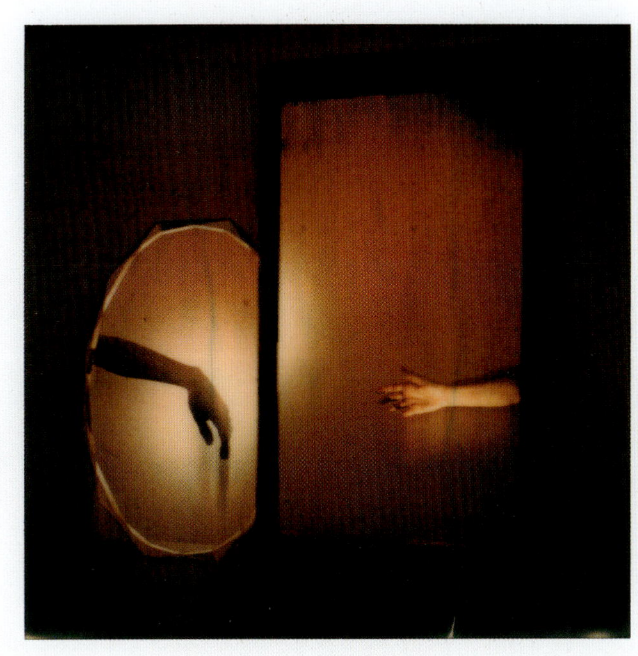

Anne Locquen, *Full Sun*   199

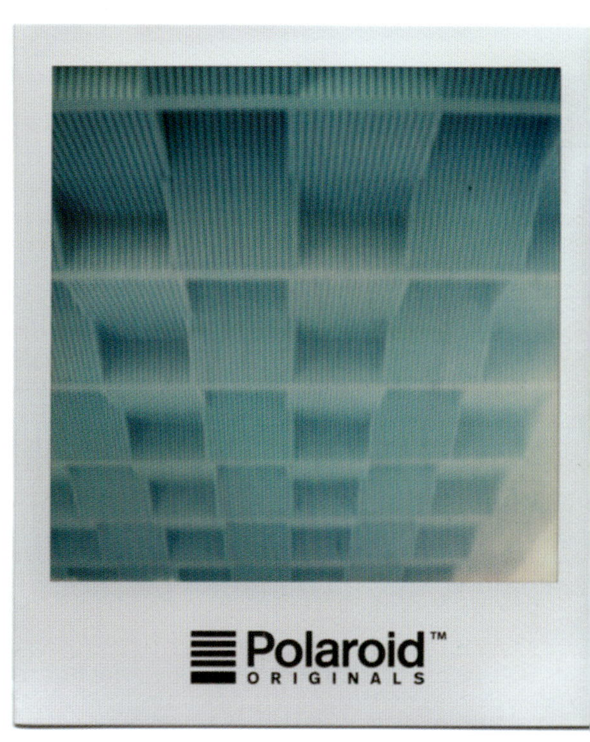

200   Marie-Sara Obrecht, *Geometric Waves*

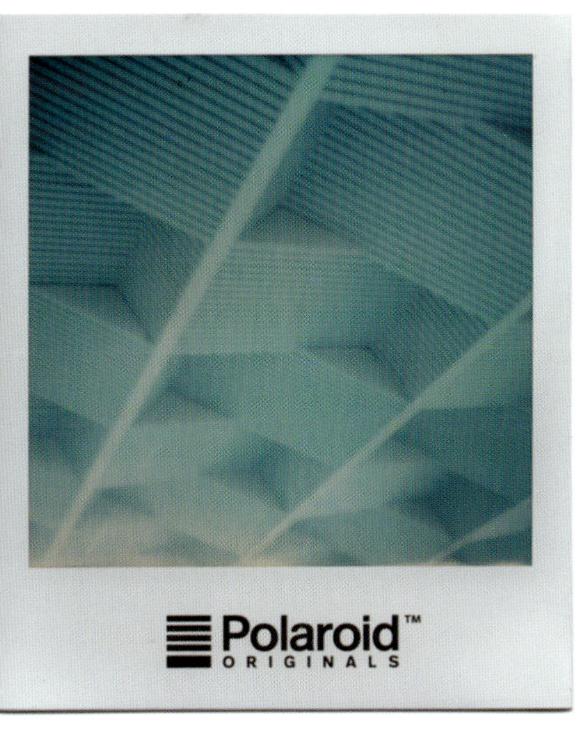

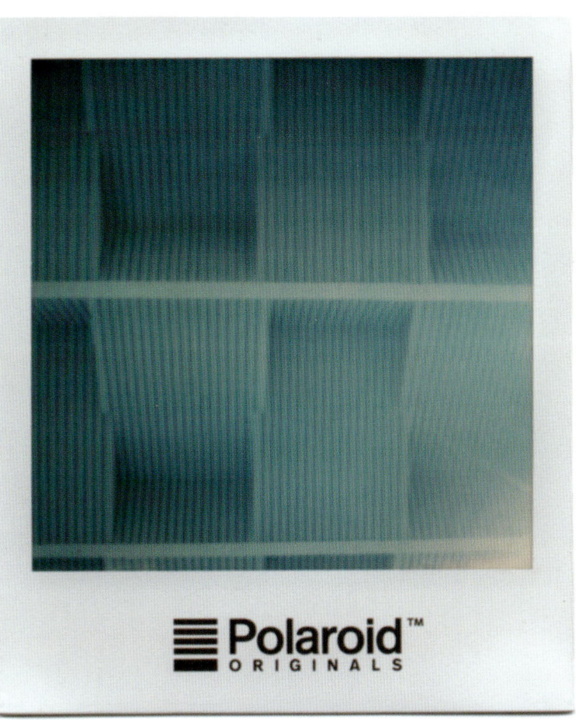

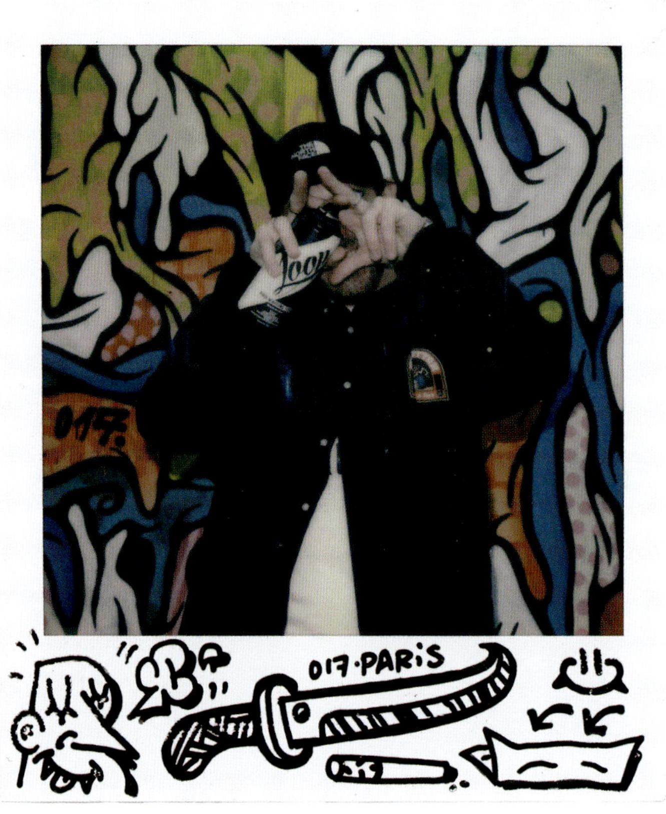

202   Samuel Limata, *I <3 Paris*

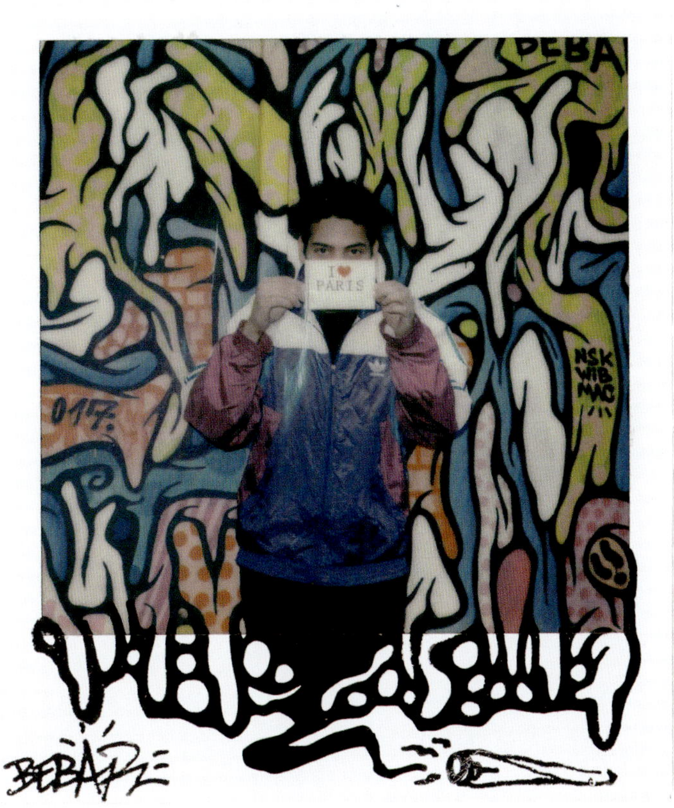

DEBA
I ♥ PARIS
NSK
WIB
MAC

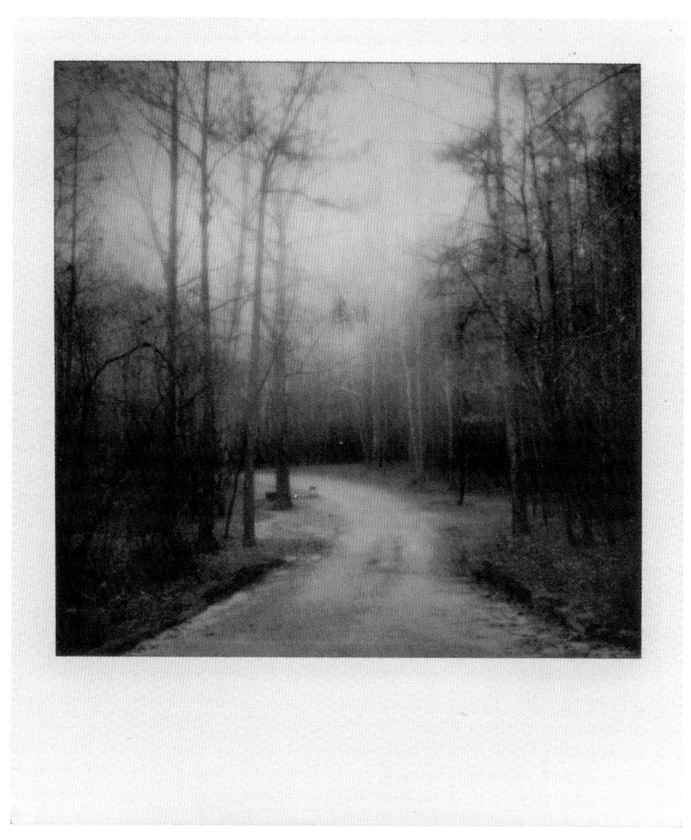

204   Scott Asano, *Untitled*

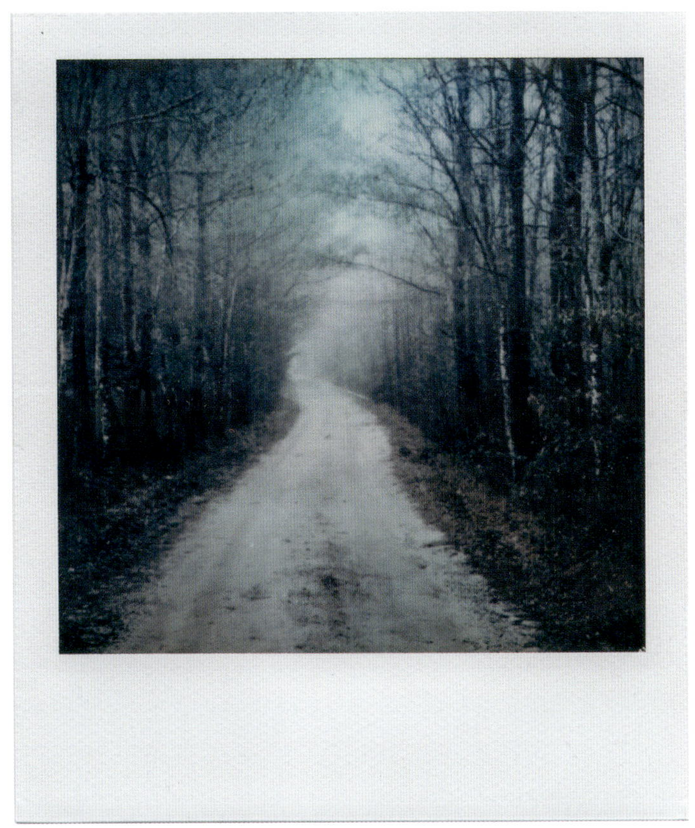

206   Grant Hamilton, *Lichtenstein*

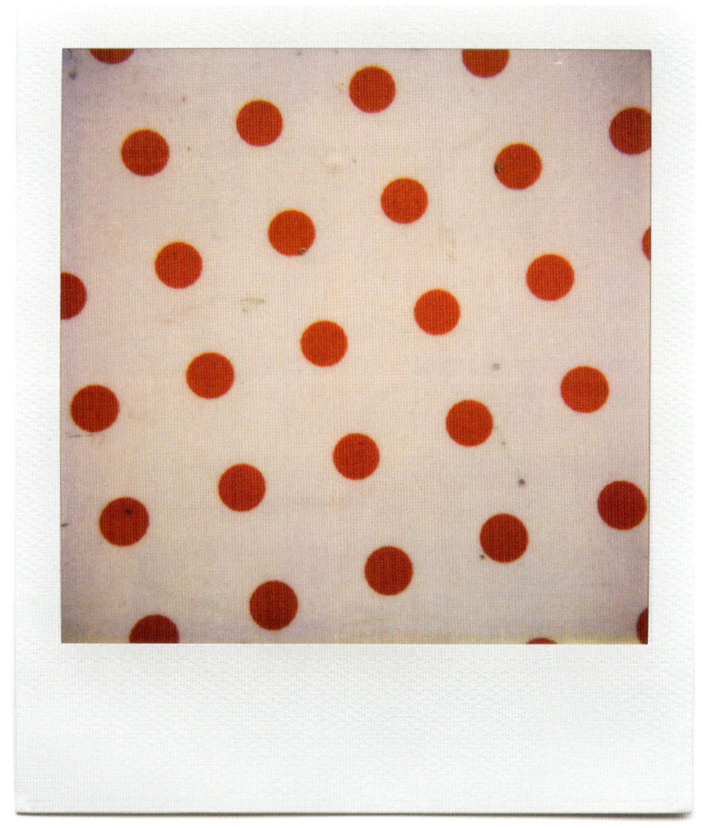

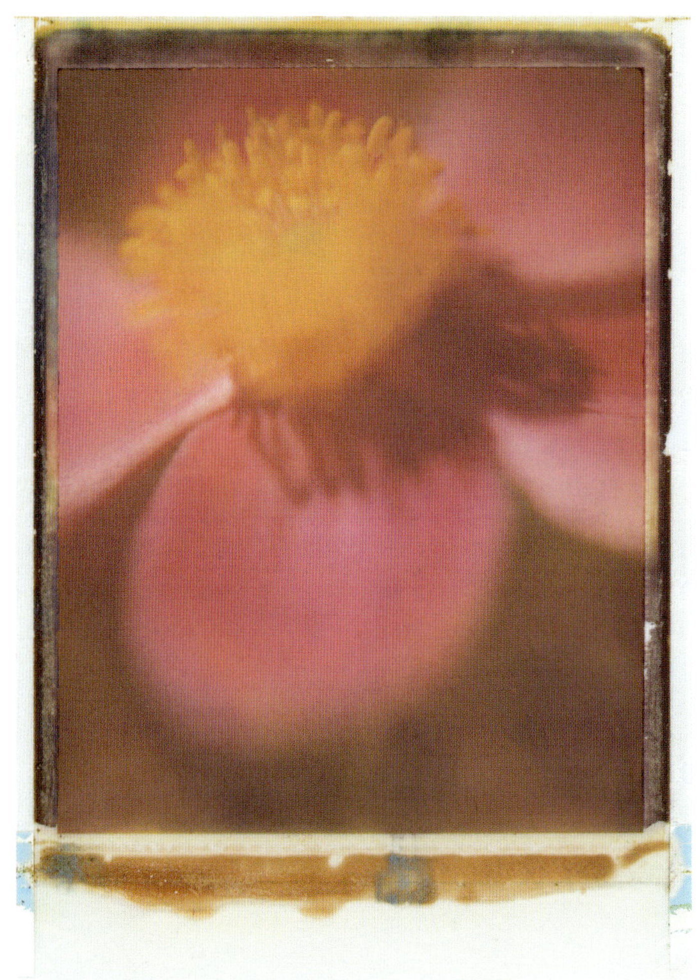

208   Lilian Wildeboer, *Beauty Anemone*

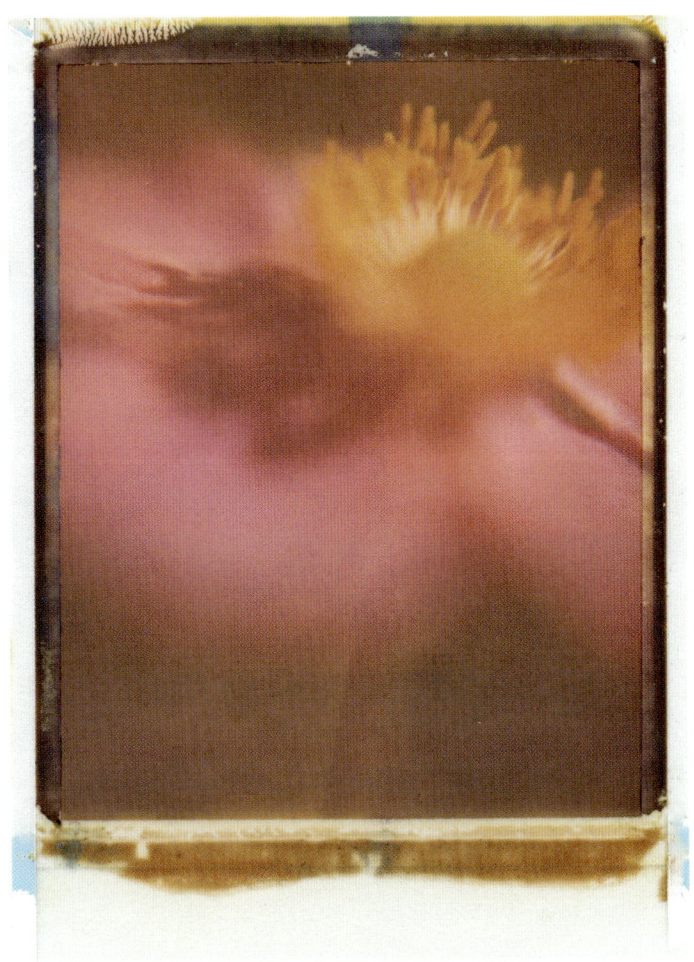

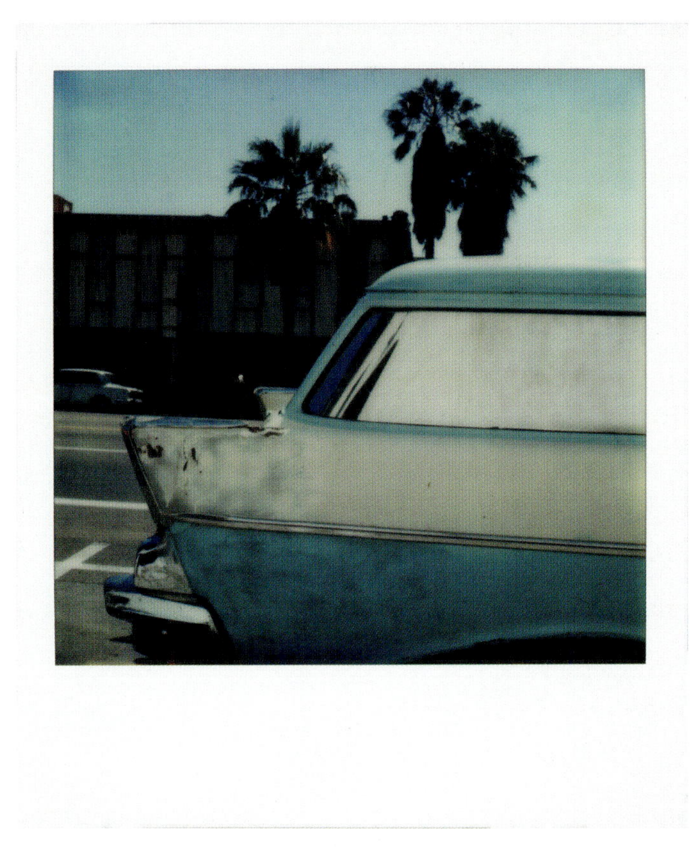

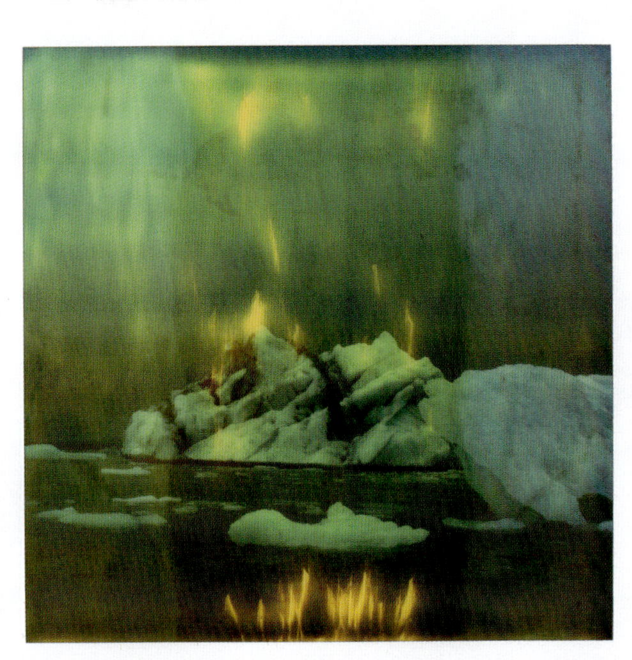

212   Jennifer Rumbach, *Burning Down the Ice*

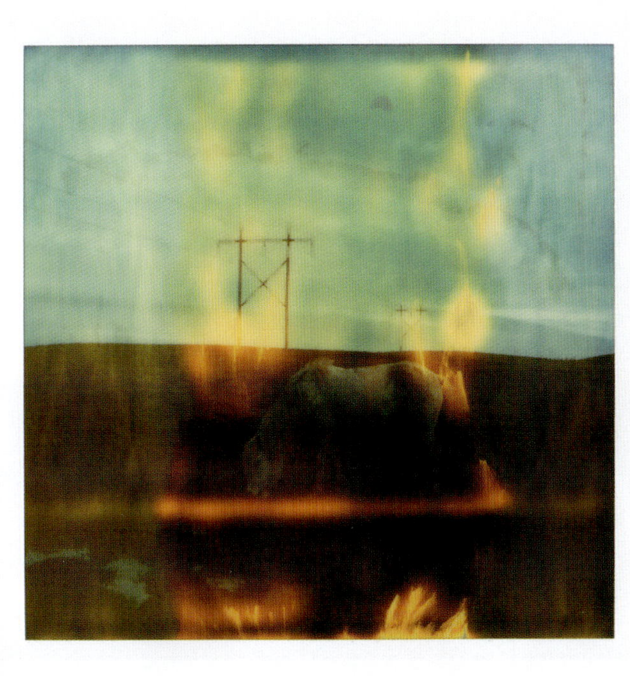

Jennifer Rumbach, *Atomic Horse*   213

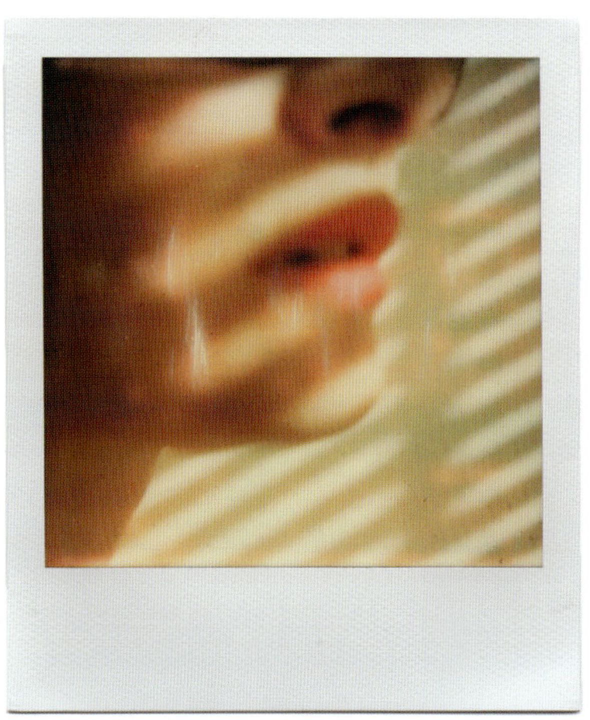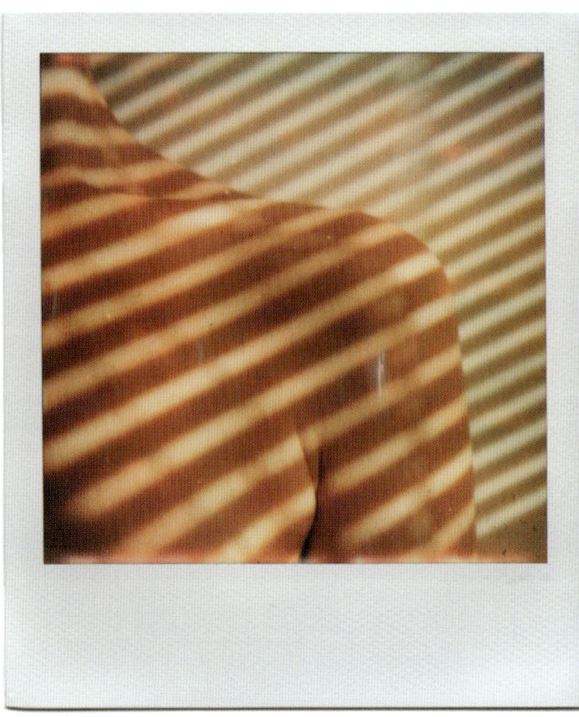

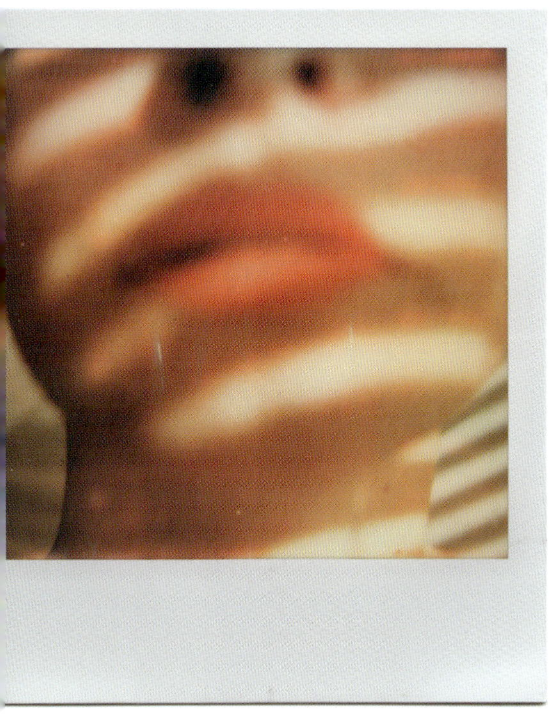

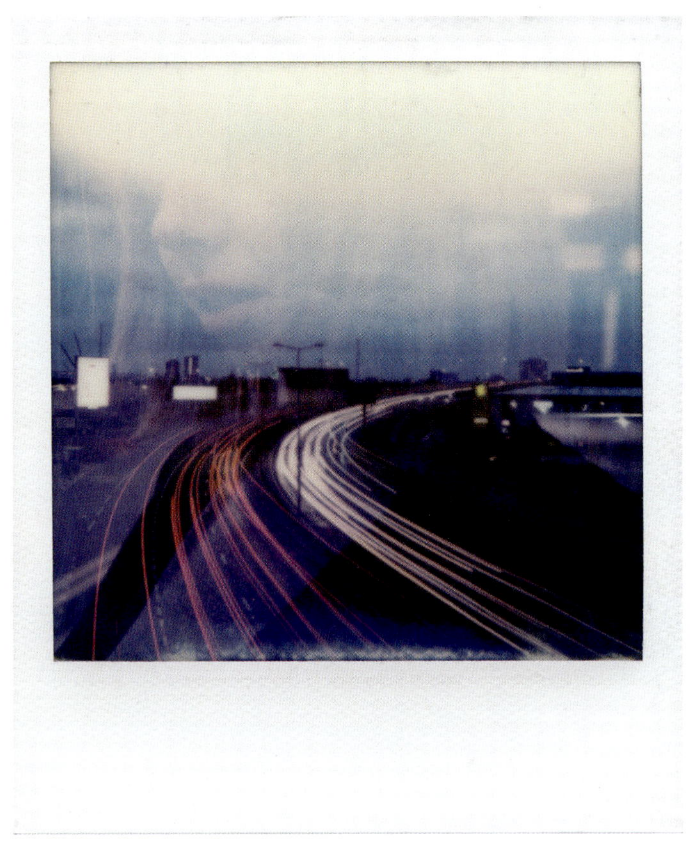

216   Ray Liu, *Untitled*

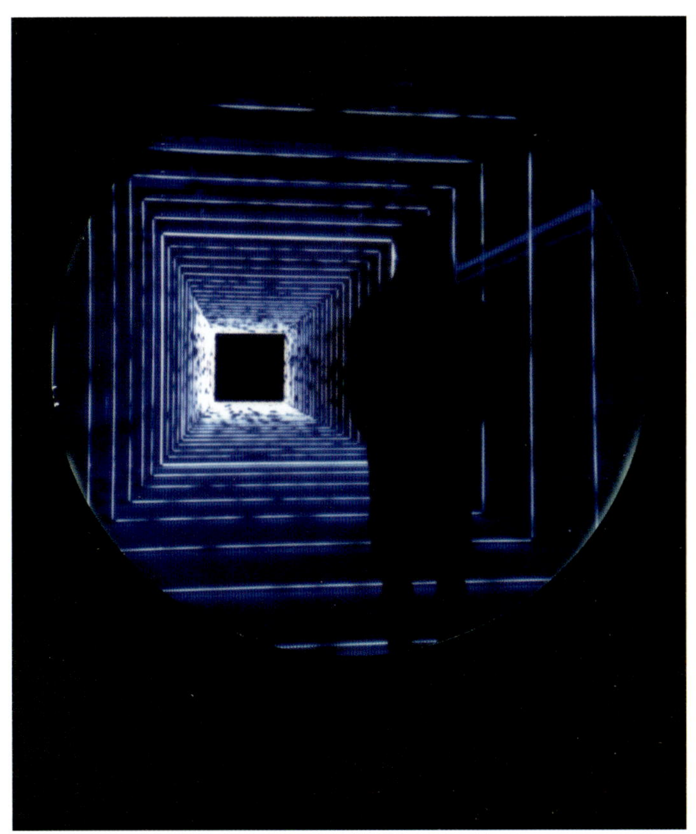

Ray Liu, *Untitled*   217

    Taylor Sheppard, *Untitled*

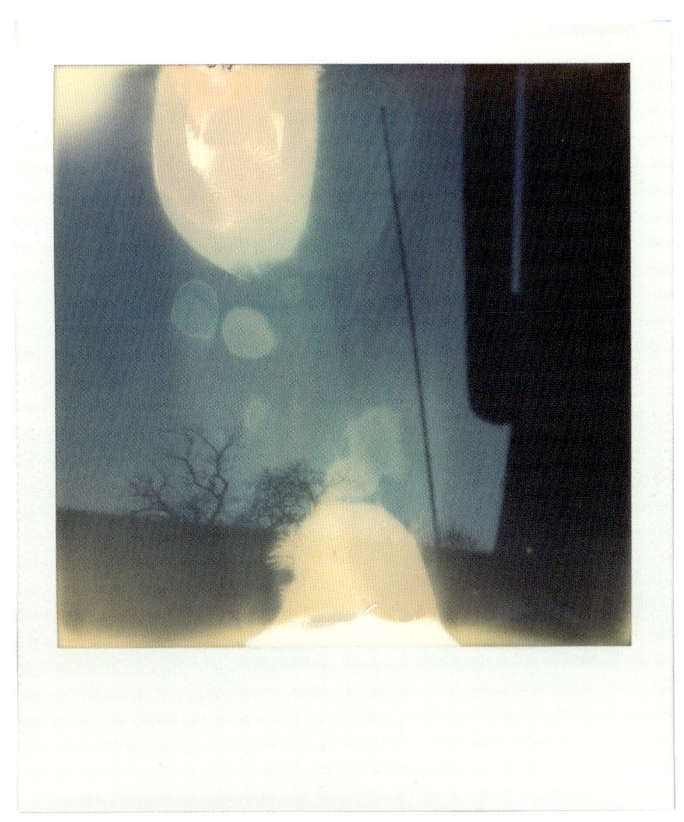

   Brian Downey, *Tessa*

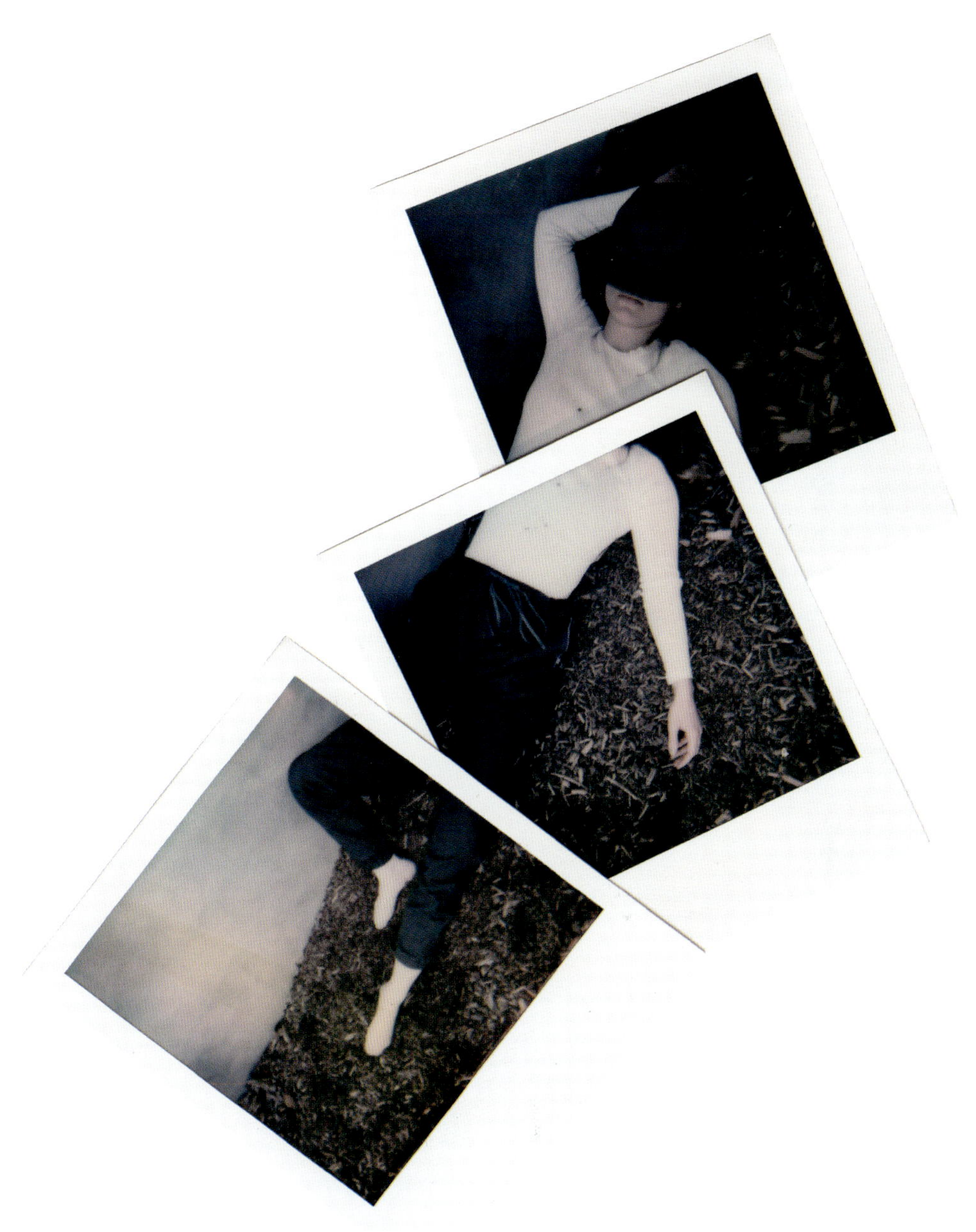

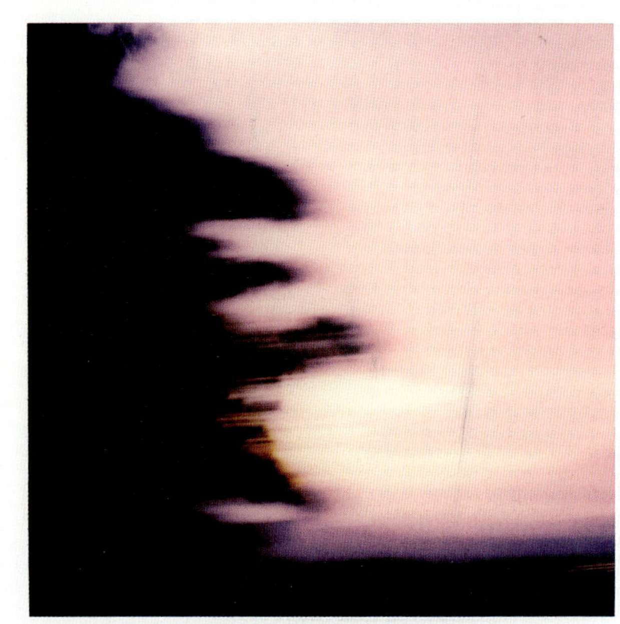

222   Rayan Nohra, *Feels Like Slow Motion (Colombia)*

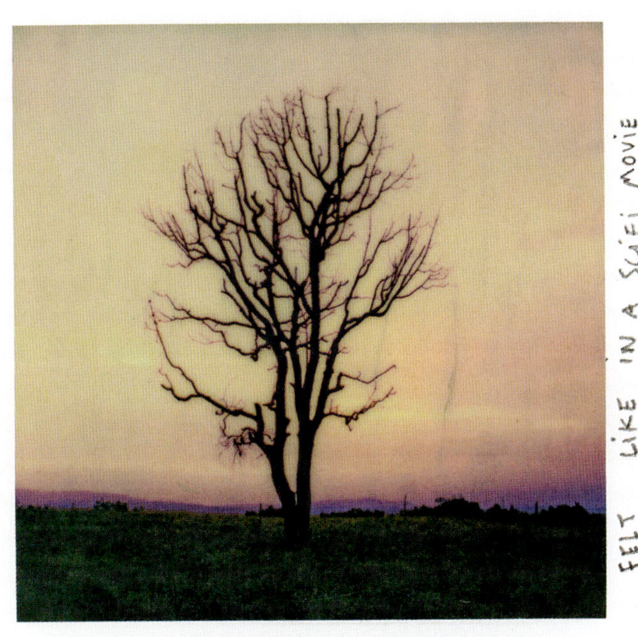

Rayan Nohra, *Tree in the Middle of a Small Field in the Jungle (Colombia)*   223

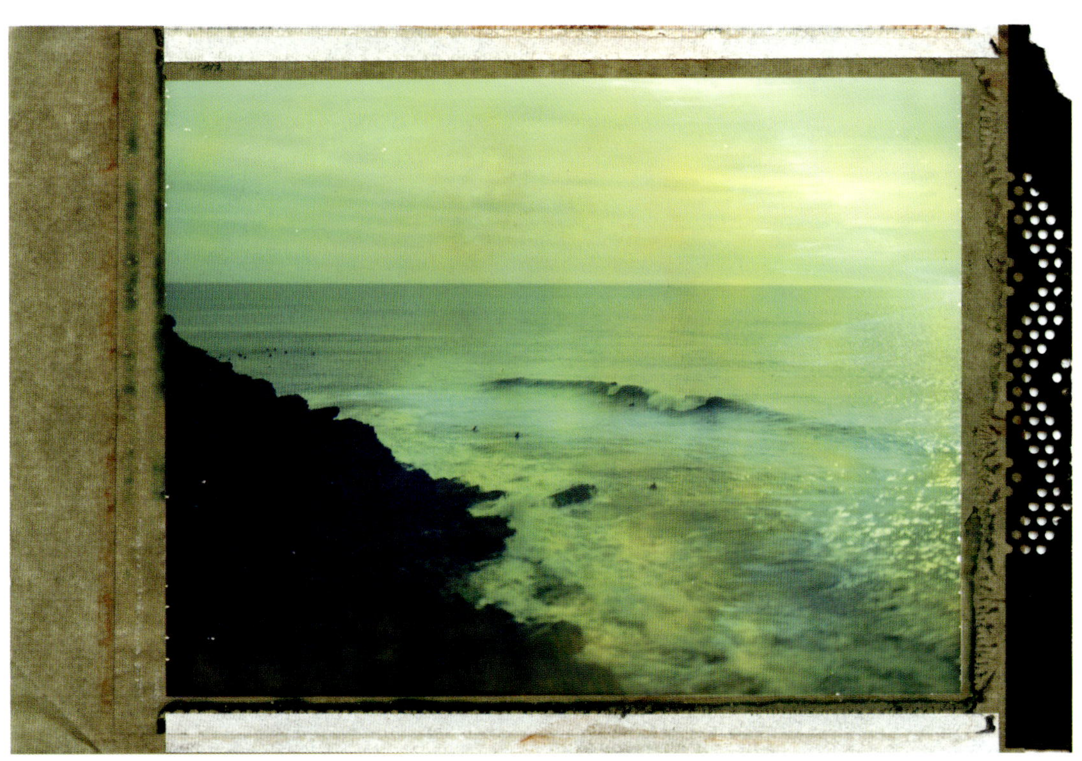

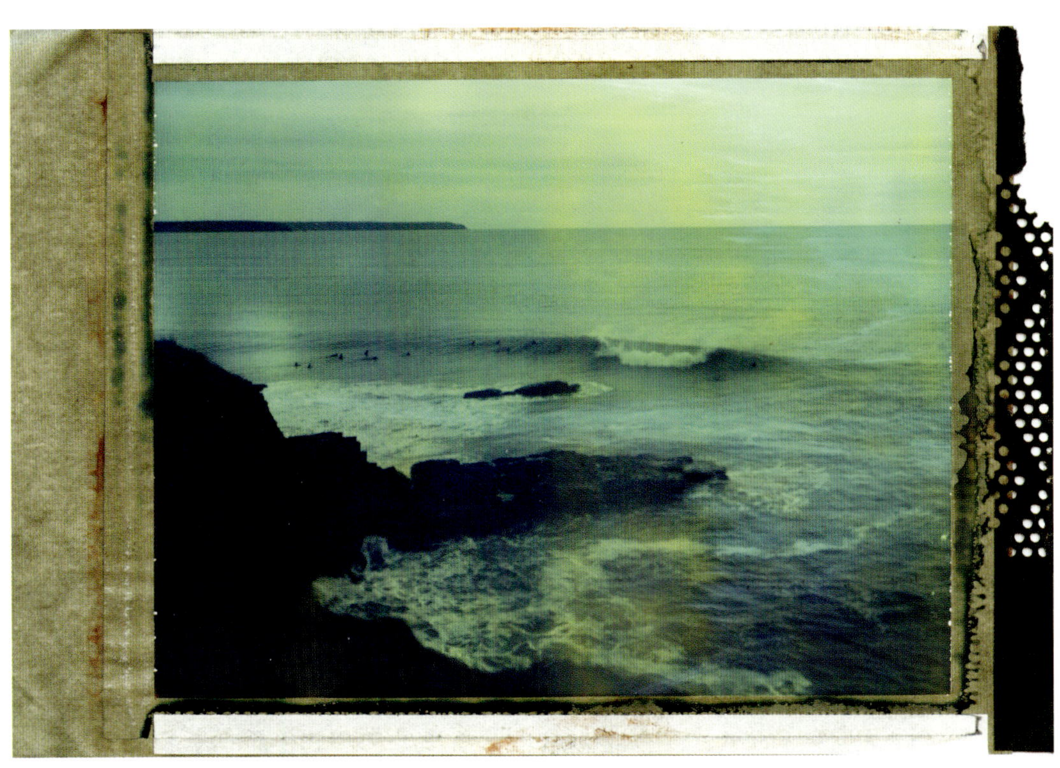

226   Grant Hamilton, *Suspicious*

LIBRE

    Dora Kontha, *Fever Dream*

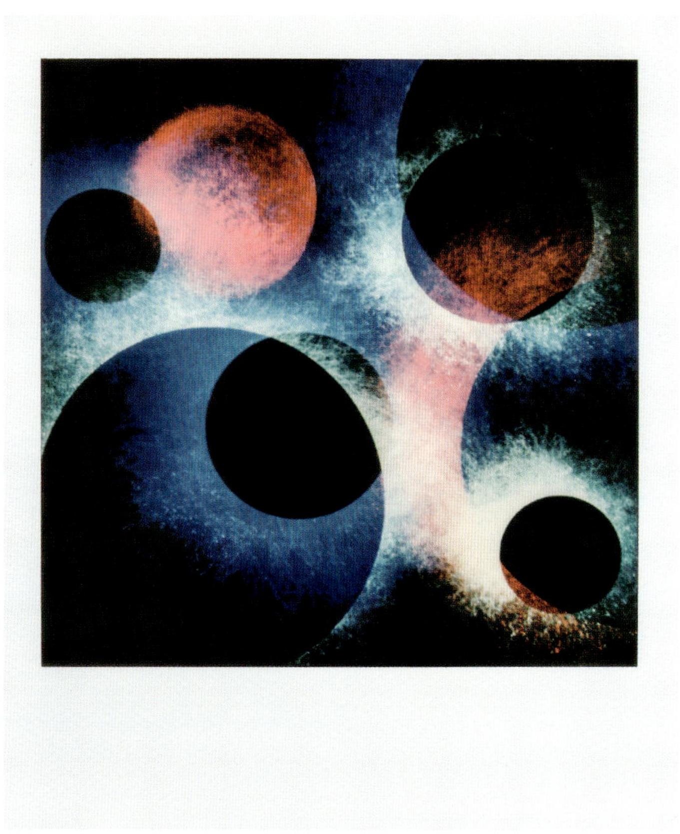

  Felicita Russo, *Exploring Negative Space*

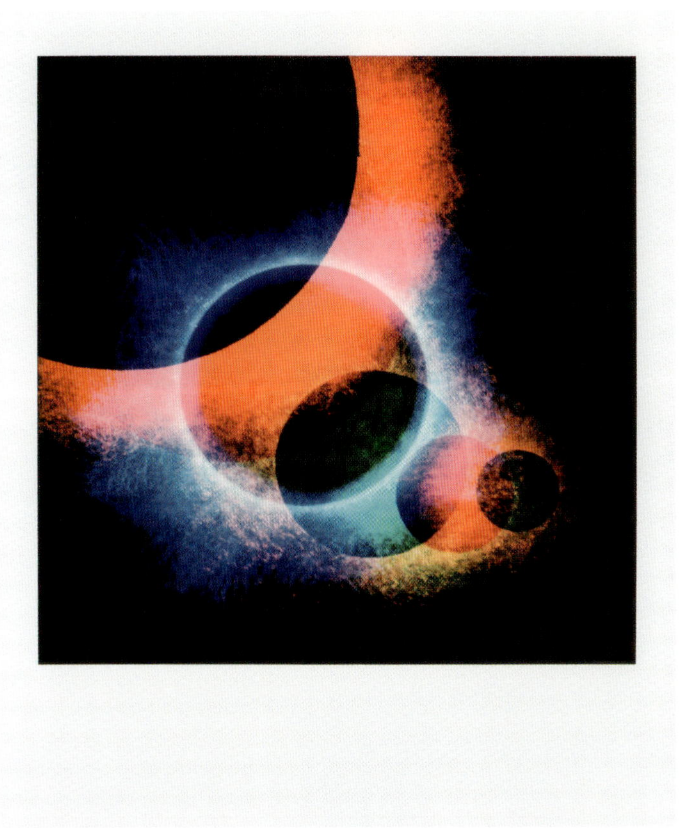

Felicita Russo, *Planet's Misalignment*   231

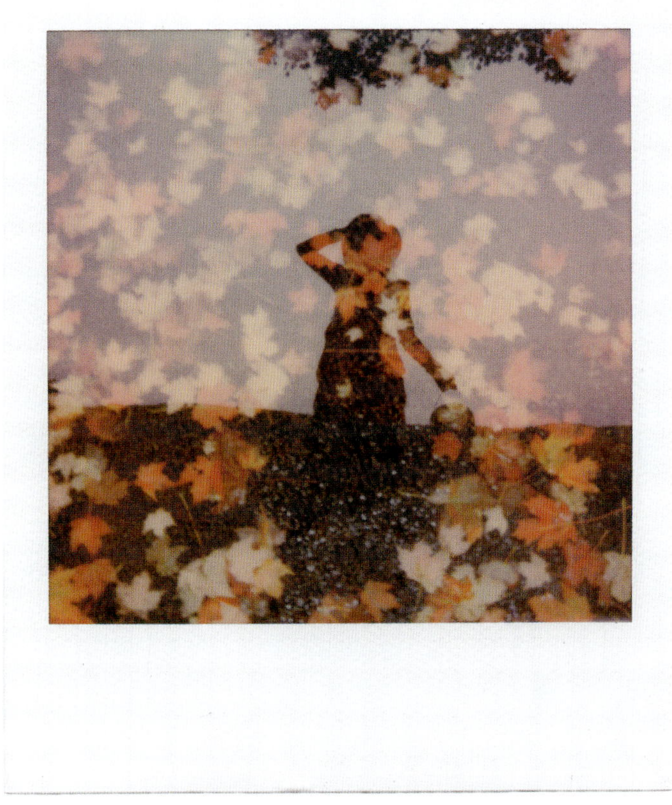

232 Tori Sviokla, *Salem Stroll*

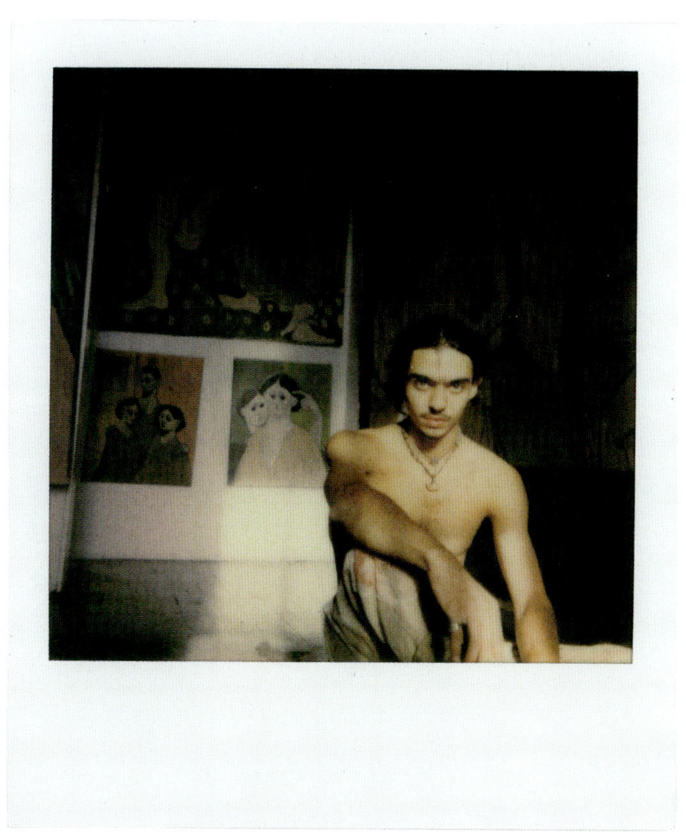

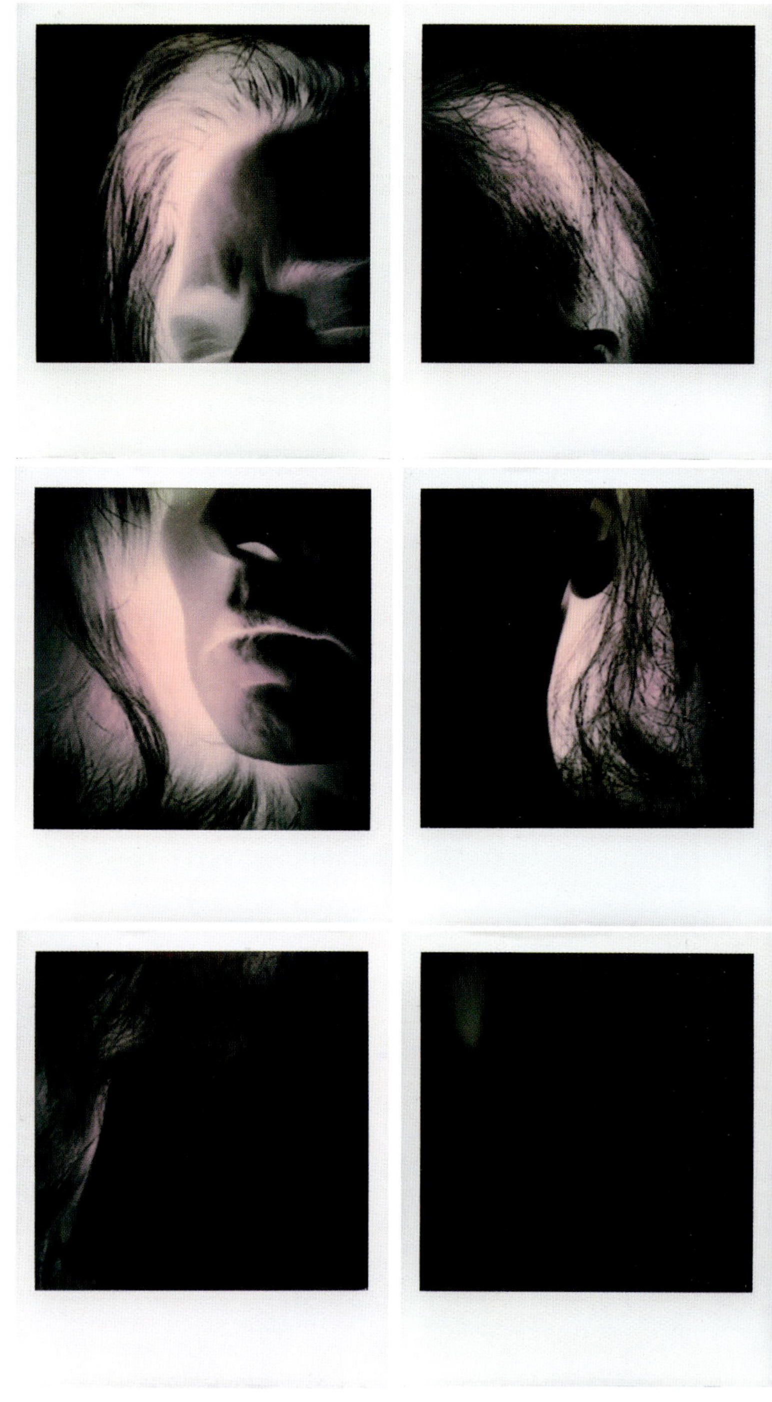

234   Kathy Rankin, *Darkness is Your Candle*

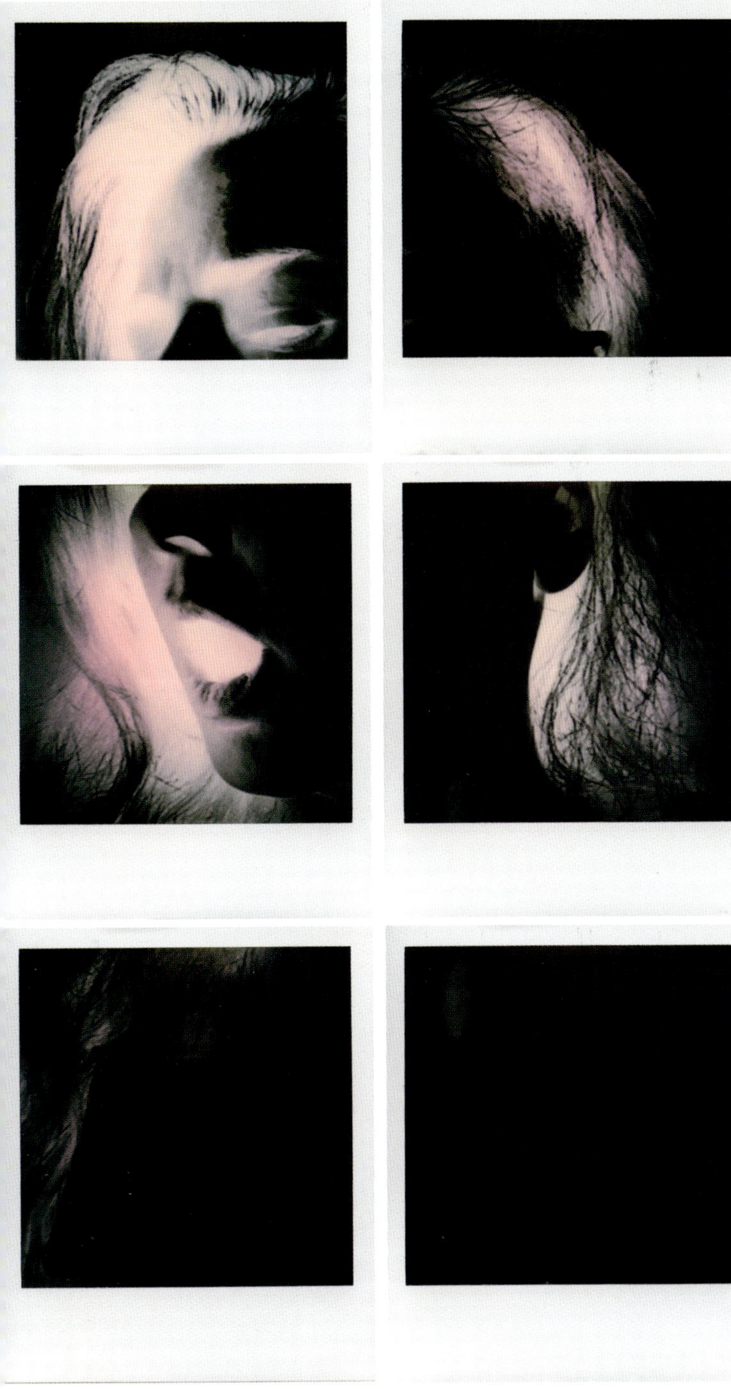

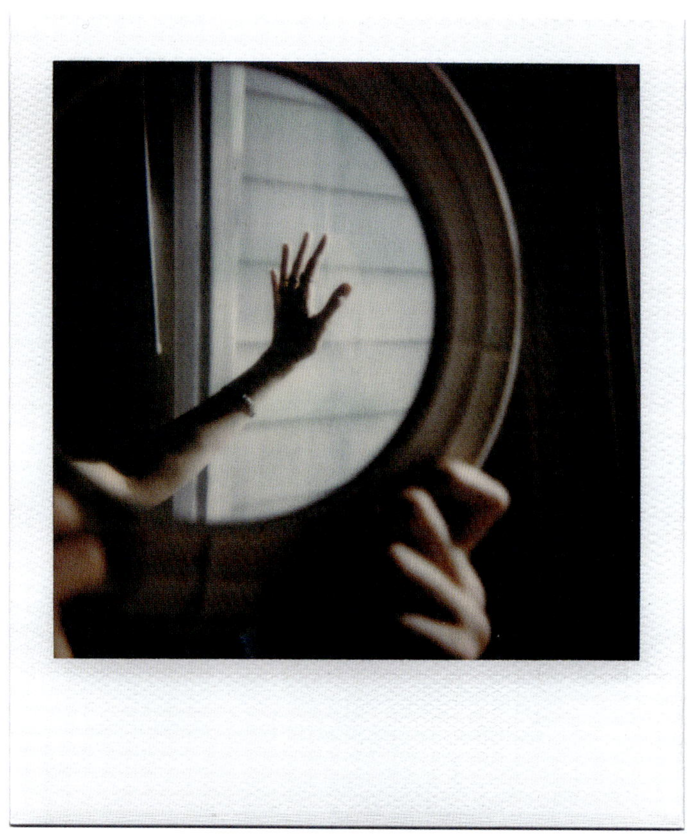

  Catherine Costanzo, *A Longing to Escape*

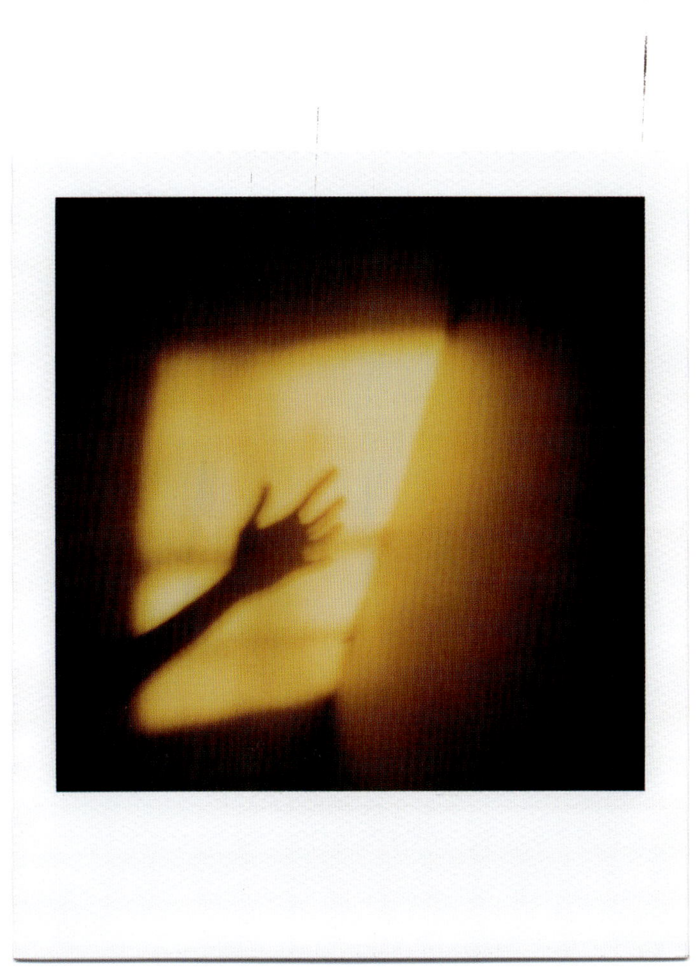

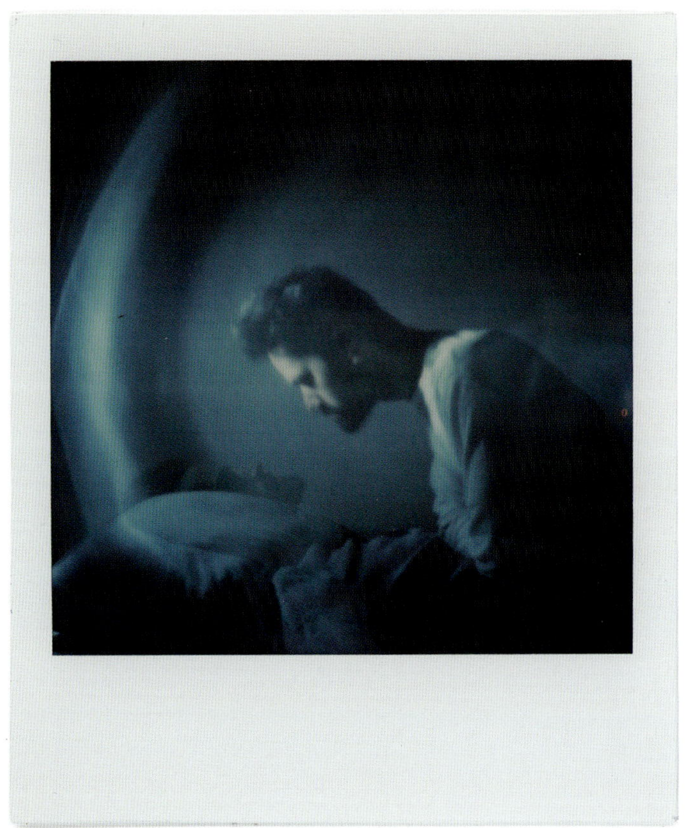

238   Ariel Shelleg, *Look At You / Self Portrait*

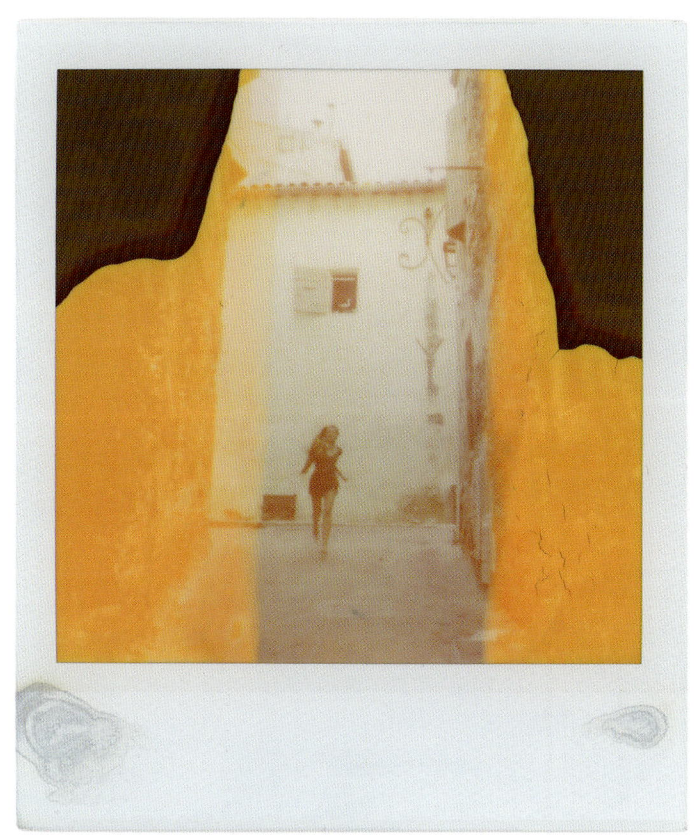

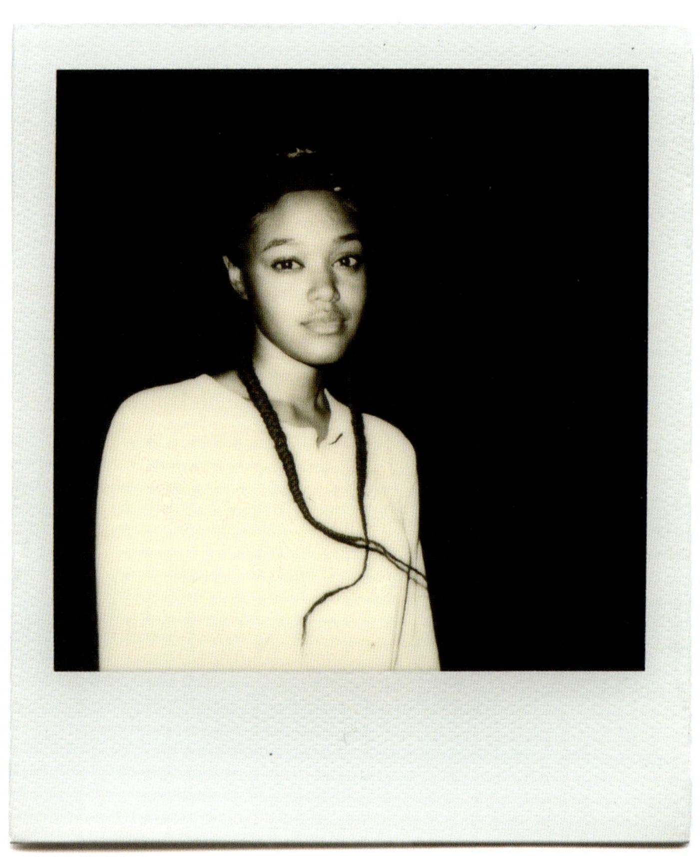

    Brock Fetch, *Chynna Rogers*

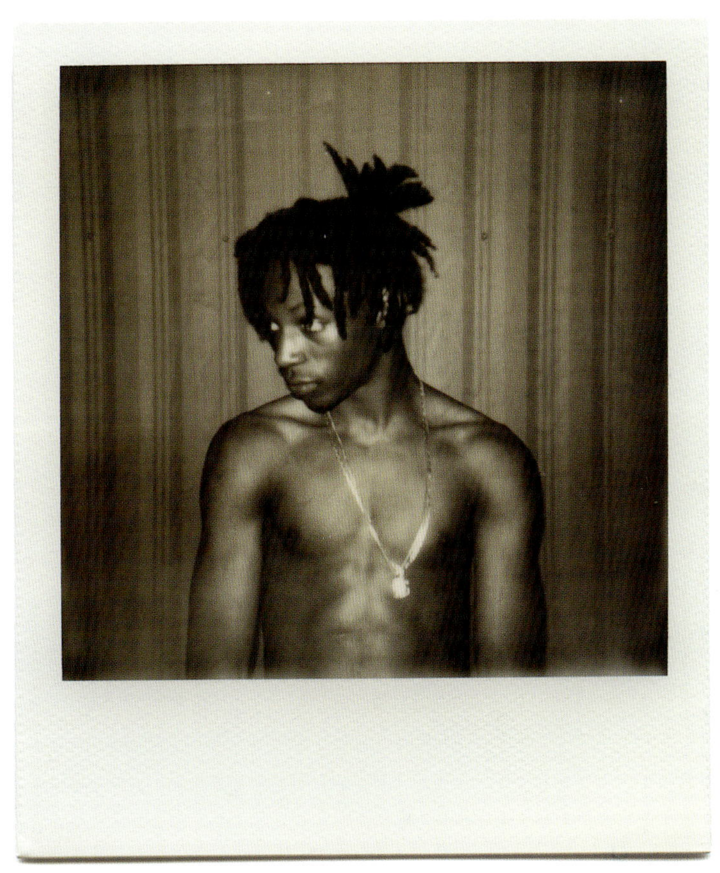

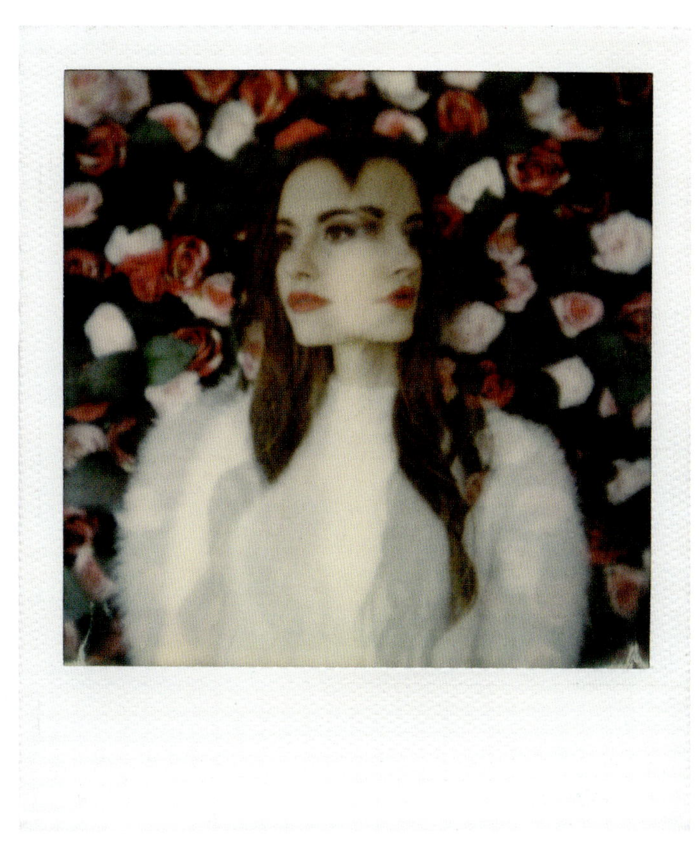

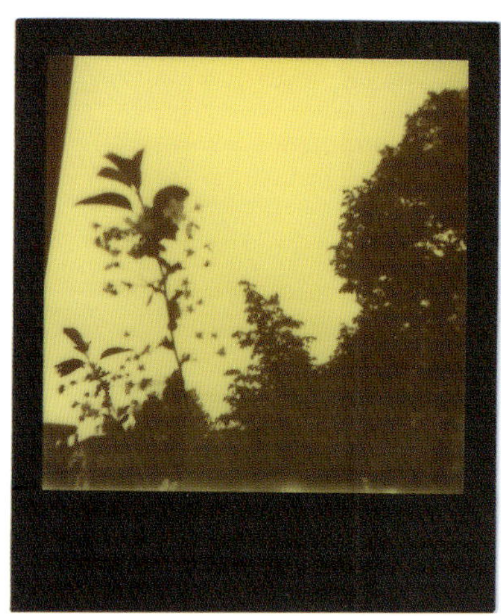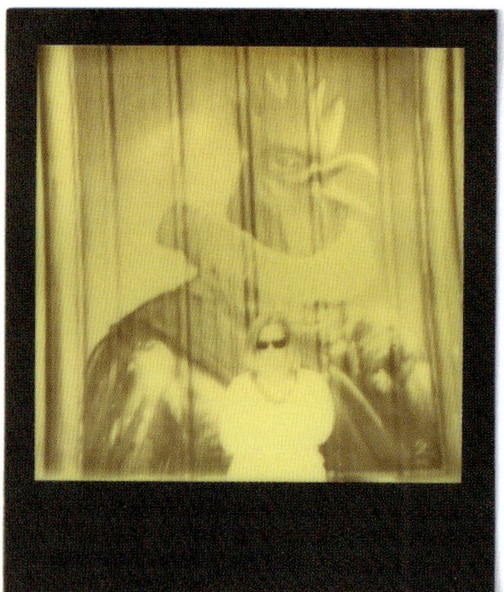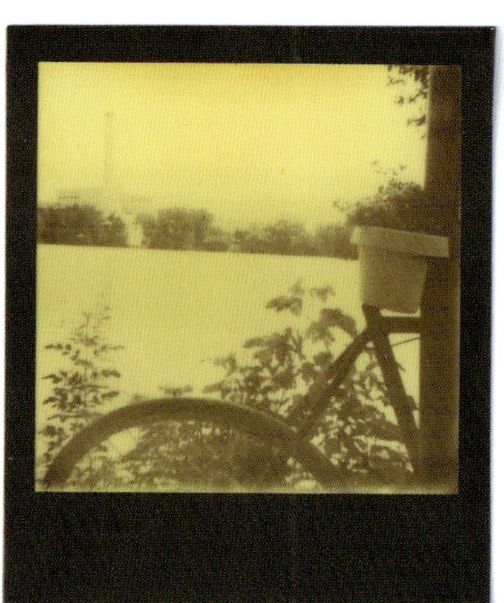

   Anke Stein, *Life Through the Yellow Lens*

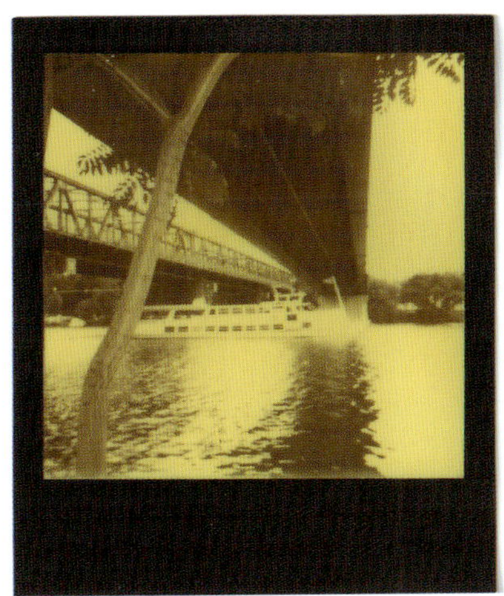 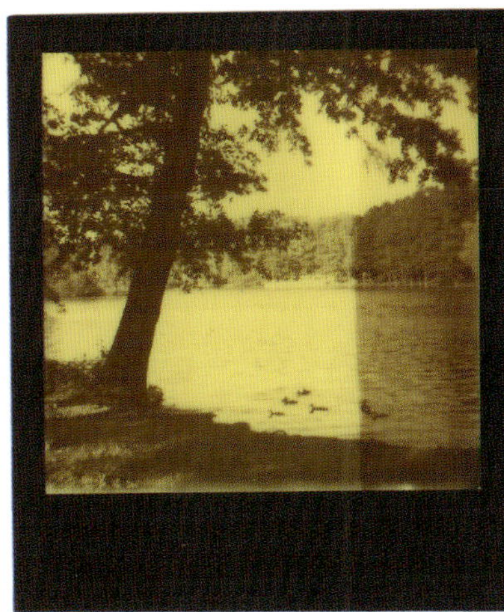 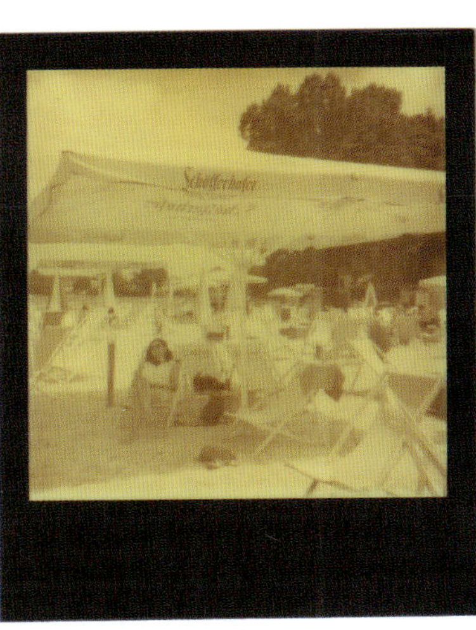

 Lilian Wildeboer, *Loss*

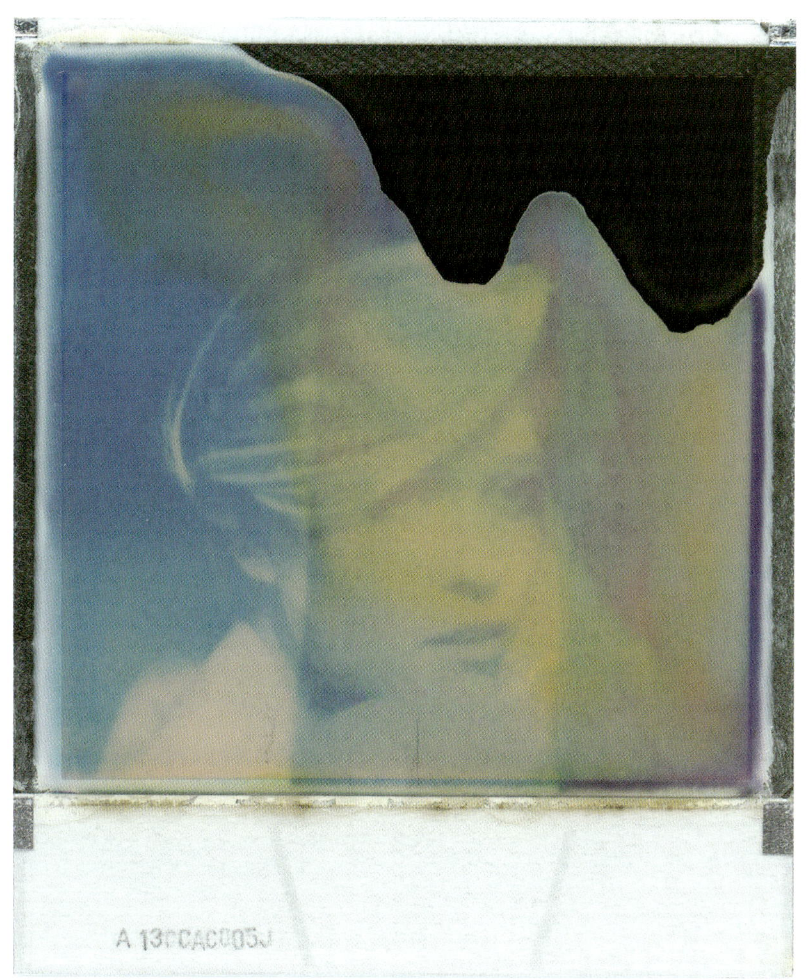

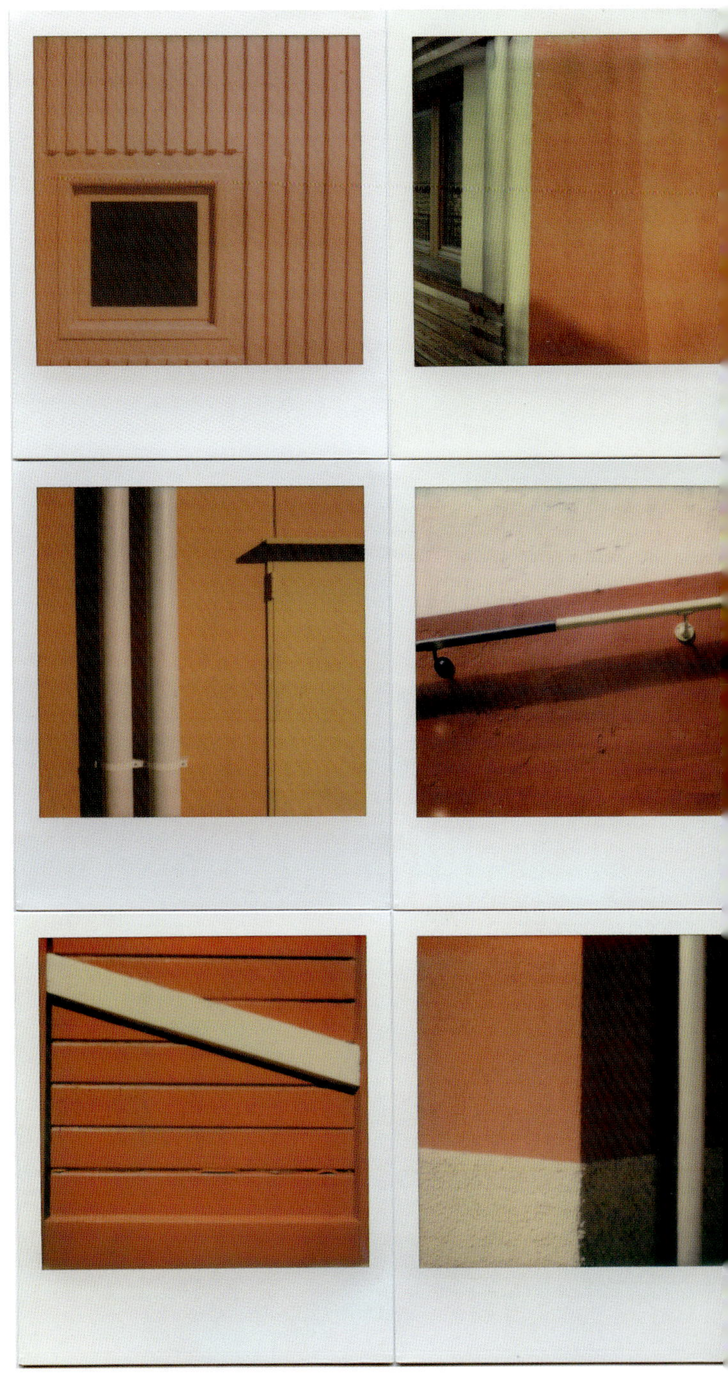

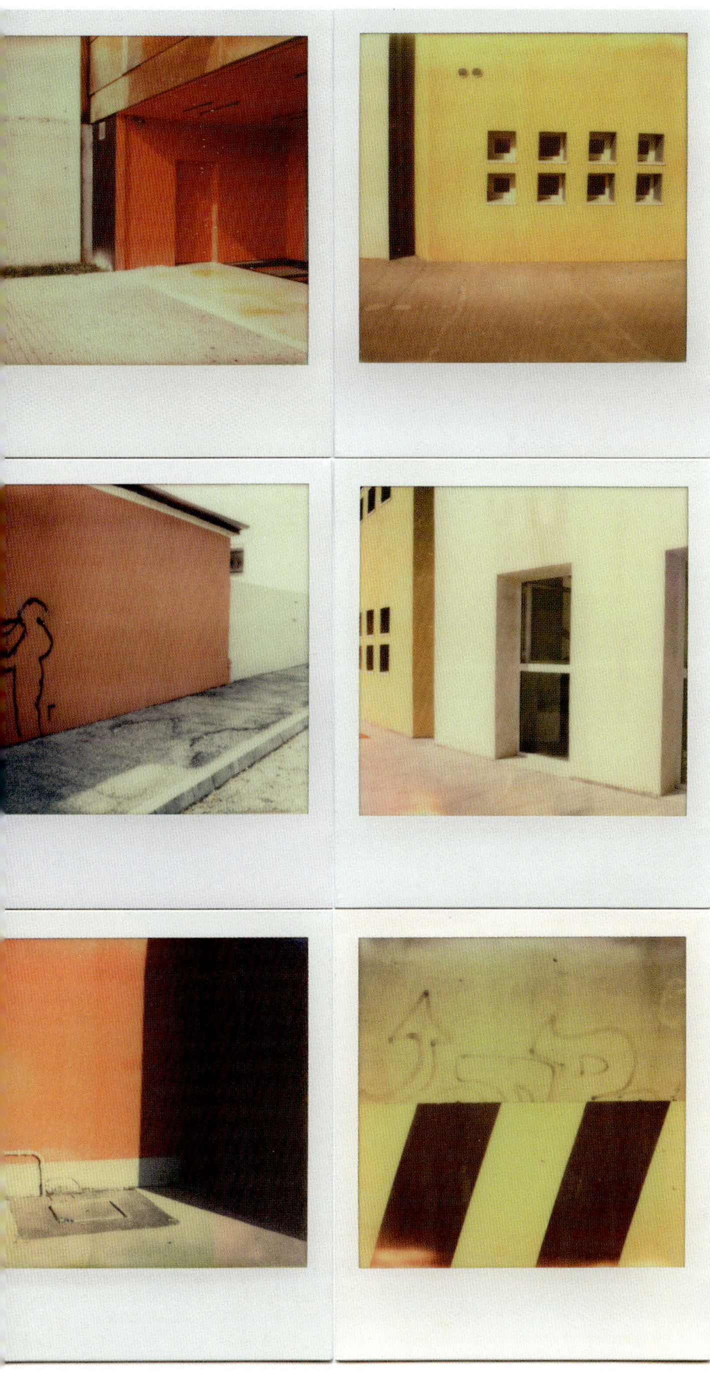

    Bizz Sjöblom, *Untitled*

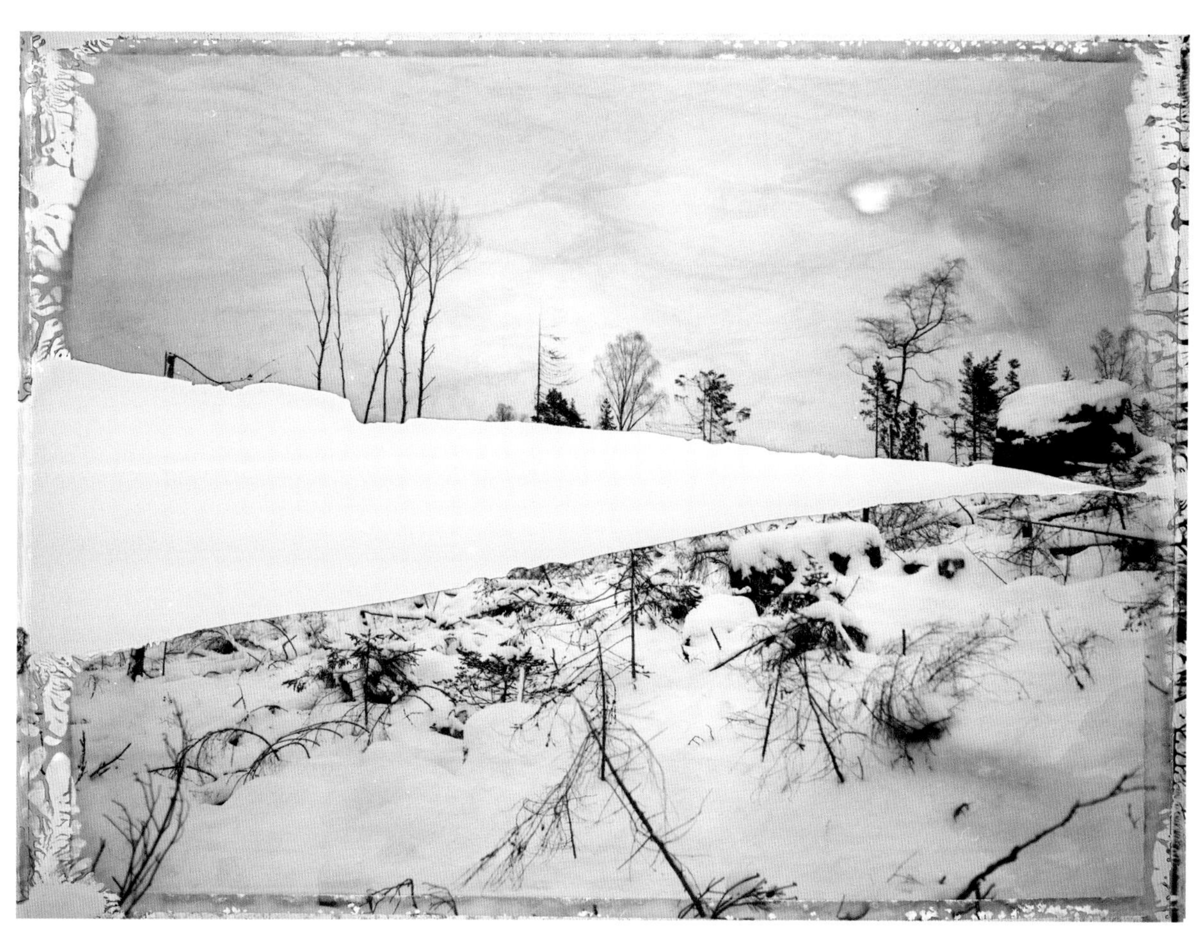

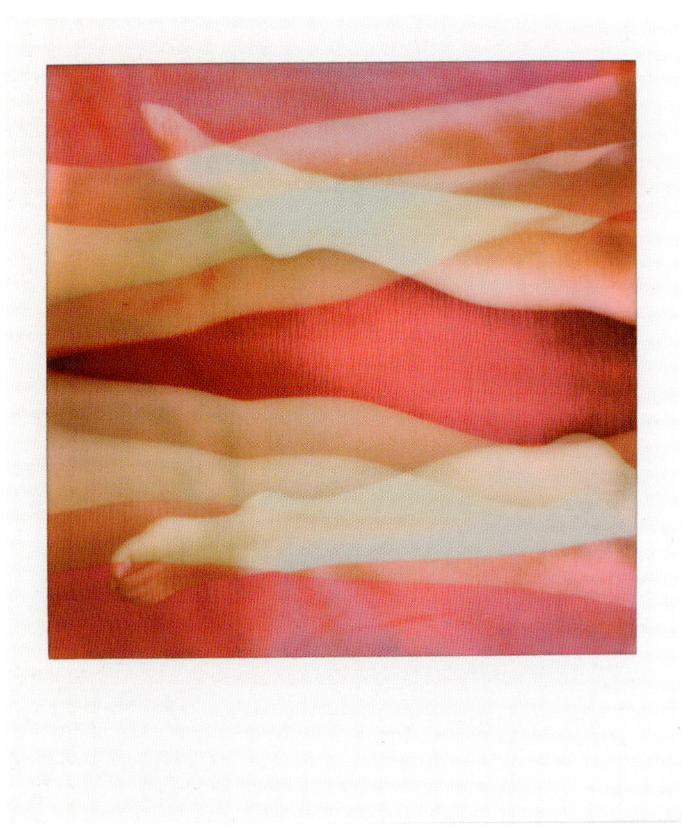

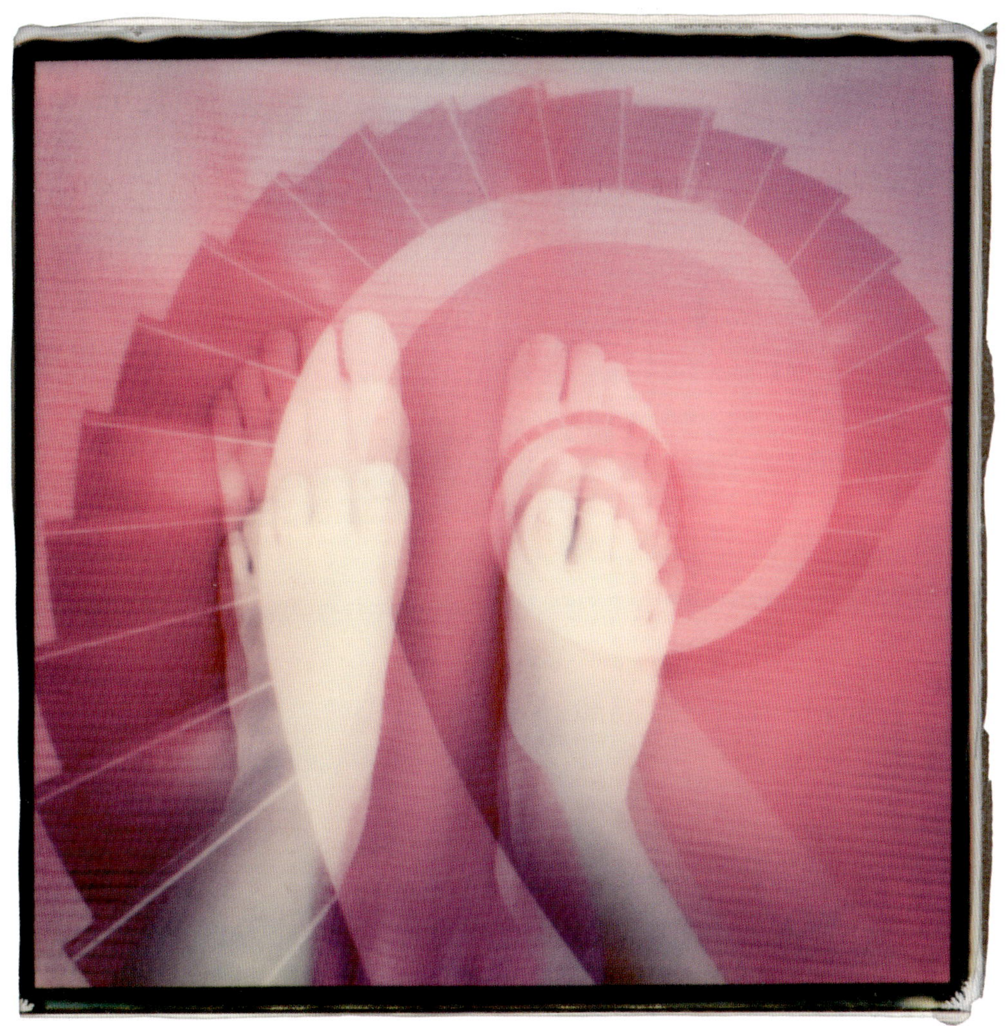

Luigi Iovane, *Vertigo*   253

    Anne Locquen, *Breathe*

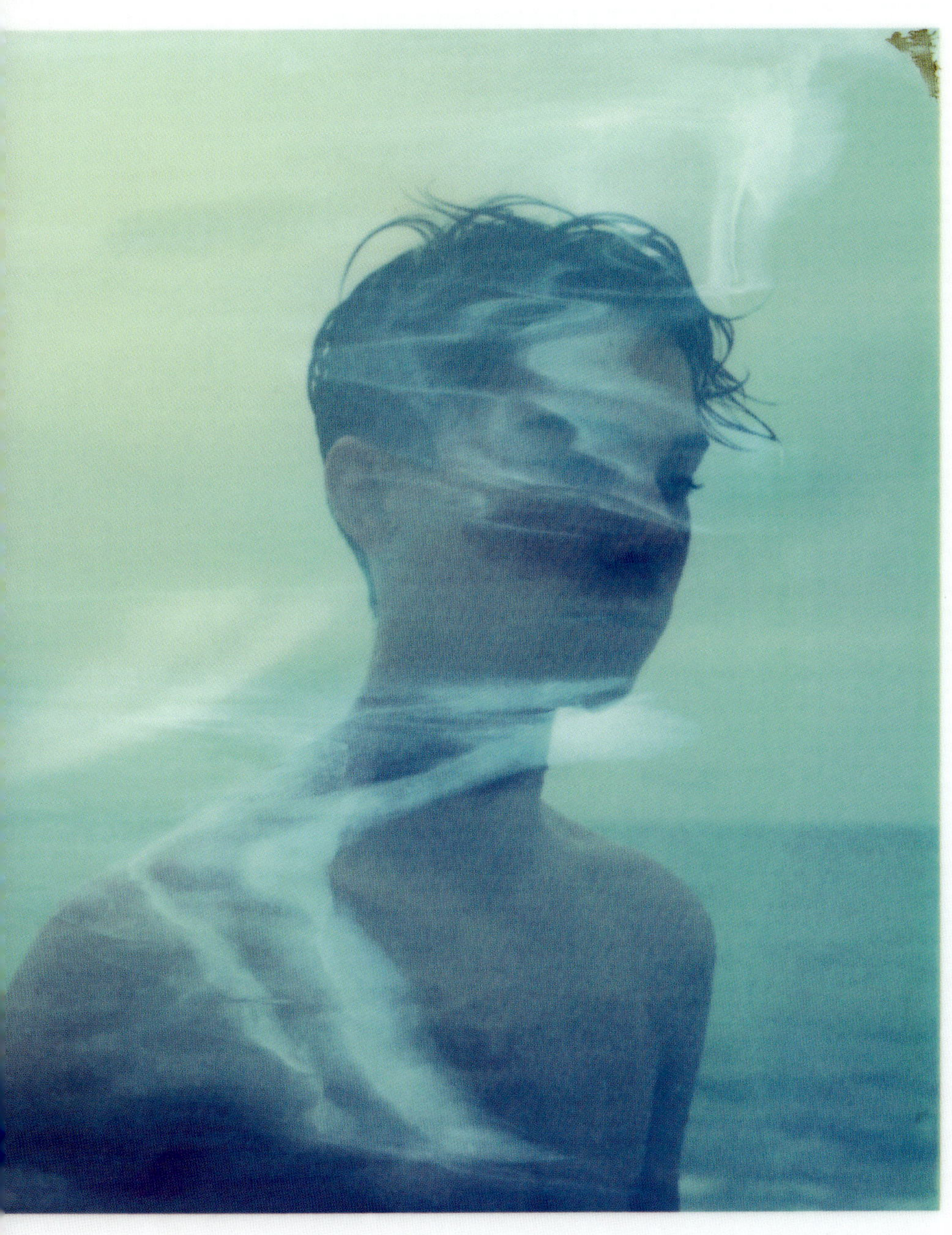

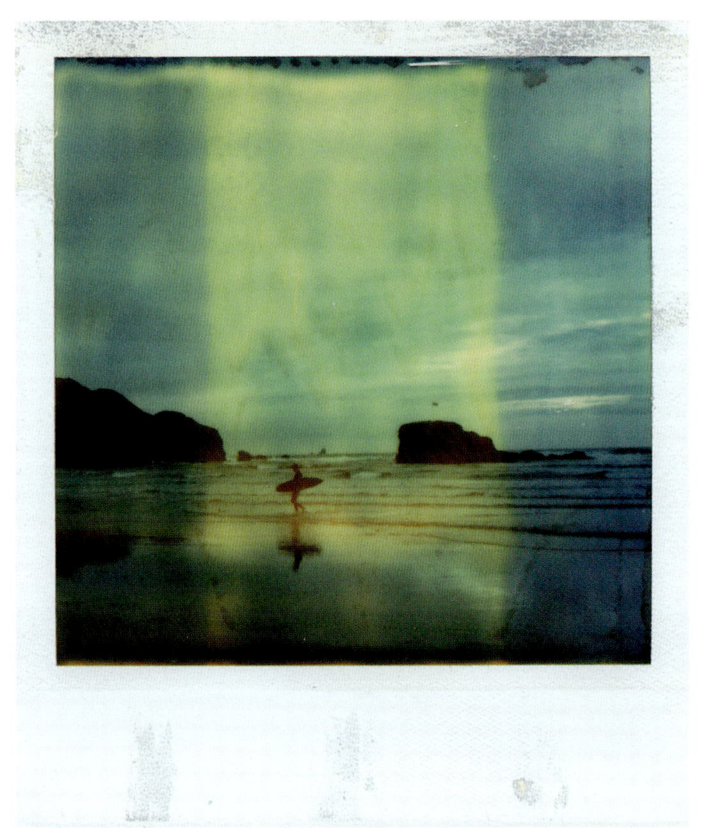

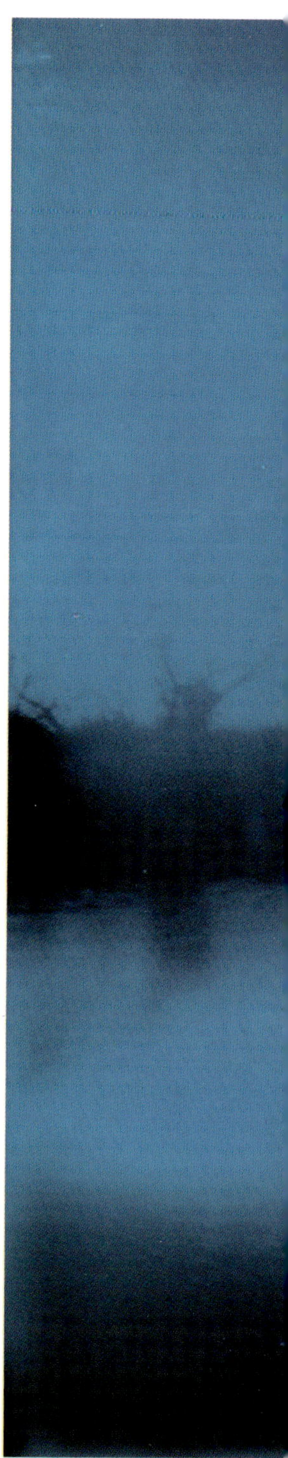

  Lisa Toboz, *Island*

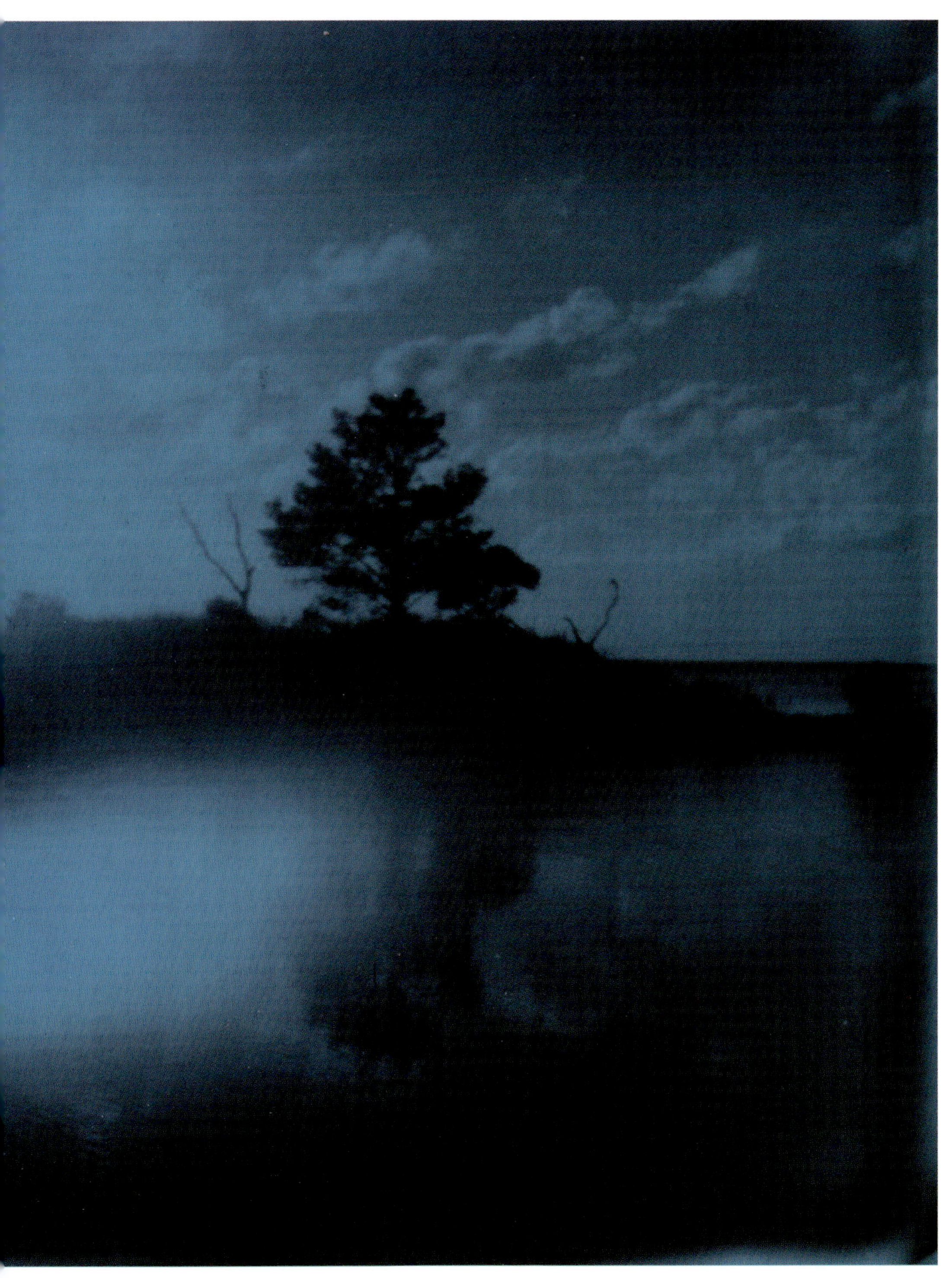

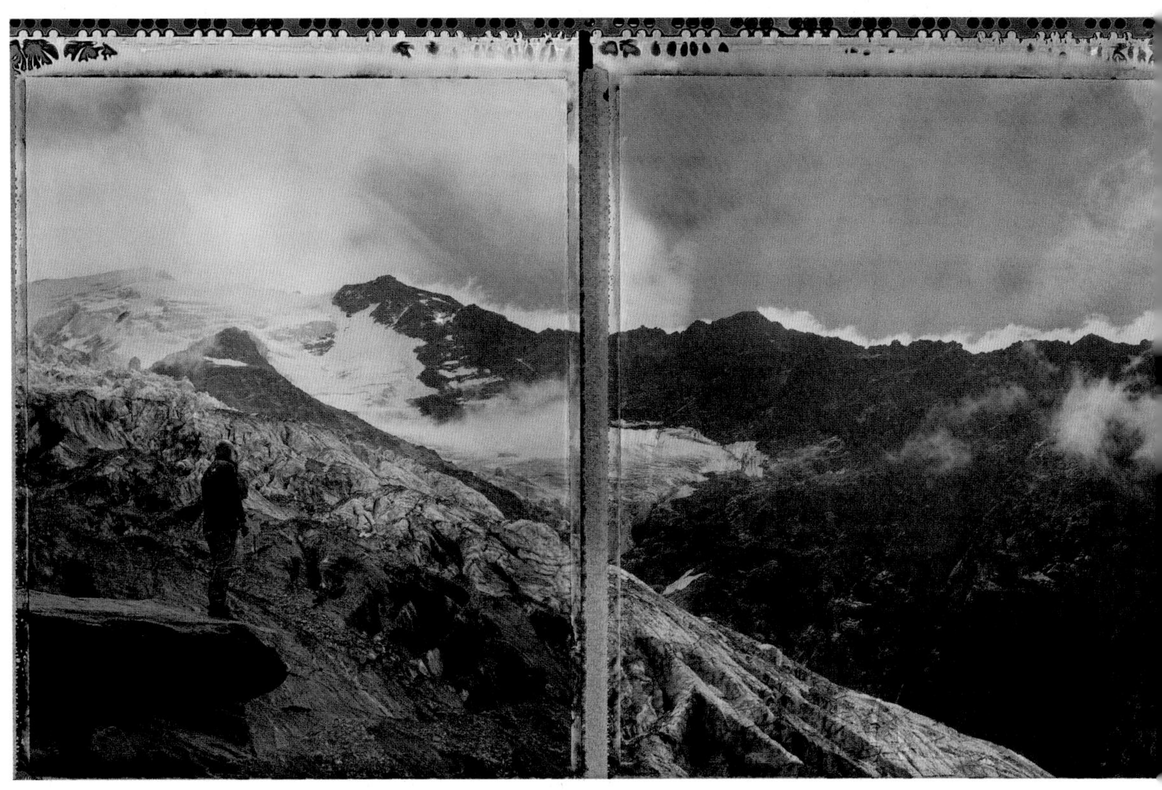

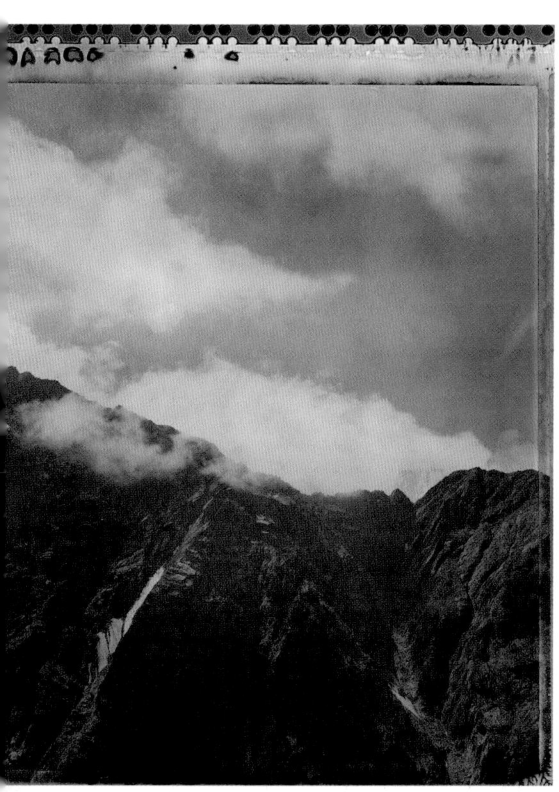

    Joshua Woodland, *Looking Through the Window*

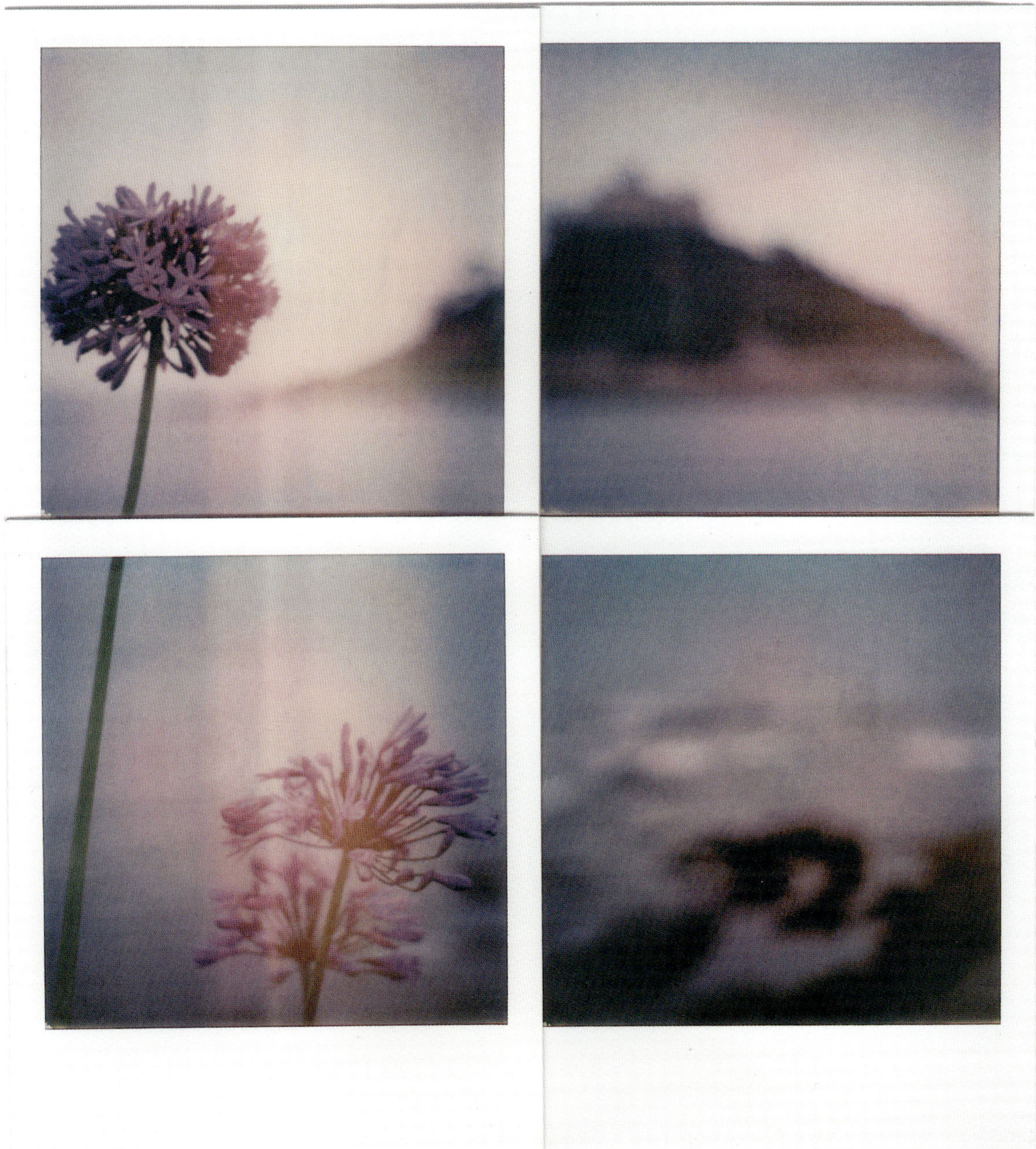

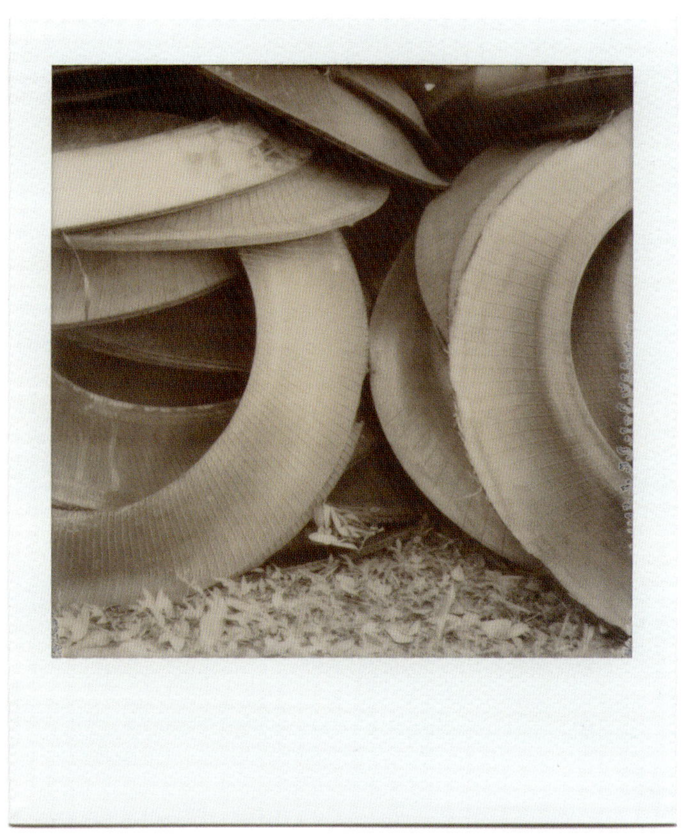

264   Steve Carlton, *Untitled*

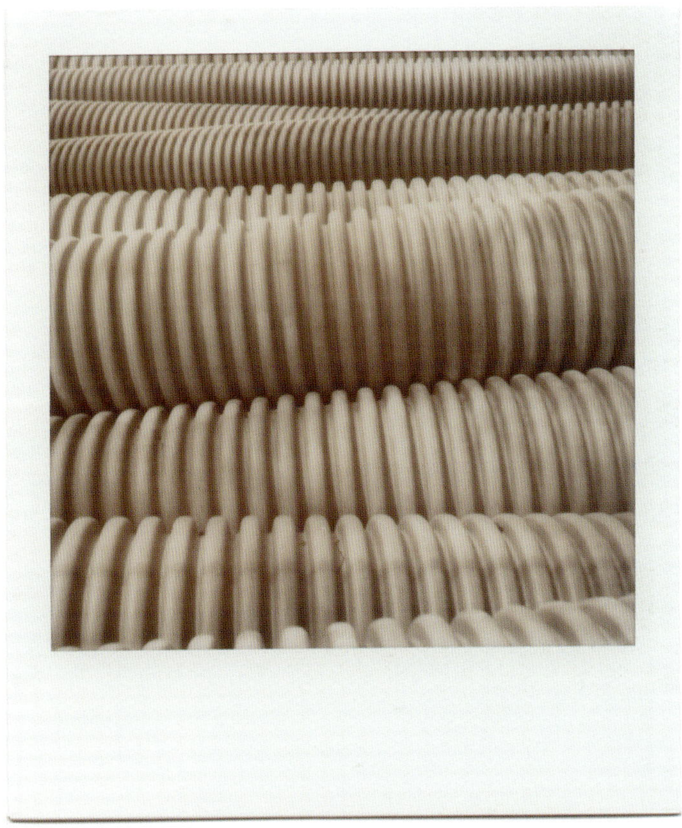

Steve Carlton, *Untitled*   265

266   Scott Asano, *Untitled*

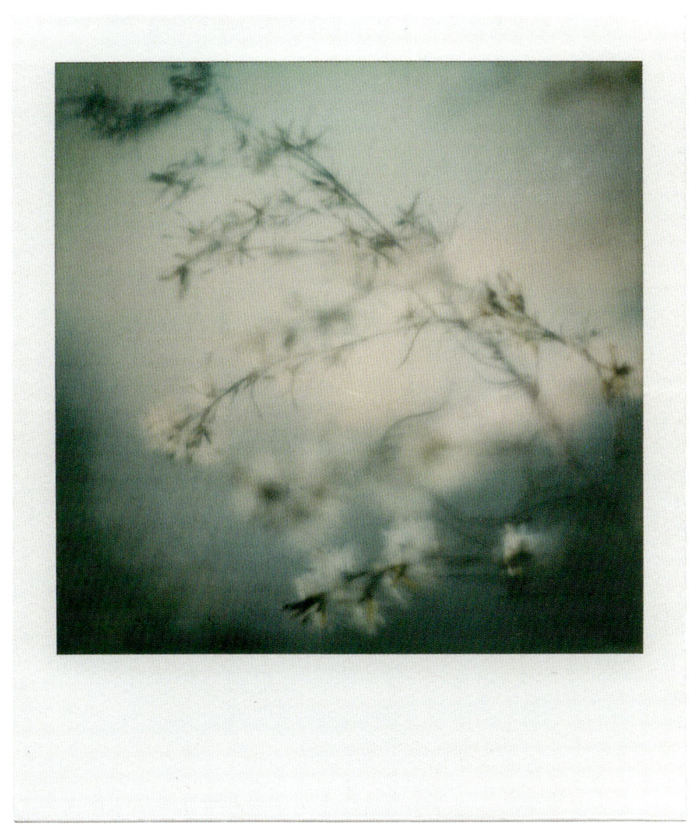

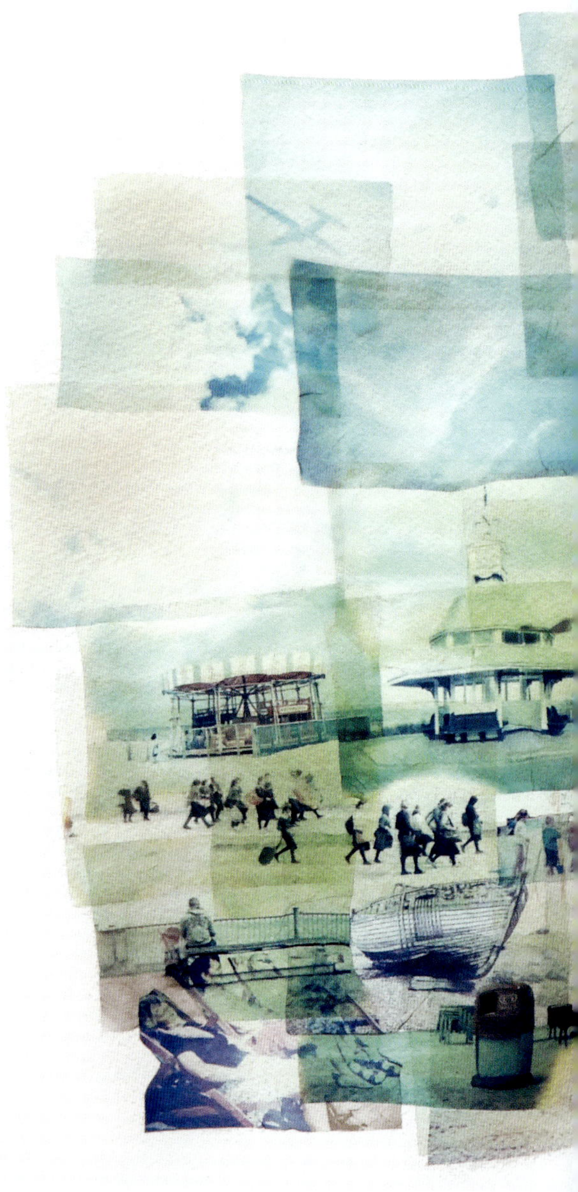

 Rhiannon Adam, *With Sand Beneath Our Feet*

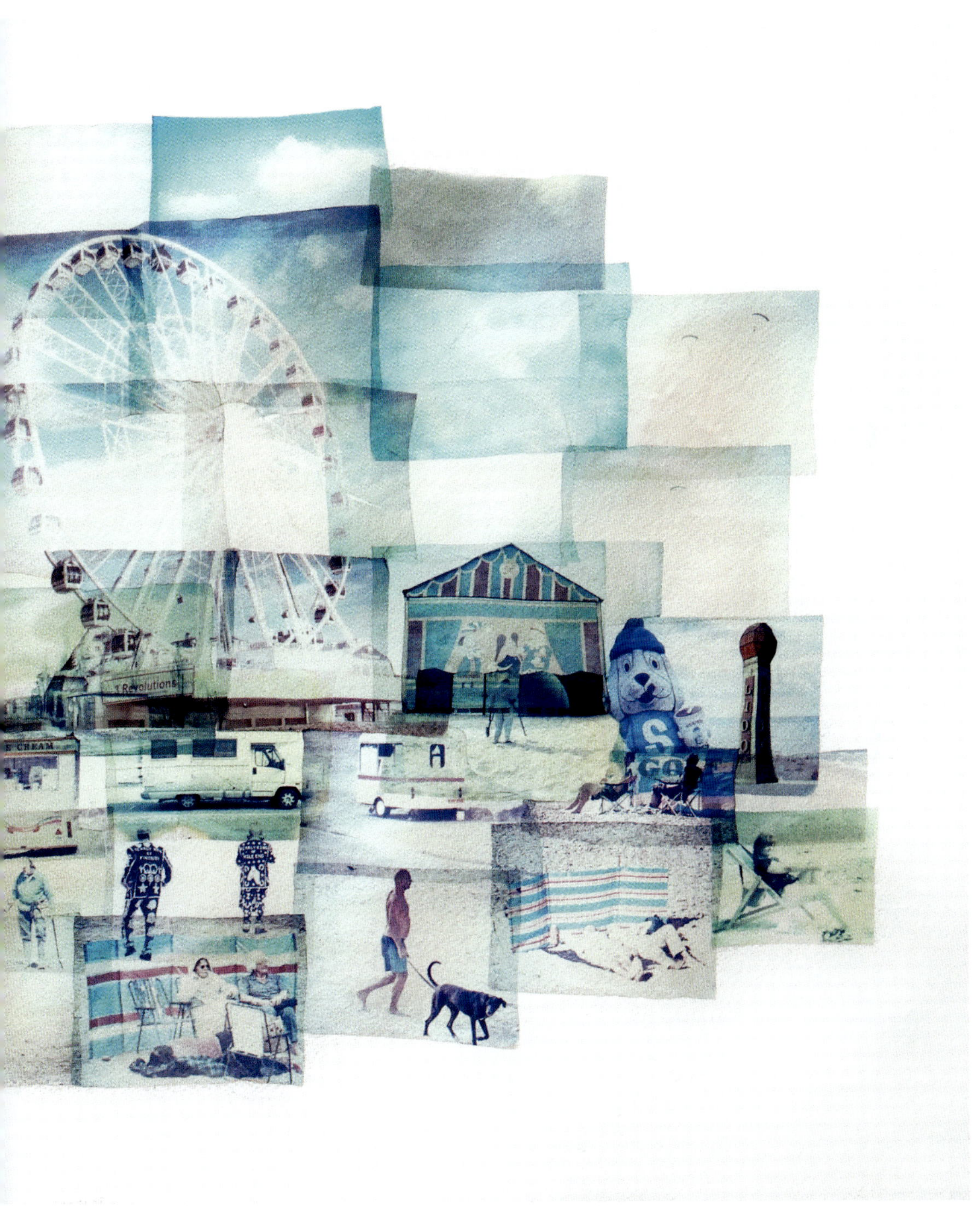
Revolutions
CREAM
GO

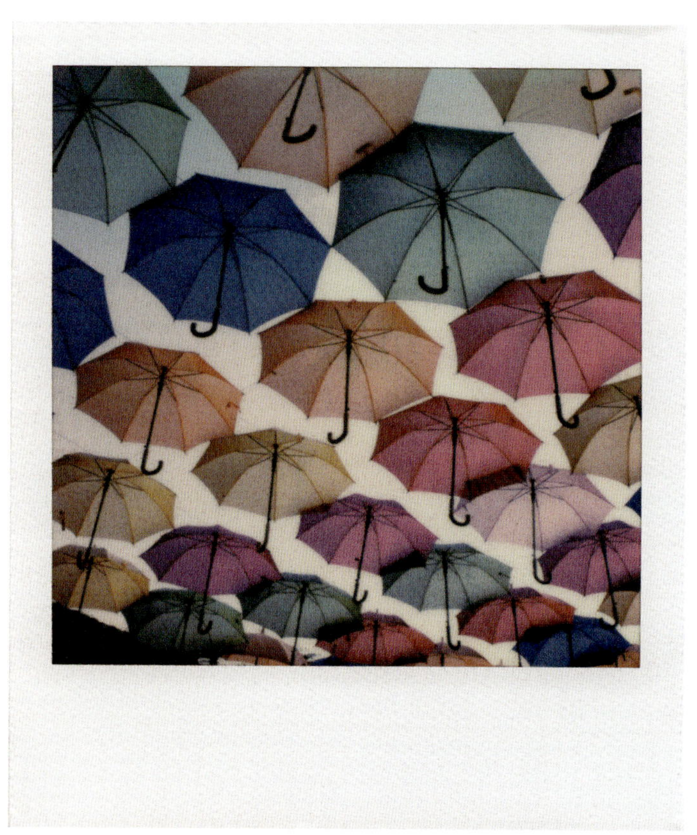

270   Bret Watkins, *In Case of Rainbows*

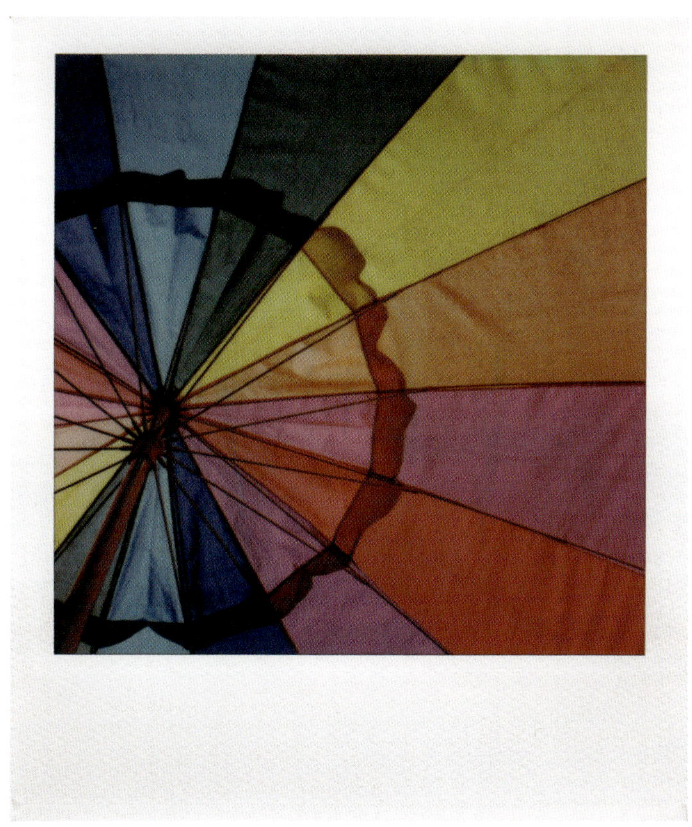

272   Erika Blumenfeld, *Untitled*

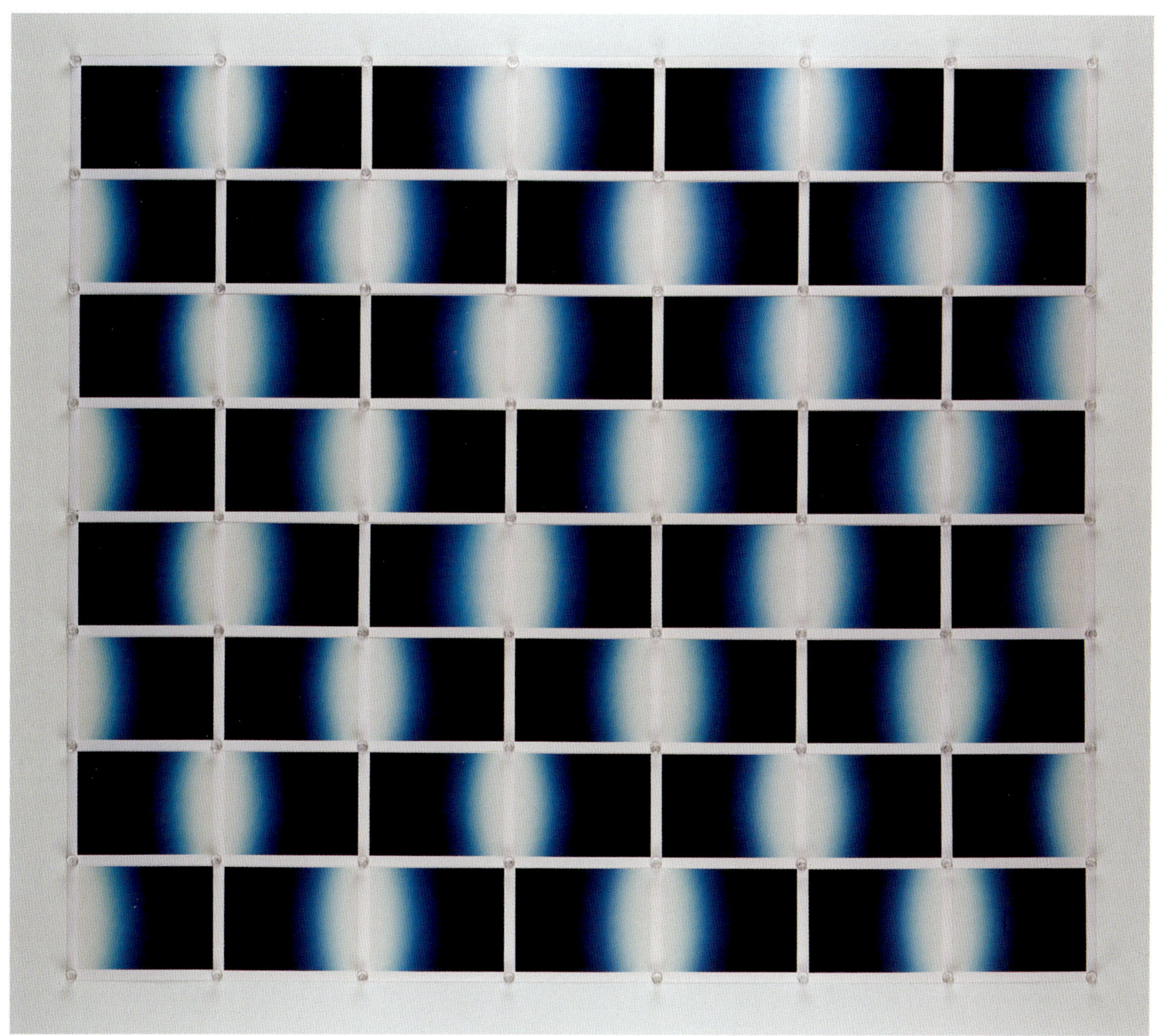

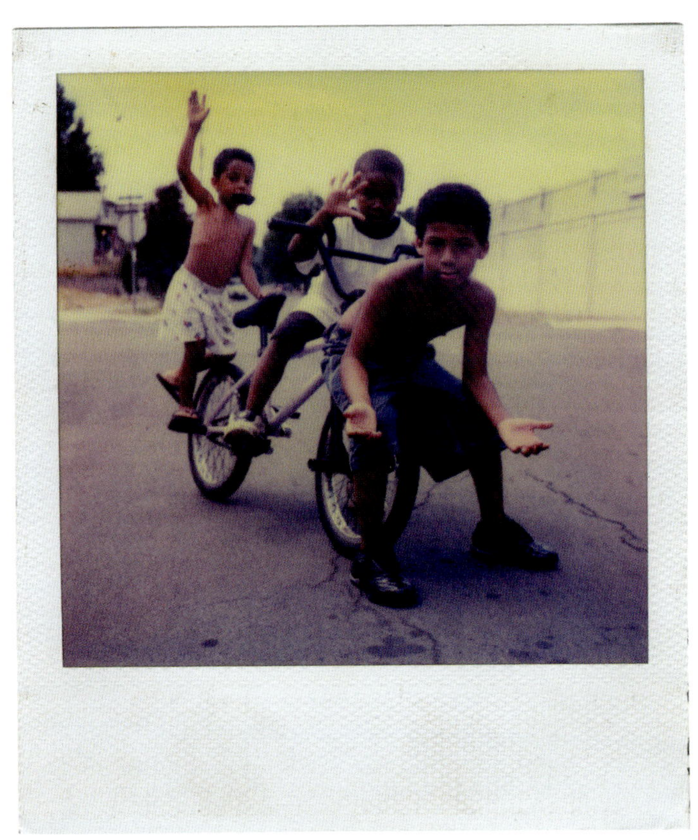

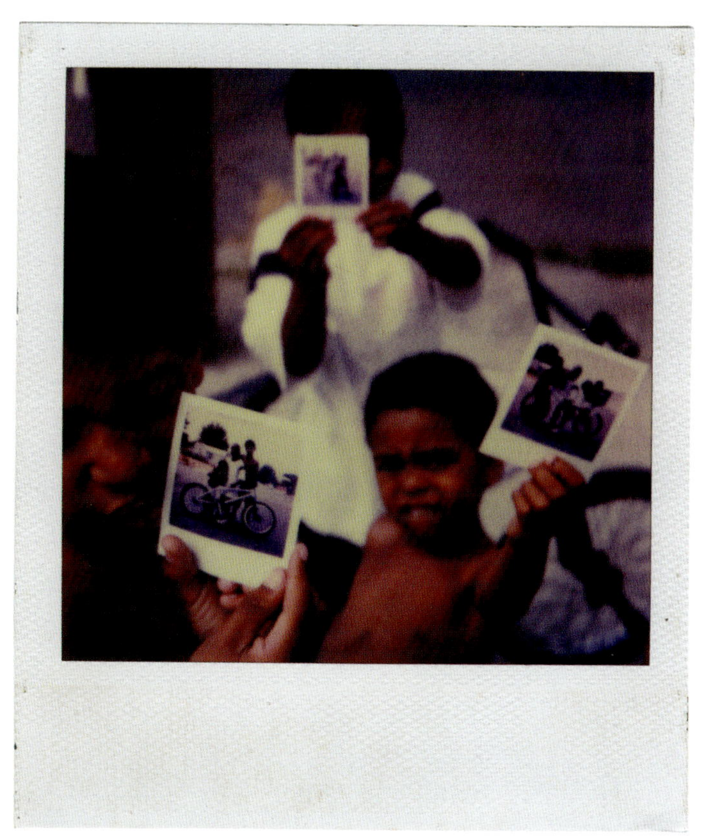

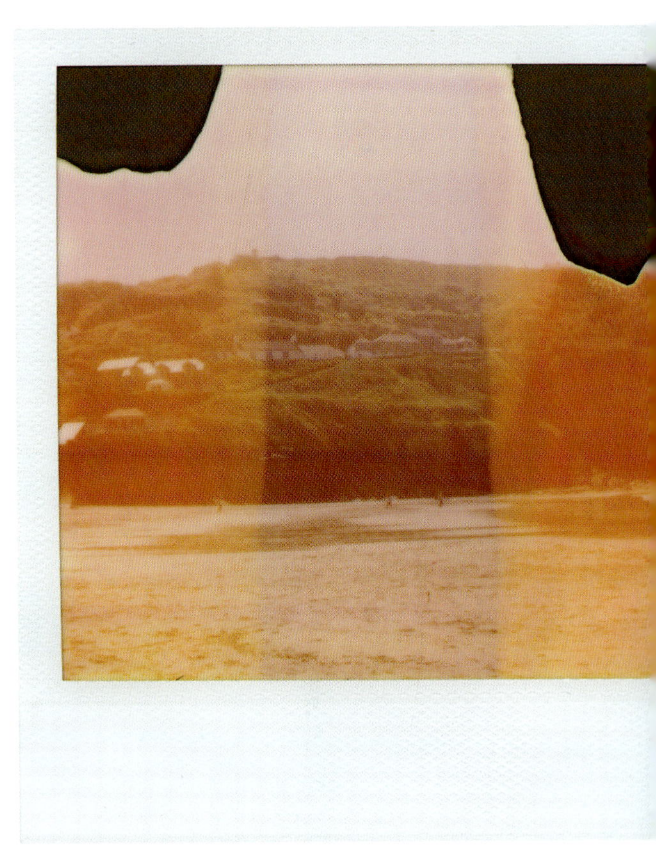

276 Matt Smith, *Untitled*

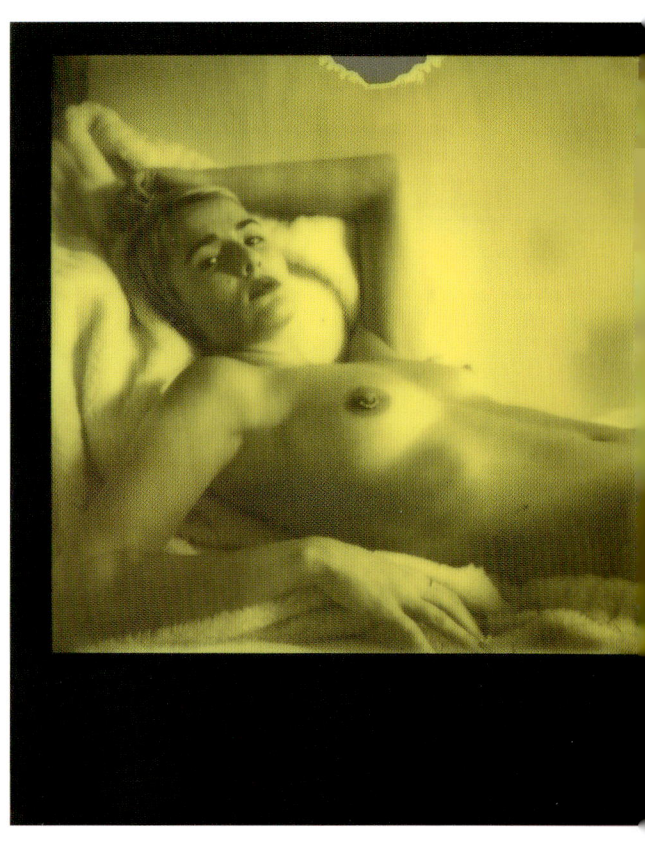

    Laurent Fouchet, *B&Y*

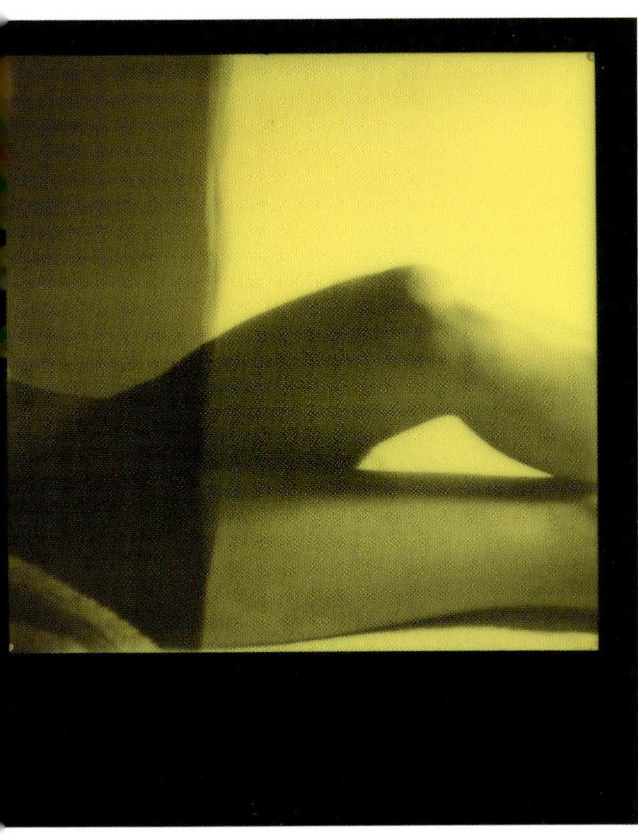

280   Giovanni Previdi, *Untitled*

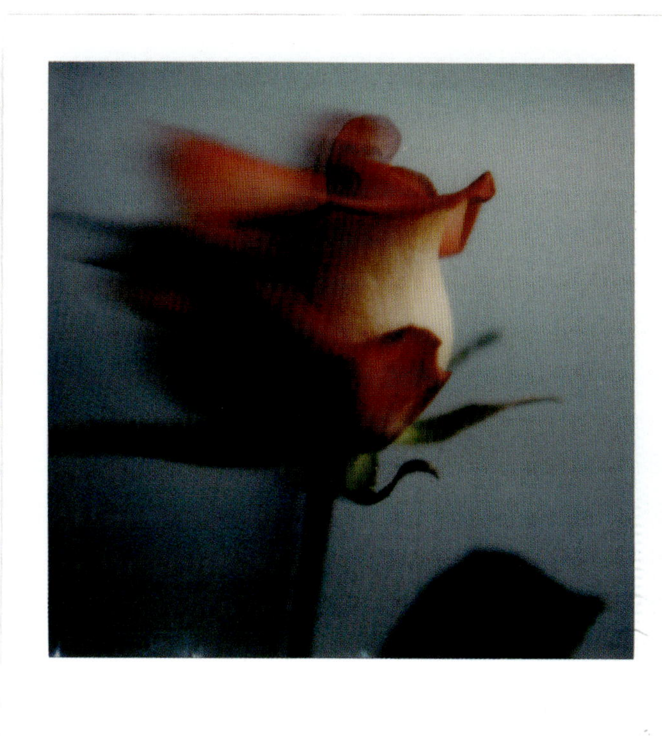

Giovanni Previdi, *Untitled*   281

282   Alex Conu, *Untitled*

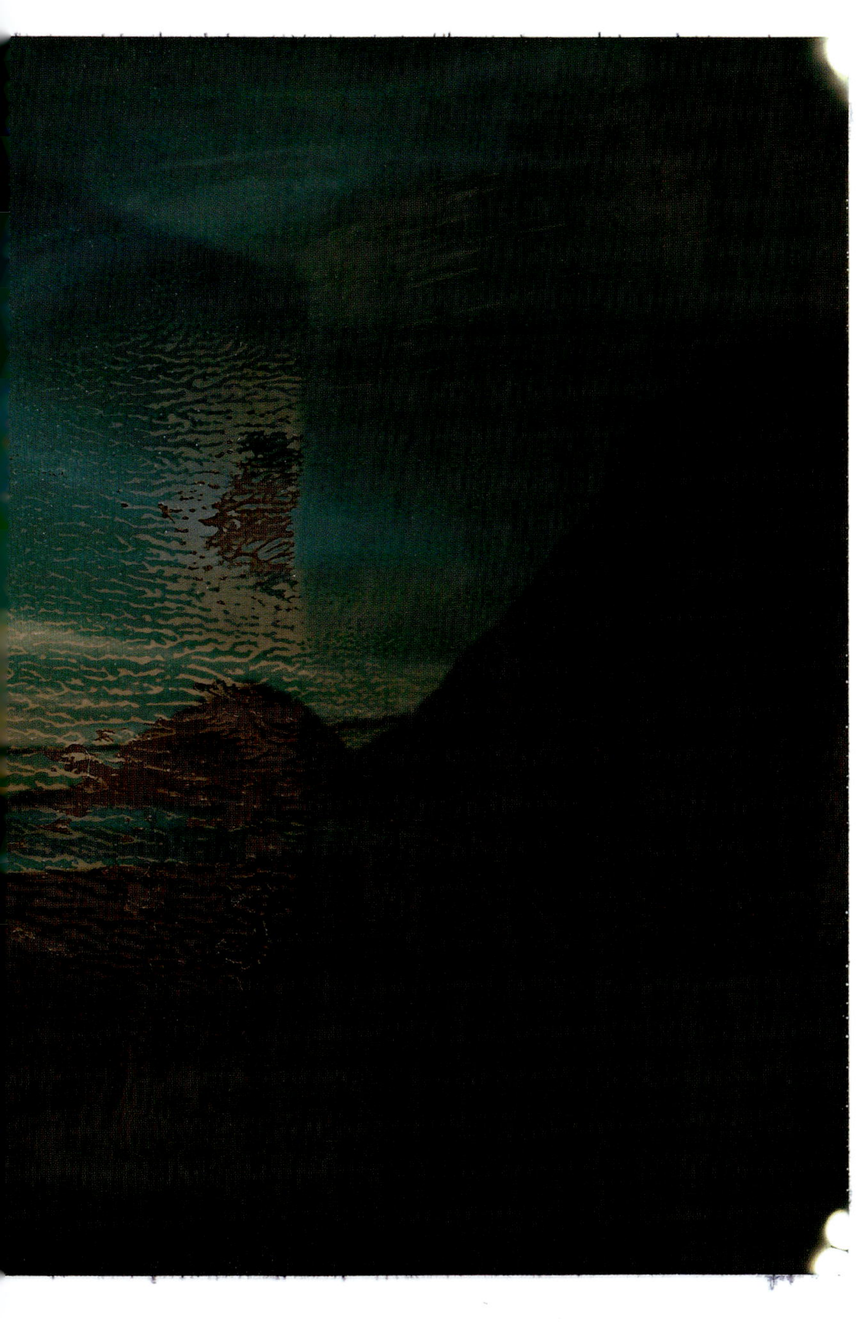

THE POLAROID
20x24
PROJECT

The Polaroid 20 x 24 Project

by John Reuter

In an unremarkable brick building on Osborn Street in Cambridge, Massachusetts, resides Edwin Land's research facilities: a labyrinthine collection of labs and offices that dates back to the earliest years of Polaroid. It is 1976, four years after Polaroid introduced the SX-70: a revolutionary instant camera system that changed photography forever.

On this day Land was meeting with John McCann, director of vision research, not to discuss SX-70 but rather the future of Polaroid's venerable peel-apart film, Polacolor. Long the backbone of the company, peel-apart film had taken a backseat to the more glamorous SX-70 film, which was a self-contained integral construction.

Polacolor remained an important product, but far out of the consumer mainstream, finding its niche in professional products and ID systems. It was still being improved, and Polacolor II, a new generation of the film, was being prepped for release into the professional market. In a bold move, Polaroid was intent on releasing the product in 8 x 10 format—once the pinnacle of professional film but superseded by advances in 4 x 5 and medium format in the editorial and advertising markets. Its release would revive the 8 x 10 camera market and introduce a whole new generation to large-format photography.

On this day, Land and McCann were discussing the upcoming launch of Polacolor 808 at the shareholder's meeting, only five weeks away. McCann recalled: "One day Land called me into his office and said he had just seen a demonstration of Polaroid's 8 x 10 system. He said he was kind of worried because—although it gave you a very nice 8 x 10 picture—since the days of SX-70, three thousand people would come to the shareholder's meeting, which was always held in this large warehouse. So, you really couldn't see an 8 x 10 picture from the back of this massive auditorium. So Land suggested, 'Why don't we go get the Optical Society camera?' That was the camera that he used to demonstrate the first use of instant film at the Optical

Society of America in 1948. 'Let's make a 20 x 24 camera that is just like the Optical Society camera.' What was surprising was that this was five weeks before the meeting instead of the usual four weeks."

That exchange typified Land's Polaroid during the glory years of the 1960s and '70s. With a robust research group that included design groups, sophisticated metal- and wood-working shops, and a bevy of engineers and craftsmen, McCann would meet Land's request—not only with a 20 x 24 camera, but also a 40 x 80 camera used to replicate impressionist paintings from the Boston Museum of Fine Arts. The new Polacolor II film, which was coated on master rolls 44 inches wide, was slit down to 22 inches to fit into this prototype system.

That shareholder's launch was a huge success, with a live portrait from the stage and a series of life-size renditions of Renoir paintings for the press and shareholders to admire. This success led Polaroid to create five 20 x 24 cameras in 1977 and 1978, as well as the 40 x 80 Museum camera (as it was informally named).

A studio complex was built on Ames Street, down the street from Land's lab. The technology was there; now what was needed was the content to match the technology.

McCann's group, who built the cameras and enabled the film stream, was located in the research division at Polaroid. The publicity and marketing groups would be responsible for attracting the artists and photographers to actually use this new medium. Sam Yanes was vice president of corporate communications at Polaroid, and his group was designated to take on this task.

Yanes soon hired JoAnn Verburg, a large-format photographer who was working with the Rephotographic Survey Project led by Mark Klett. This project utilized Polaroid's Type 55 positive/negative film to rephotograph the sites in the American West covered a century before by the likes of Edward Curtis and Timothy O'Sullivan. Verburg's connections to the photography and museum worlds led her to connect with the first group

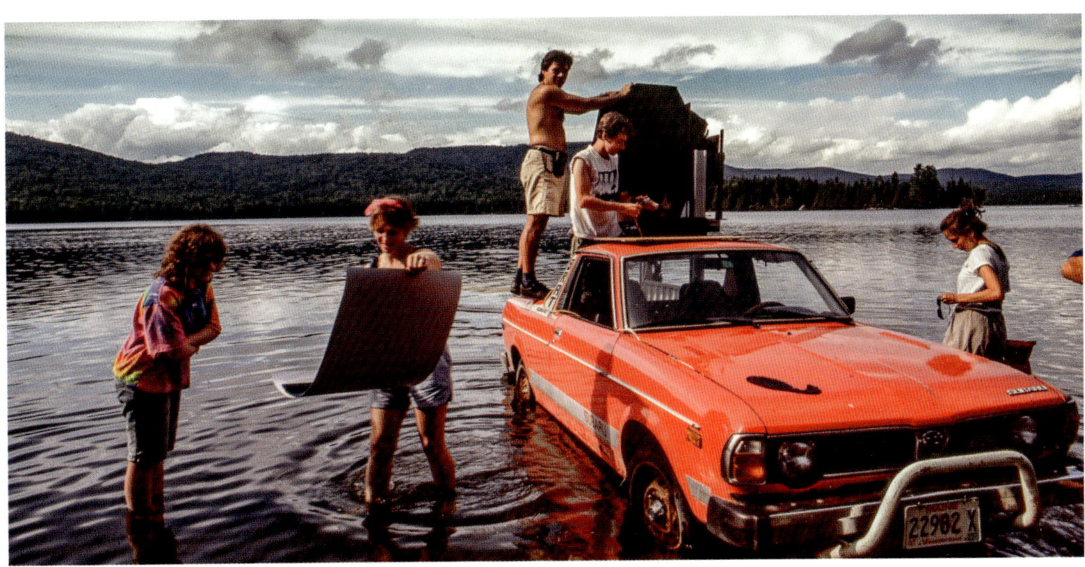

20 x 24 camera with William Wegman, Rangeley, Maine.

of artists to ever use the 20 x 24. These included John Pfahl, Carl Chiarenza, Chuck Close, William Wegman, Betty Hahn, and Jan Groover, among others.

Polaroid expanded its artist support during the next decade and appeared in exhibits in galleries and museums all over the world. Polaroid-sponsored studios were set up in Cambridge, Massachusetts, Amsterdam, and Tokyo, expanding the aesthetic as artists learned what the system and film could do. The project was costly, however, and despite the enormous publicity it provided to Polaroid, there was internal pressure to start making the project pay for itself. In the US, the Boston photo market proved to be too small, and soon the company's sights were set on New York, the capital of the professional and art markets.

In 1986, the Polaroid 20 x 24 Studio set up shop in the SoHo district of Manhattan under the direction of John Reuter. Located in the midst of dozens of photo galleries and commercial studios, the SoHo location was instrumental in its success. Acceptance was swift, and soon projects followed with Barneys, Mikimoto Pearls, Pirelli Calendar, Kohler, *The New York Times Magazine*, *Esquire*, and Tommy Hilfiger, among others.

The Artist Support Program continued in earnest boosted by the New York location, and it became a

prized accomplishment to be invited to use the camera. The European studio was equally active with projects at numerous film festivals and trade shows, and an annual presence at the Les Rencontres de la photographie d'Arles. The studios remained popular throughout the 1990s, and even the bankruptcy in 2001 did little to diminish the enthusiasm for the medium. As the company traded hands in the early 2000s, the New York studio remained viable and somewhat immune from the troubles Polaroid experienced. By 2004, decisions were being made to exit the film business in several years, and it became apparent that the studio would have to go it alone at some point.

Plans were made in 2007 to set aside a significant amount of 20 x 24 film to last beyond the planned phaseout of all other instant films. By 2008, a new company was formed—with the utilitarian name of 20 x 24 Holdings LLC—to take the 20 x 24 project outside of Polaroid. Initiated by conversations between Elsa Dorfman, Dan Stern, John Reuter, and Polaroid, the plan was to begin operations just as Polaroid would officially exit the film business in the first quarter of 2008.

Bizarre realities intervened as Tom Petters, the then owner of Polaroid, was indicted on criminal charges just as the financial crisis of 2008 was in full bloom. Polaroid declared bankruptcy for a second time that

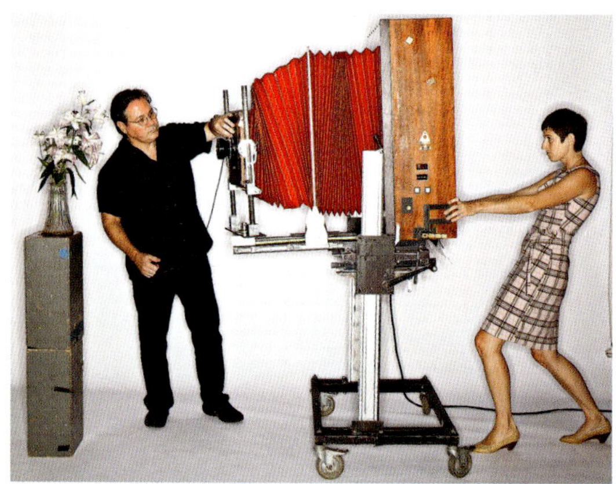

John Reuter and Jennifer Trausch in the 20 x 24 Studio, New York.

decade, and it took until the middle of 2009 before the dust settled and the contract agreed to in early 2008 was finally realized. The film, chemicals, and production equipment—all stored in a warehouse outside of Boston—were finally released to the new company.

The new challenge was to set up facilities after this long delay to continue production. It is often misunderstood just what was needed to keep the 20 x 24 film stream going. It is far from simply storing boxes of film in the refrigerator and taking them out as shoots arise. The film is stored in master rolls of 200 meters that must be spooled into the smaller rolls the 20 x 24 cameras utilize. These rolls are 150 feet for the negative and 50 feet for the positive. Creating a case of film involves one roll of negative and three rolls of positive. The negative master rolls are stored off-site in a refrigerated warehouse and are acquired on an as-needed basis. The positive rolls, which do not require refrigeration, are stored in the warehouse along with the chemicals and production equipment. Polaroid provided an elaborate mixing machine (called a reactor) to create the reagent liquid that is eventually inserted into the pods to develop the 20 x 24 image. The reagent is a complex recipe of sixteen different chemicals, some quite hazardous, that are mixed in a several-hour process in the reactor under nitrogen and finally transferred into holding tanks.

The original recipes supposed to be provided by Polaroid were seemingly misplaced or lost in the one-year gap while the legal issues were sorted out for the

transfer. It was only the ingenuity of Theo McLelland, brought on as director of reagent manufacturing, that saved the project from ending before it began. Theo was able to reconstruct initial recipes from his and some colleague's notes; and by the late fall of 2009, the first reagent batch was produced, nearly a year and a half after the last batch was produced in Polaroid's Waltham plant.

These recipes would have to be monitored and adjusted constantly as the clock was now running on the natural shifting that all film emulsions encounter. They are essentially living entities that change with age with shifting color balance and moving points of maximum density. The reagent recipes have been adjusted almost every three months for ten years to try and stay in sync with the moving target of the negative. Some of the individual chemicals have not lasted as expected and had to be replaced. At one point, nearly 100 gallons of potassium hydroxide had to be disposed of, as it prematurely degraded. It was intended to last for at least five years and instead failed after two—an unexpected and expensive setback.

The final step in the production process is the seemingly simple process of injecting the reagent solution into the foil packets known as pods. For this process, a sixty-year-old, 1-ton Rube Goldberg of a machine is employed. Known simply as the Pod Machine, it is a series of heated laminating and injection stations which employ a large roll of specialized foil with a heat-initiated red strip that seals the foil after the reagent has been injected under pressure and a nitrogen blanket to keep out oxygen. With sealing temperatures of up to 400°F, this mechanical masterpiece can produce about 600 pods in two hours—with constant testing in a nearby 20 x 24 camera system to ensure quality and correct opening. The complexity of the red-stripe seal is that it must break open under the pressure of the camera rollers but stay sealed tightly enough to keep out oxygen for months, until it is used. Over the years, the pod production has been the most complex and stress-inducing part of this process.

Only three people, the entire staff of 20 x 24 Holdings, accomplish the entire production process. A rotating cast of employees at Polaroid once did this with as many as twenty employees participating in the entire film-production process, albeit not on a full-time basis. Each had expertise in a specialized part of the process and brought their skills to bear when needed.

Only Theo McLelland had manufacturing experience, and the other two, Nafis Azad and John Reuter, were trained as photographers. A company this small requires an all-hands-on-deck approach as each of them takes a role in the reagent manufacture and podding process. Azad has an undergraduate degree in electrical engineering, which comes in handy considering the sixty-year-old pod machine is an electrical spaghetti puzzle. Reuter has a PhD in worrying, which is critical to every run.

The film and reagent production is only one aspect of the post-Polaroid world. Finding and supplying customers is the other side of the coin. For the first eight years after exiting Polaroid, the New York studio accounted for 90 percent of all activity, even though there were cameras still scattered around the world. Of the five original cameras Polaroid built, four were still active.

For many years, only Elsa Dorfman's camera was active, as she continued her unique portrait business. The European camera, once a substantial part of Polaroid-supported activity, became virtually inactive as Jan Hnizdo, the owner and operator, essentially retired. Nevertheless, the New York camera continued with projects with long-time practitioners such as Chuck Close, Ellen Carey, Jack Perno, and Mary Ellen Mark.

The camera also took residency at Lincoln Center in New York, participating in the annual New York Film Festival, photographing film greats such as Martin Scorsese, Béla Tarr, Frederick Wiseman, Jonas Mekas, Liv Ullmann, Steven Spielberg, Carrie Fisher, Pedro Almodóvar, and many others. Rotating exhibits of these portraits are on constant view in the theater complexes at Lincoln Center.

In 2019, the European studio was revived when Markus Mahla, former Polaroid marketing manager and one-time assistant to Jan Hnizdo, established a new 20 x 24 studio in Berlin. For the first time in ten years, there was now a companion studio to New York to provide access to the still-viable Polacolor film. When they met at a shoot in Vienna, Mahla was able to convince the reluctant Hnizdo to sell him his camera instead of offering it at auction. The Berlin studio quickly picked up important projects with Formula One Car Collections, a return to Les Rencontres de la photographie d'Arles, and a portrait project—One Shot Rankin—with famed artist Rankin in Milan.

Mahla describes his continued enthusiasm for the project he first encountered nearly thirty years ago: "What all groups, clients, and partners have in common is that they adore what we do. The 20 x 24-inch size is simply overwhelming; it gives you goose bumps and makes you overjoyed. I have never seen anybody who was not blissfully happy about his image; and people who watch and follow the photography process are enthusiastic. This process was, and is, magic and attracts everyone in its spell. Taking a single photograph is an event in itself, but peeling this huge image apart in front of an audience, literally a minute after pulling it out of the huge camera, is a ball. People are moaning, applauding, screaming, they get goose bumps—we had folks who were in tears when their portrait was peeled off. It's always a very special moment. Even me being around this wonderful piece of art for quite a while, I'm getting excited while I tell all this to you."

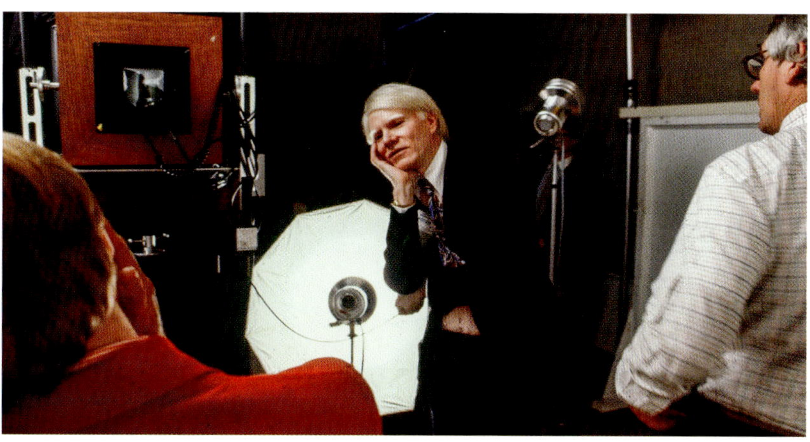

Andy Warhol in Polaroid Ames Street Studio, 1979.

Cameras

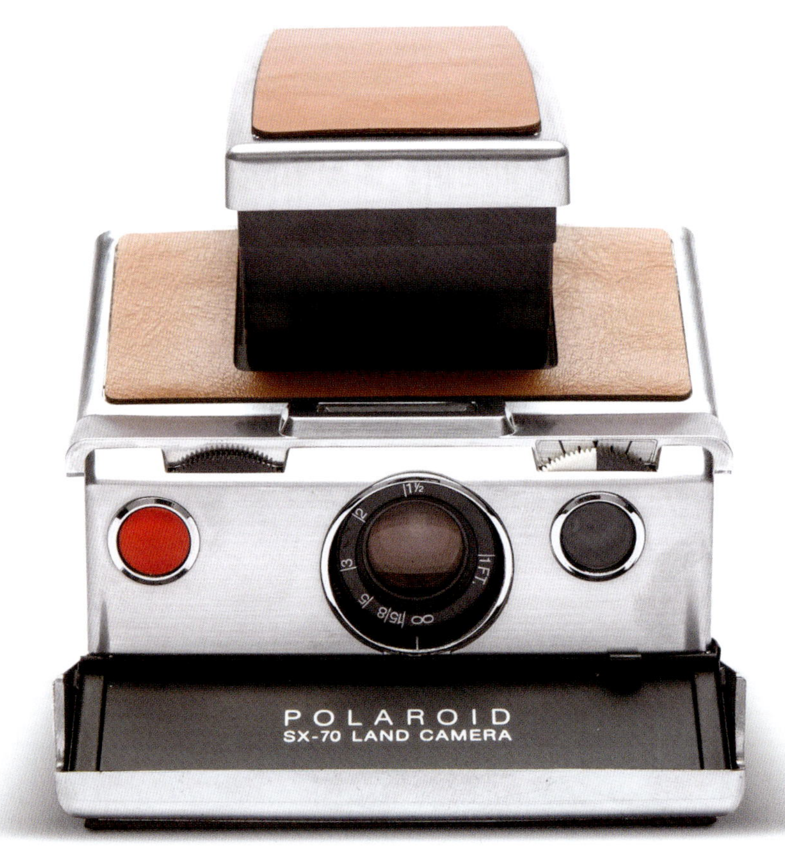

POLAROID
SX-70 LAND CAMERA

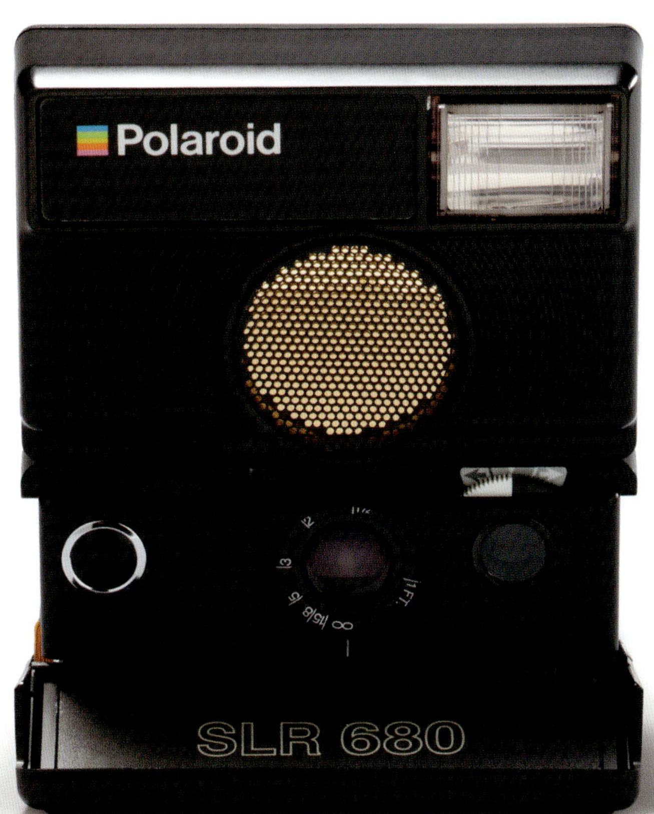

Polaroid
SLR 680

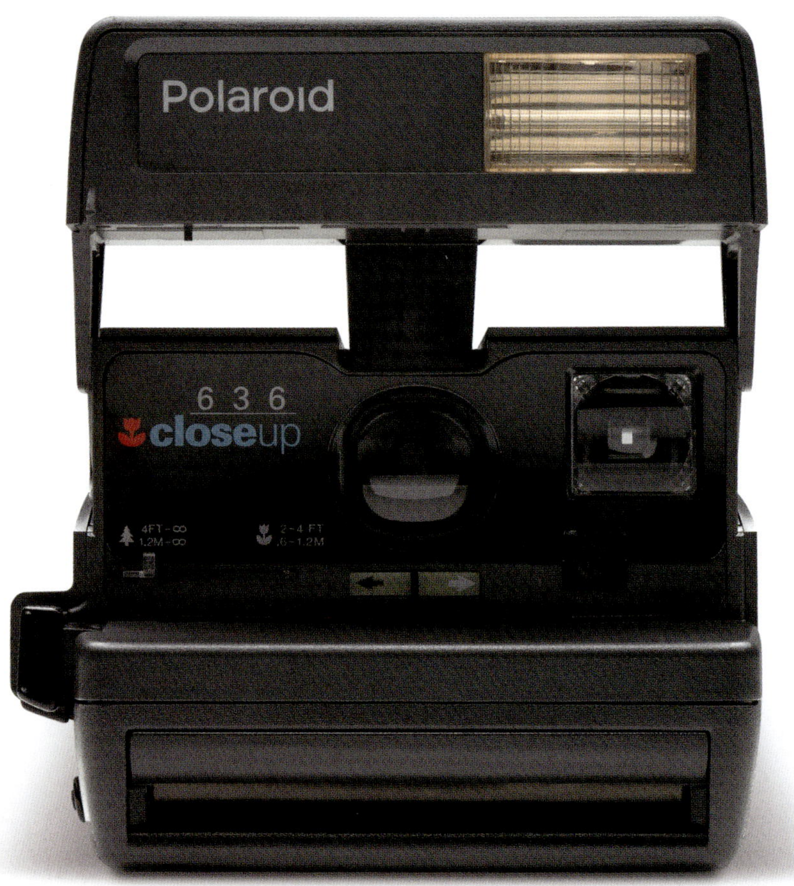

Polaroid
6 3 6
closeup
4FT – ∞
1.2M – ∞
2–4 FT
.6–1.2M

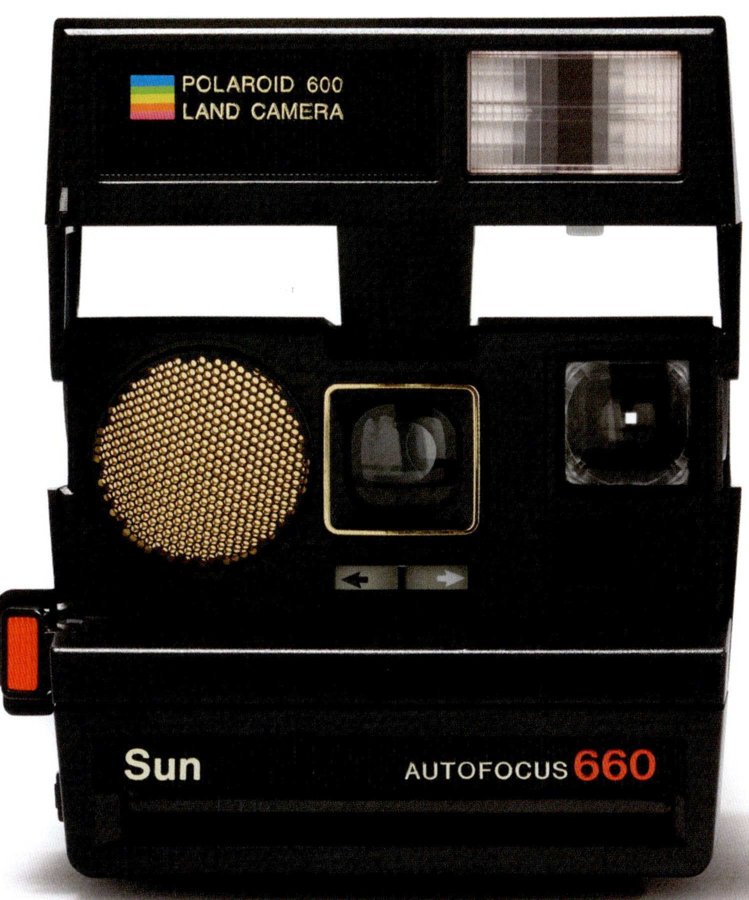
POLAROID 600
LAND CAMERA
Sun
AUTOFOCUS 660

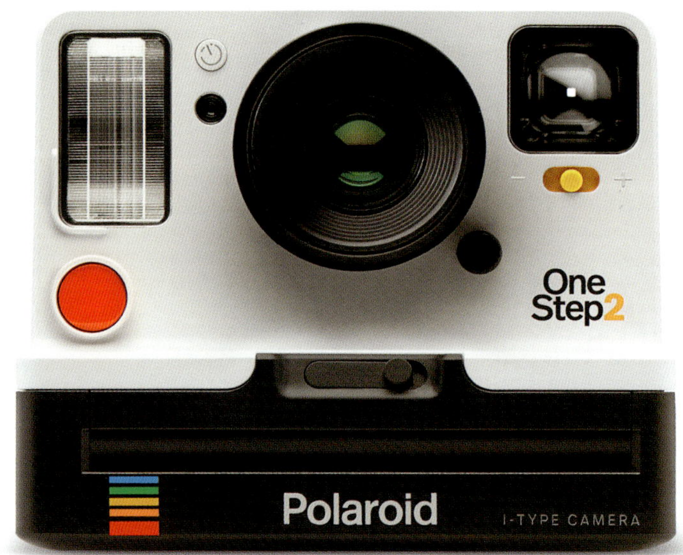

One
Step2
Polaroid
I-TYPE CAMERA

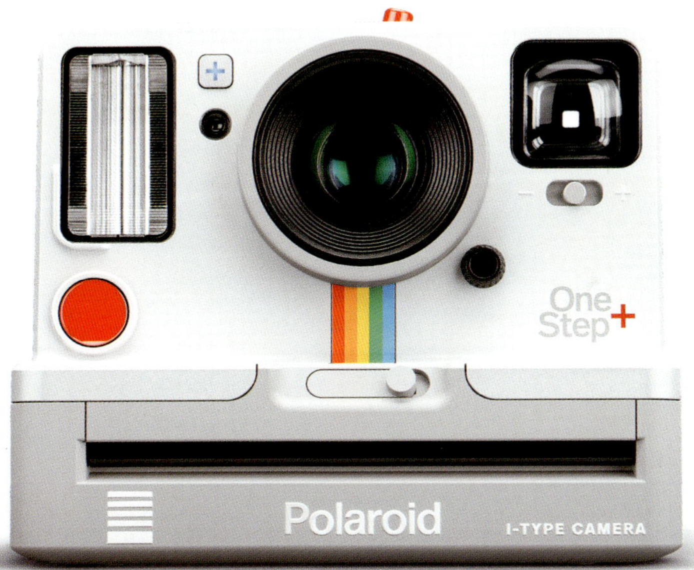

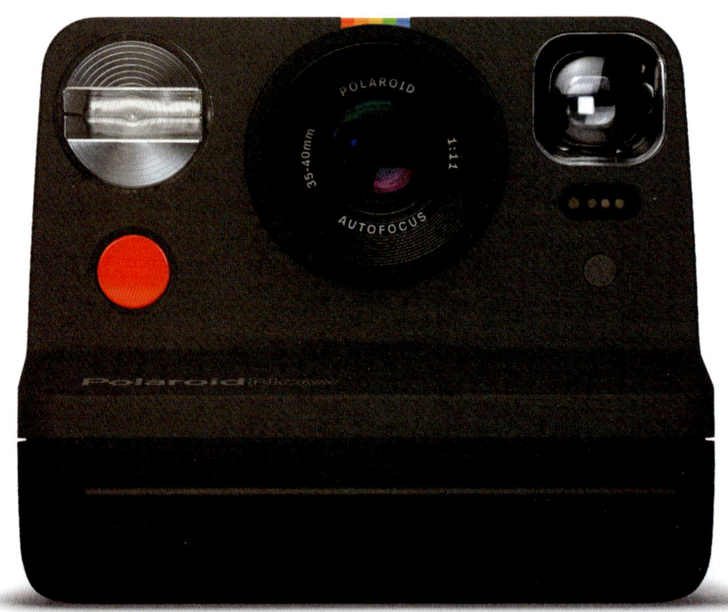

298   i-Type series camera, Now

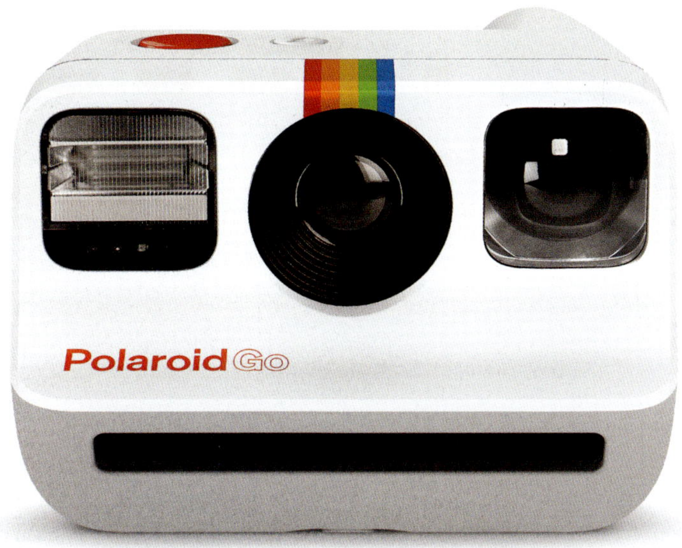

Lindus, Alek
Pages 80–81, *Neither Subject nor Object*, 2020, 669 film
© 2021 Alek Lindus
IG: @aleklindus
aleklindus.com

Liu, Ray
Page 34, *Lightstreams on Tower Bridge*, 2016, i-Type film
Page 35, *Untitled*
Page 216, *Untitled*, SX-70
Page 217, *Untitled*
Page 243, *Untitled*
© 2021 Ray Liu
IG: @rliu
rayliu.co.uk

Locquen, Anne
Page 198, *Pink Time*, SX-70
Page 199, *Full Sun*, SX-70
Pages 254–255, *Breathe*, 669, 180 film
© 2021 Anne Locquen
IG: @annette1817
annettelo.tumblr.com

Lussana, Leonardo
Page 83, *Vertical Square*, Bergamo, Piazza Vecchia, 2019, i-Type film
© 2021 Leonardo Lussana
IG: @leonardo_lussana

Manning, Duncan
Pages 84–85, *Isolation*, 2020, 669
© 2021 Duncan Manning
IG: @ds_manning

Marcheselli, Alan
Pages 146–147, *My Dreams are Heavy*, 2019, B&W 600 film
© 2021 Alan Marcheselli
IG: @alan_marcheselli
alanmarcheselli.com

Meyer-Rassow, Steven
Page 130, *Study in Yellow, Part 1*, 2019, SX-70
Page 131, *Study in Yellow, Part 2*, 2019, SX-70
© 2021 Steven Meyer-Rassow
IG: smrphotoart
smrphotoart.com

Mokline, Jeannette
Page 99, *Dissociate / Enter My World*, 2020, SX-70
© 2021 Jeannette Mokline
IG: @instantorious

Müller, Robby
Page 86, *Kensington Motel*, Santa Monica
Page 87, *While shooting To Live and Die in L.A.*
Page 112, *Winter Trees*
Page 113, *Untitled*
Page 144, *While shooting Falsche Bewegung*
Page 145, *While shooting Honeysuckle Rose*
Page 210, *While shooting To Live and Die in L.A.*
© 2021 Robby Müller
IG: @annetgelinkgallery
annetgelink.com

Nakai, Akio
Pages 132–133, *Blue the Sleepy, no.1, 2, and 3*, 2018, Blue 600 film
© 2021 Nakai Akio
IG: @nakaiakio
NakaiAkio.com

Nalin, Guillaume
Pages 90–91, *Narcisse*, 2020, 600 film
© 2021 Guillaume Malin
IG: @guilomme.n

Neese, Anika
Page 227, *Maybe I Just Need to Clean My Glasses*, 2020, i-Type film
© 2021 Anika Neese

Nohra, Rayan
Page 182, *Camera*
Page 183, *Distortion With A Glass (Paris Night Time)*
Page 222, *Feels Like slow Motion (Colombia)*
Page 223, *Tree in the Middle of a Small Field in the Jungle (Colombia)*
© 2021 Rayan Nohra
IG: @rayannohra
rayannohra.com

Obrecht, Marie-Sara
Pages 200–201, *Geometric Waves*, Piscine St Georges, Rennes
Pages 214–215, *Through the light*
© 2021 Marie-Sara Obrecht
IG: @pola_woman

Polley, Heather
Page 77, *Self Portrait (Eye)*, 2016, 600 film
© 2021 Heather Polley
IG: @hpolleyphotography
heatherpolley.com

Previdi, Giovanni
Page 280, *Untitled*, SX-70
Page 281, *Untitled*, SX-70
© Giovanni Previdi
IG: giovanni_previdi

Questorio, Stefano
Page 36, *Ocean*, 2019, 88 film
Page 37, *Hidden Portrait*, 2019, 88 film
Pages 92–93, *The Day I Tried to Climb the Sky*, SX-70
Page 94, *The Second Adventure of Mr. Q / Is Such a Small World*, 2019, SX-70, 600 film
Page 116, *The Philosophy of Mr. Q / Optimism*, 2020, SX-70, 600 film
© 2021 Stefano Questorio
IG: @stefanoquestorio_polaroids
stefanoquestorioinstantphotography.com

Rankin, Kathy
Pages 234–235, *Darkness is Your Candle*, Lab, 600 film
© 2021 Kathy Rankin
IG: @kathy_rankin

Reader, Robert
Page 38, *Blue No.1*, 2009, SX-70
Page 39, *Orange No.7*, 2009, SX-70
© 2021 Robert Reader
IG: @cameraandcompass
robertreader.com

Reuter, John
Page 287, 20 x 24 with William Wegman in Rangeley, Maine
Page 289, Andy Warhol in Polaroid Ames Street Studio, 1979
Photos courtesy John Reuter.
20 x 24 Studio
© 2021 John Reuter

Rumbach, Jennifer
Page 212, *Burning Down the Ice*, 2018, SX-70
Page 213, *Atomic Horse*, 2018, SX-70
© 2021 Jennifer Rumbach
IG: @jennifer_rumbach_polaroids
jennifer_rumbach.de

Russo, Felicita
Page 230, *Exploring Negative Space*, 2019, i-Type film
Page 231, *Planet's Misalignment*, 2019, i-Type film
© 2021 Felicita Russo
IG: @felicitarusso
felicitarusso.it

Salgado H., Eduardo
Page 237, *Dreaming Of*, 2019, 600 film
© 2021 Eduardo Salgado H.
IG: @___________edouard_

Sambati, Francesco
Pages 96–97, *Bonaccia series*, 2015, SX-70
Page 129, *Bonaccia series*
© 2021 Francesco Sambati
IG: @francesco.sambati
francescosambati.com

Santiago, Sabrina
Page 233, *Vincent in his Studio*, 2017, i-Type film
© 2021 Sabrina Santiago
IG: @__sabrinasantiago
sabrina-santiago.com

Shelleg, Ariel
Page 184, *Idle Hands & Busy Minds* / self portrait
Page 185, *Luxuria* / self portrait with Pauli
Page 238, *Look At You / Self Portrait*, 2017, SX-70

Page 239, *RUN*, 2018,
779 film
© 2021 Ariel Shelleg
IG: @shelleg
arielshelleg.com

Sheppard, Taylor
Page 219, *Untitled*, 2014,
600 film
© 2021 Taylor Sheppard
IG: @taylorsheps
taylorsheppard.com

Sjöblom, Bizz
Page 251, *Untitled*, 2017,
55 film
© 2021 Bizz Sjöblom
IG: bizzsjoblom
Bizzsjoblom.com

Smith, Matt
Pages 224–225, *Porthleven*,
2019, 59 film
Page 256, *Chapel Rock
Reflections*
Pages 276–277, *Untitled*
© 2021 Matt Smith
IG: @instant_surf
instantsurf.co.uk

Stein, Anke
Page 244–245, *Life
Through the Yellow Lens*,
2017, Impossible Third
Man Records Edition film
© 2021 Anke Stein
IG: @ankespicures

Storey, Ruth
Page 71, *Sometimes when
you look at me it's more than
I can stand. I'm not good
enough for you to look at me
like that*, 2017, 600 film
Page 104, *We're all going
somewhere. I hope I'm
going there with you*, 2018,
600 film
© 2021 Ruth Storey
IG: @roo_roo_s

Surfleet, Leanne
Page 105, *Self Portrait*,
2012, Impossible Project,
PX-70
© 2021 Leanne Surfleet
IG: @leannesurfleet
Leannesurfleet.co.uk

Sviokla, Tori
Page 232, *Salem Stroll*,
2018, i-Type film
© Tori Sviokla
IG: torisviokla
torisviokla.com

**Thys Van Den Audenaerde,
Kirsten**
Page 110, *Come Fly With Me*,
2020, 600 film
Page 111, *Salt On My Skin*,
2017, 600 film
© 2021 Kirsten Thys Van
Den Audenaerde
IG: ___polaroidlives___

Toboz, Lisa
Pages 40–41, *Mirror Image*,
2018, Spectra film
Pages 164–165, *Dwell*,
2017, Spectra film
Pages 258–259, *Island*,
2018, i-Type film
© 2021 Lisa Toboz
IG: @lisatoboz
lisatoboz.com

Tonellotto, Andrea
Pages 248–249, *Hot
Composition*, SX-70
© 2021 Andrea Tonellotto
IG: @andreatonellotto
andreatonellotto.com

Toscani, Oliviero
Front and Rear Endpapers,
Andy Warhol
© 2021 Oliviero Toscani
IG: @olivierotoscanistudio
olivierotoscanistudio.com

Warhol, Andy
Page 4, *Debbie Harry*, 1980,
Polacolor Type 108
Page 5, *Jean-Michel Basquiat*,
1982, Polacolor ER
© 2021 The Andy Warhol
Foundation for the Visual
Arts, Inc. / Licensed by Artist
Rights Society (ARS)
warhol.org

Watkins, Bret
Page 270, *In Case of
Rainbows*, 2018, SX-70
Page 271, *Rainbow
Protection*, 2019, 600 film
© 2021 Bret Watkins
IG: @intothepolaroid

Wildeboer, Lilian
Pages 174–175, *Swan of
the Lake*, 2015, SX-70
Pages 208–209, *Beauty
Anemone*, 2007, 690 film
Page 247, *Loss*, 2011,
Impossible Project PX
Push film
© Lilian Wildeboer
IG: @lilian.wpolaroidphotog-
raphy
l.wildeboer@live.nl

Wilson, Meredith
Page 118, *Untitled*, 2020,
250 Land, 669 film
Page 119, *Dog Beach*,
Ruislip Lido, 2016, 250
Land, 669 film
© 2021 Meredith Wilson
IG: @merrimayhem
flickr.com/photos/
mawphotography

Winfield, Patrick
Pages 32–33, *Origin 5*,
SX-70
Page 55, *Origin 14*, SX-70
Pages 64–65, *Sleep*, SX-70
Pages 188–189, *Origin 15*,
SX-70
© 2021 Patrick Winfield
IG: @patrickwinfield_art
patrickwinfield.com

Woodland, Joshua
Page 263, *Looking Through
the Window*, 2020, i-Type
film
© 2021 Joshua Woodland
IG: polaroids_of_
turnips____________

Zamolo, Thomas
Pages 260–261, *Triptych Did
D'Aigles*, 2017, 55 film
© 2021 Thomas Zamolo
IG: @thomaszamolo_
photography
thomaszamolo.com

Zyla, Noah
Pages 120–121, *Twins of
Leda I and II*, 2018, Spectra
© 2021 Noah Zyla
IG: @noahandhisshadow

Polaroid **Now**

THE HISTORY AND FUTURE OF POLAROID PHOTOGRAPHY

Essays by Steve Crist, Oskar Smolokowski, and John Reuter

Edited by Steve Crist and Gloria Fowler

Design: Carrie Worthen and Ben Pope, ThirdThing

Production: Kayleigh Jankowski

Research: Lola Crist

Rights Clearance: Mallory Farrugia and Alex Colombino

Copy Editor: Sara DeGonia

Thank you to Oskar Smolokowski, John Reuter, Matthew Antezzo, Ruth Bibby, Stephanie Gamache Tungseth, and all the Polaroid Artists who contributed to this book.

ISBN: 978-1-7972-0137-5
Library of Congress Cataloging-in-Publication Data available.

Manufactured in China

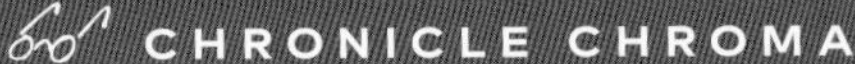

Chronicle Chroma is an imprint of Chronicle Books
Los Angeles, California

chroniclechroma.com

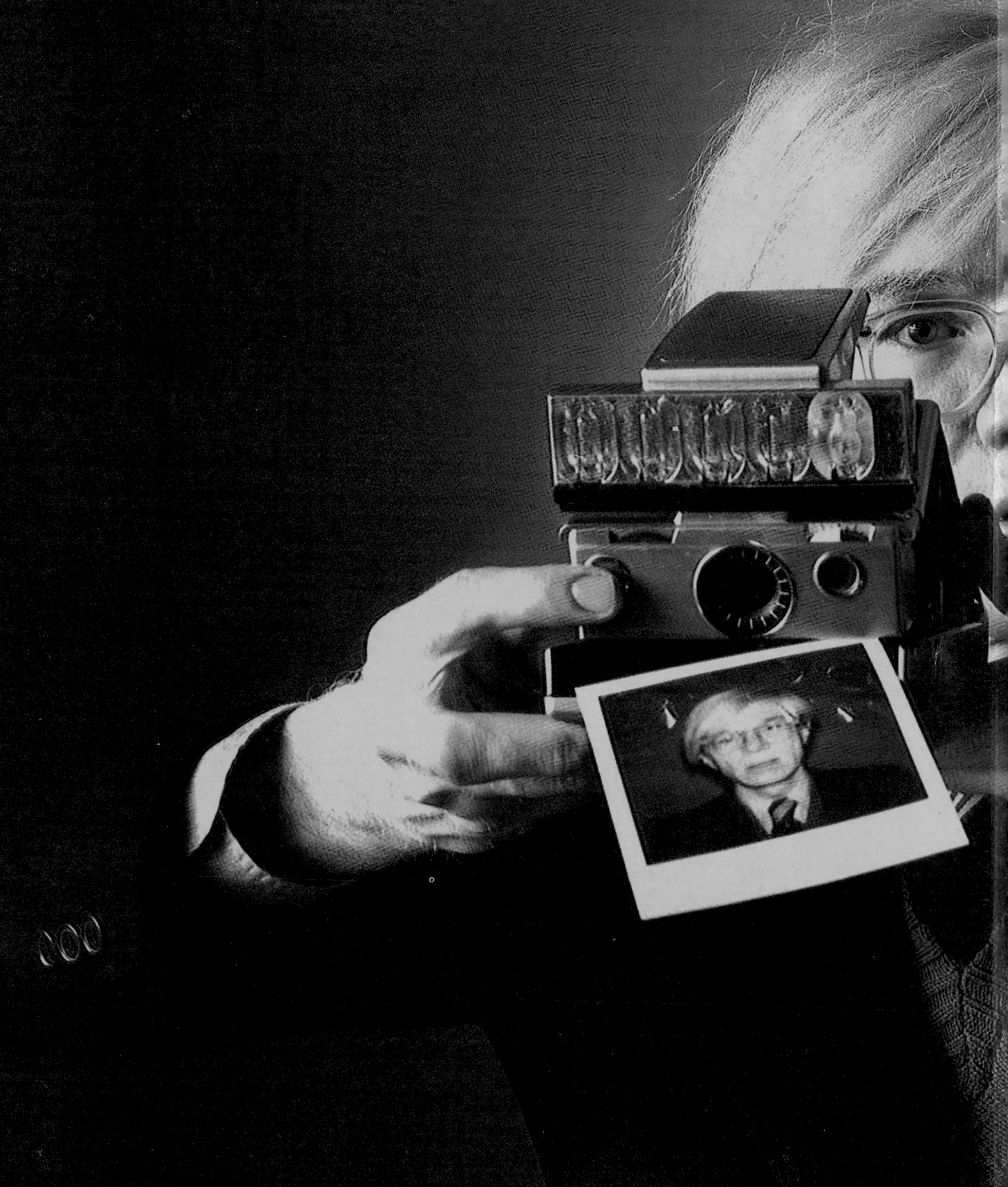